Woman
and the
Demon

Perhaps women were once so dangerous
that they had to have their feet bound

—Maxine Hong Kingston
  The Woman Warrior

Woman
and the
Demon

The Life of a
Victorian Myth

Nina
Auerbach

Harvard University Press
Cambridge, Massachusetts
and London, England

Library of Congress Cataloging in Publication Data

Auerbach, Nina, 1943–
    Woman and the demon.

    Includes index.
        1. English fiction—19th Century—History and criti-
cism.   2. Women in literature.   3. Feminism and literature.   4. Women—England—History—19th century.
5. England—Popular culture.   I. Title.
PR878.W6A9   1982   823'.8'09352042   82-9298
ISBN 0-674-95406-8 (cloth)   AACR2
ISBN 0-674-95407-6 (paper)

Acknowledgments

THE LIFE of my wide-ranging myth depends upon unorthodox associations. So did the life of this book, thanks to the diverse interests and approaches of the friends and colleagues
with whom I discussed the material as it was taking shape.

The talk, travel, reading, viewing, and thought that fed my
writing, as well as the writing itself, were all made possible by a
generous grant from the Guggenheim Foundation during the
1979–80 academic year. The department of English under
Stuart Curran's chairmanship and the Faculty of Arts and Sciences of the University of Pennsylvania kindly granted me an
additional semester of sabbatical leave in which the book was
completed.

I am grateful to the curators and staffs of the following mu-
seums for their courtesy in making their wonderful collections
available to me: the Birmingham Museum and Art Gallery; the
British Museum and Library; the Fogg Art Museum; the Lady
Lever Art Gallery, Port Sunlight; the Leeds City Art Museum;

the Lilly Library, Indiana University; the City of Manchester Art Galleries; The Tate Gallery; the Walker Art Gallery; and the Victoria and Albert Museum.

An abridged portion of Chapter V appeared in 1980 in *Nineteenth-Century Fiction;* an abridged version of Chapter I appeared in 1982 in *Critical Inquiry.*

The following friendly advisers shared with me their books, knowledge, and ideas: Sharon Bassett, Jerome H. Buckley, Marilyn Butler, Rachel Blau DuPlessis, Roland Frye, Susan Gubar, Edward Guiliano, Carolyn Heilbrun, Arlene Jackson, Victoria Kirkham, Sally Mitchell, Helene R. Roberts, Lee Sterrenburg, Joanne Walsh, and, as always, Carl Woodring. Martha Vicinus deserves a sentence to herself, for without her learning and the extraordinary colleagiality that led her to share her files, there would have been no fourth chapter. Justine Auerbach, Elaine Showalter, Carole Silver, Lee Sterrenburg, Alexander Welsh, and Ruth Yeazell read various first drafts, in whole or in part. All saw the book within and, with patience and incisiveness, led me toward it. Once the manuscript was apparently complete, an anonymous reader for the Harvard University Press delivered a magnificent series of final suggestions, carrying the myth into areas I had not charted. Any errors and eccentricities in the resultant text are of course my own responsibility.

The old maid and the fallen woman found their first incarnations as courses at the University of Pennsylvania. I am grateful to students too numerous to enumerate for finding the subversive life within these stereotypes.

My parents, Arnold and Justine Auerbach, have always believed in the woman and the demon. For that, and for much else, they have my thanks and my love.

N. A.

Contents

Illustrations

Woman
and the
Demon

Introduction

THIS BOOK grows out of feminist criticism, but neither woman nor women are its sole protagonists: my subject is the Victorian cultural imagination, in the chaos of its apparent inconsistency and the intensity of its underlying coherence. This imagination is essentially mythic, though it tries to be scientific, moral, and "real"; its most powerful, if least acknowledged, creation is an explosively mobile, magic woman, who breaks the boundaries of family within which her society restricts her. The triumph of this overweening creature is a celebration of the corporate imagination that believed in her.

The demon that accompanies the woman of my title exists in the broadest sense: as that disruptive spiritual energy which also engorges the divine. This demon is first of all the woman's familiar, the source of her ambiguous holiness, but it is also the popular—and demonic—imagination that endowed her with this holiness in defiance of three cherished Victorian institutions: the family, the patriarchal state, and God the Father. At its most intense this seditious dream bestows the joy of a new religion. It has become commonplace to label Victorian England as an age of doubt, but a vibrant new belief infuses its most resonant vehicles of popular mythology, literature and art. Today it is academic dogma to commiserate with the Victorian "loss of faith," but it may be that we have looked for faith in the wrong places.

My myth finds its strength in its centrality. I began this book looking only for "feminism" in secret pockets of the age, and completed it finding a "feminism" so pervasive—in the broad power of this many-faceted myth of a mobile presiding woman—that the word had lost its meaning. For this myth animates not merely the literature, but the lives, of women and men alike, providing new icons, new shapes for the self, new sources of belief. In its social structure Victorian England was sharply divided, but its imaginative iconography united class and gender. In the alacrity with which our empowered outcast adapts herself to conventional paradigms of womanhood, she assumes the binding power of England's own fiercely proper, yet irremediably alien, little Queen.

I want to point out one way in which the decorous clash of Victorian cultures coalesced in a myth that was never quite formulated but that recurs incessantly in literature and art, a myth crowning a disobedient woman in her many guises as heir of the ages and demonic savior of the race. I do not mean to suggest that woman is the sole vehicle of transcendence in a century thrown open to unorthodox beliefs; the end of my book shows the expansiveness of the myth into peculiarly Victorian visions of the self-transfiguring, eternally vital literary character. I am suggesting that we need a freer context for understanding the complex life of woman in culture, one which welcomes any society's capacious avenues of power, as well as excoriating its particular conventions of oppression.

In this instance, both iconoclastic feminists and their more sedate (and generally older) antagonists have agreed in condescending to popular mythology, so if this book about a myth succeeds, it may offend as well as enlighten both sorts of readers. In the early 1970s feminist criticism began its life pinioning just such myths. Gleefully, in the classroom and in print, we identified pernicious "myths" and "images" of women, certain that we knew what the reality was: it was us, solid, sullen, and victimized. The allegiance of feminism in the early 1970s was to the social sciences, whose demographic charts and statistics affirmed the reality of our half-life in society—and nothing else. But lives are inspired by beliefs before they are immortalized in statistics. It may be time for feminists to circle back to those "images" of angels and demons, nuns and whores, whom it seemed so easy and so liberating to kill, in order to retrieve a less tangible, but also less restricting, facet of woman's history than the social sciences can encompass.

More traditional scholars have been equally dismissive of the myths and images of popular culture, particularly as these manifest themselves in a belief in aggrandized womanhood. Walter E. Houghton's *The Victorian Frame of Mind,* a classic guide to the British nineteenth century, speaks only slightingly of the female "angel in the house" as a pallid substitute for authentic, and thus presumably orthodox, belief. Later spokesmen for the Victorian religious crisis have followed Houghton in examining only traditional forms of religion, ignoring the unifying vitality of popular myth. But a living belief cannot be reduced to conventional forms. It was not only churchgoing Victorians who could believe, with Lewis Carroll's White Queen, "as many as six impossible things before breakfast"; a study of Victorian faith should encompass the many Victorians who believed in the White Queen herself. The permutations and the intensity of such a belief are my subject.

My method is in part that of the archaeologist: to reconstruct a lost world of belief through fragments and shards of popular artifacts. I want to piece together in new ways a rich composite of verbal and visual images from Victorian culture; many of these have been forgotten today, but all were compellingly popular in their time. Through this collage of texts and pictures, we can discern a myth that functioned above all as a shaping principle, not only of fictions, but of lives as well. My association of biography and autobiographical self-presentations with fictions shows one way in which a cultural myth interacts with history, by giving shape to the lives that are history's substance.

I hope the reader will not merely watch the reconstructive process of this book, but assist it as well. The texts and the works of art I have selected are representative, not exhaustive. The Victorians left behind a wealth of material from which the collaborative reader is urged to cull her or his own demons, fallen women, mermaids, and so on, to enhance the paradigms each chapter constructs. I wrote with the help of an imagined reader providing new authors and images that added dimension to mine. Ideally the book each reader reads will emerge as a richer portrait than the book I wrote.

My vision of this book is Carlylean, and thus inexhaustible. Carlyle's hero fades before the power of the woman with the demon, but like him I want to recover a new mythos, one with which male and female Victorians alike countered a crisis of faith, and one which may provide women today with an unexpectedly empowering past. Like Carlyle, too, I want to recover history as the creation of inspired lives. But unlike the austere, indistinguishable army of Carlyle's *On Heroes and Hero Worship*, my female hero is a single vivid creature of seemingly endless mutations and personae. This book defines her mobile life by subdividing her.

Text and illustrations compose a series of paradigms of representative Victorian womanhood. The book begins with a polarity revealing a fundamental identity: that of the victim and the queen. This first, essential definition of woman ignores traditional femininity for a clash of extremes of powerlessness and power. Science in these chapters interweaves with romance, realism, and moralism as disparate genres converge into a single, if mutable, vision of the special sorts of power with which woman confronts her apparent master.

The next chapter, on angels and demons, moves from this peculiarly Victorian blend of science, romance, and magic to a more conventionally theological perspective. As all clean-minded Victorians knew, a normal, and thus a good woman, was an angel, submerging herself in family, existing only as daughter, wife, and mother. Virginia Woolf claimed that no woman can write without first killing this self-renouncing angel; I shall reanimate her to show her revolutionary ardor and her dangerous mobility, for the angel's otherworldly power translates itself imperceptibly into a demonism that destroys all families and all houses.

Chapters on the old maid and the fallen woman uncover this cyclonic theological energy within actual Victorian society. Both old maid and fallen woman find identity in exclusion from family; each rises through pathos to find mythic incarnation in a grand supersession of family as she leads the race toward new modes of transcendence. Popular mythology in these chapters shapes itself within social mores, as myth provides the energy that becomes historical.

At this point my galvanized woman moves outward into the large and diverse sphere of popular Victorian mythologies. As formal religion dwindled into Victorian duty, daily life provided new and inexhaustible forms of belief. The powers of women amalgamate with the dynamism of art, sharing their energy with portraits, with Shakespearian performers, and, especially, with those demi-divinities who brought eternity into Victorian temporality—characters in literature. In the end, Victorian culture is revealed less as a prelude to our modern wasteland than as a pageant of mythic promises.

Like ourselves, Victorians did not always believe where they approved, and so it is possible to trace the convergence of both sexes, of many sorts of writers, and of many varieties of audiences in a belief that was spontaneous, disobedient, and uniquely their culture's own.

1. The serpent-woman's face as seen by Edward Burne-Jones.

I

The Myth
of Womanhood:
Victims

WHILE RIGHT-THINKING VICTORIANS were elevating woman into an angel, their art slithered with images of a mermaid. Angels were thought to be meekly self-sacrificial by nature: in this cautiously diluted form, they were pious emblems of a good woman's submergence in her family. Mermaids, on the other hand, submerge themselves not to negate their power, but to conceal it. The subject of Burne-Jones's haunting "Head of a Mermaid" (Figure 1) thrusts her face at us with serpentine suddenness, a demon's magic glimmering within it. The mermaid is a more aptly inclusive device than the angel, for she is a creature of transformations and mysterious interrelations, able to kill and to regenerate but not to die, unfurling in secret her powers of mysterious, pre-Christian, prehuman dispensation.

The crisis of belief that characterized the nineteenth century brought with it unorthodox, and sometimes frightening, new vehicles of transfiguration. An ethos of religious humanism exhorted man to stretch to godhood; many good citizens did their uneasy and self-deceiving best to obey. But while Victorian man strove loudly to be good and a god, the mermaid exemplified the secrecy and spiritual ambiguity of woman's ascribed powers. Fathomless and changing, she was an awesome threat to her credulous culture. The social restrictions that crippled women's lives, the physical weaknesses wished on them, were fearful attempts to exorcise a mysterious strength. Hans Christian Andersen's beloved tale "The Little Mermaid" is one allegory of a good woman's mutilated power.

The little mermaid inherits timeless magic, but she forfeits her birthright for love of a callow Prince. She renounces her flexible tail to dance for him on bleeding feet; she allows her tongue to be amputated and her unearthly song to be lost; she abandons her home in the immortal sea for the possession of a problematic soul only the Prince's caprice can bestow. Were she to kill the Prince, her wounds would be healed and her native magic restored; but like many actual women, she refrains from this murderous self-restoration. Andersen's mermaid clings winsomely to her dispossession, but her choice is a guide to a vital Victorian mythology whose lovable woman is a silent and self-disinherited mutilate, the fullness of whose extraordinary and dangerous being might at any moment return through violence. The taboos that encased the Victorian woman contained buried tributes to her disruptive power.

Not all mermaids were obediently mangled. Thackeray's Becky Sharp keeps her tail judiciously submerged and subdues all assaults, including her author's, with inexhaustible vitality. Becky Sharp's compelling self-possession animates fin-de-siècle art: Gustav Klimt's Viennese "Watersnakes" and their sinuous kin peer coolly beyond their frames as if appropriating the viewer and his terrestrial sphere to themselves. The lamias who invade British fiction possess societies with similar ease. These serpent-women, terrestrial cousins of the hybrid mermaid in their secret self-transformations, their power over social life and its laws, exude a power that withers patriarchs: George Eliot's lamialike Rosamond and Gwendolen, Tennyson's Vivien, Sheridan LeFanu's Carmilla, all find their greatest triumphs in displacing male authorities. The ramifications of the mermaid in the nineteenth century are one manifestation of a mythography of womanhood without which our understanding of the age is truncated.

The mermaids, serpent-women, and lamias who proliferate

in the Victorian imagination suggest a triumph larger than themselves, whose roots lie in the antiquity so dear to nineteenth-century classicists. These creatures' iconographic invasion may typify the restoration of an earlier serpent-woman, the Greek Medusa. In Hesiod's account, the paralyzing Medusa was decapitated by Perseus, who became a hero when he refused to look in her face. Burne-Jones and his Victorian associates force us to look into the serpent-woman's face and to feel the mystery of a power, endlessly mutilated and restored, of a woman with a demon's gifts.

My aim in this book is to become the Frankenstein of this seeming monster, reconstructing her outcast grandeur from paintings, from essays, from the buried structures of literary texts, and from the letters and memoirs that hint at the shapes of past lives. From the unity shaping these seemingly disparate genres and materials I want to resurrect the central female paradigms that presided over the Victorian imagination and structured its apprehensions, abandoning domestic confinement to unfurl their awesome capacity for self-creation. Seen together, these interdependent and mutually sustaining character types infuse restrictive social categories with the energy of the uncanny. Once we restore the integrity of these types, we see that they intensify power rather than limiting it. The very rigidity of the categories of victim and queen, domestic angel and demonic outcast, old maid and fallen woman, concentrates itself into a myth of transfiguration that glorified the women it seemed to suppress.

From the power of character types I shall move to the mythic alliance between woman and that potent, intensely Victorian abstraction: character itself. As a vehicle of mobile immortality that leaped free from the imperfections of its text and the eventual death of its author, the literary character was the triumphant fulfillment of its century's last prayer: its boundless vitality recreated itself in endless freedom from time. Woman's power of self-transformation, her home in the mermaid's realm of magic and infinite change, associate her with a literary dream in which personality and eternity meet. Her grand incarnation in character types enables her to incarnate character itself, the nineteenth century's most potent vision of humanity made perpetual.

This myth that animated so many Victorian achievements

must be pieced together as it surfaces unconsciously but persistently in the scattered fragments of a culture's life. Once we have reconstructed the Victorian woman and restored to her her demon, I hope we shall find that we have not, after all, stitched together a monster from fragments of bodies, but that we have resurrected a hero who was strong enough to bear the hopes and fears of a century's worship.

Victorian Myths

A cultural myth thrives in large part because it lives below the formulated surface of its age; rarely does it crystallize into explicit gospel or precept which the conscious mind can analyze and reject. "Myth" is, or should be, an uncomfortable word, poised uneasily between rejection and embrace, apocrypha and dogma, arousing our trust and dispelling it simultaneously, remaining with us longer, perhaps, than do those things we know to be lies and truth. For this reason, such eminent and self-conscious Victorian sages as Thomas Carlyle and Matthew Arnold say little about women when they attempt to formulate new systems of belief adequate to the jaded secularism of the age. The myth of womanhood flourishes not in the carefully wrought prescriptions of sages, but in the vibrant half-life of popular literature and art, forms which may distill the essence of a culture though they are rarely granted Culture's weighty imprimatur.

But myth, though it may have a secret life below the official doctrines of its age, cannot survive if it uproots itself from the history of that age and from the lives its age shapes and is shaped by. In Victorian England, where national life was flattered each day by mighty reflections in the popular press, myth and history so fueled each other that we disjoin them at our peril. Disraeli's foreign policy cannot be extracted from the myth he made of himself as chief magician to "the Faery," his Queen; Gladstone's later political career is inspired by his faith in the popular myth of himself as England's Grand Old Man, chopping down trees.[1] Nineteenth-century political realities take substance from mythic creations of character, imaginations of giants on the earth.

In woman's history as well, mythic projection is inseparable from political achievement. Such ideologically conservative but inspiringly grandiose exaltations of domestic womanhood as

Sarah Lewis' *Woman's Mission* (1839), a long-lived best-seller hymning the potency of woman's special, mystic influence as the source of all good, fed the Amazonian imagery, the over-weening confidence in the inspiration guiding their social mission, of later feminist activists. Aggrandizement of the True Woman, sanctifying family, fueled the legislative triumphs of the New Woman, galvanizing society, for conservatives and radicals alike believed in woman's transforming power. In relation to both men and women, history was the stuff of myth while myth in turn gave form to history; but myth has a different impact in relation to women and to men. We begin to see these differences in the Arthurian poems of Alfred, Lord Tennyson, Victorian England's Poet Laureate and chief consoling counselor.

Most of us know how we are expected to respond to the blameless Arthur of Tennyson's *Idylls of the King,* the paragon who is humanity's noblest antidote to an absent God. Tennyson's attempt at a constructive heroic response to a crisis of faith is a laudable and forgettable attempt to create a king worthy of our belief; we grasp the well-meant intention and substitute it for the man, just as we do with those equally therapeutic but lifeless Victorian abstractions, Thomas Carlyle's hero and Matthew Arnold's critic. All three exemplary leaders are postulates in whom we will to believe rather than living objects of spontaneous faith.

We find it more difficult to define the imaginative status of Tennyson's vivid Lady of Shalott. We may allegorize her into the artist, the poet's anima, a fragile divinity, an heretical anti-divinity, and a great deal more, but she carries a suggestive resonance beyond these classifications, weaving a myth that belongs to herself alone, though its moral and spiritual status remains elusive. Perhaps because her myth is solely her own, not an exemplary tale into which she must fit herself, it is not King Arthur but this difficult creature who became a haunting icon in her own day. The Pre-Raphaelites painted her with obsessive, virtually incantatory repetition. Like Andersen's Little Mermaid, she assumed compelling life as a mysterious amalgam of imprisonment and power. This woman who appropriated the bard's function to make her own myth wove a spell over artists and readers that spread beyond her destiny in one particular poem or its source in Malory. It is this sort of heightened, resonant, and self-creating life, transcending conventional categories of value, that is the stuff of artistic and cultural mythologies.

Until recently feminist criticism has depreciated this interaction between myths of womanhood, literature, and history, seeing in social mythology only a male mystification dehumanizing women. The myth of womanhood was reduced to manufactured fantasies about woman's nature (inferior brain weight, tendency to brain fever if educated, ubiquitous maternal instinct, raging hormonal imbalance) meant to shackle female experience to male convenience.[2] More recently, as feminist criticism gains authority, its new sense of power involves not the denial of mythology but the impulse toward it. *The Madwoman in the Attic,* Sandra M. Gilbert and Susan Gubar's compendious exposure of the wounded rage of nineteenth-century woman writers, begins by echoing Virginia Woolf's exhortation that we kill the male projections of angel and monster; but it ends half in love with its antagonist's images, weaving them into a rhapsodic and sibylline myth of its own. Woman's freedom is no longer simple initiation into historical integrity, but the rebirth of mythic potential.[3] The mythologies of the past as well have become stronger endowments than oppressions. When properly understood, the angel in the house, along with her seemingly victimized Victorian sisters, is too strong and interesting a creature for us to kill.

Just as feminist critics today are rediscovering myth as a source of contemporary strength, so did Victorian commentators. Prosaic as the age may seem on the surface, the barest facts of its history and social history, as well as its supposedly realistic fiction, are amenable to mythic glosses we are just beginning to learn to read.[4] With a bold flexibility we have lost, the clearest-minded rationalists often spoke most effectively for the animating power of myth, clearing away its oppressive veneer to celebrate its liberating energy. Thus, Frances Power Cobbe, progressive feminist, exposes her culture's myth of marriage to corrosive reason before paying homage to the awesome primacy of the mythmaking faculty itself.

Cobbe's scathing "Criminals, Idiots, Women, and Minors" (*Fraser's Magazine* 78 [December 1868], 777–794) anatomizes the legal insanity couched within the Prayer Book's "Solemnisation of Holy Matrimony" by demonstrating that total union between husband and wife engorges and maims the woman. Sacramental myth took social shape in the iniquitous Matrimonial Property Laws, forcing wives into the category of the dispossessed and bestowing on husbands the legal identity of the tarantula spider who gobbles his mate, "making [the mate] thus, in a very literal manner, 'bone of his bone' (supposing tarantulas to have any bones) 'and flesh of his flesh.' The operation being completed, the victorious spider visibly acquires double bulk, and thenceforth may be understood to 'represent the family' in the most perfect manner conceivable" (p. 789). In images of cannibalism, of the perverse pregnancy of a male insect, Cobbe forces on us the social monstrosity to which the logic of romantic mythology leads. She is a ruthless opponent of the oppressive role of mythology, exposing it as a monster whose absurdities are easily expelled by the well-honed mind, which thereby redeems civilization from the animal burden of eating and being eaten.

But in "Dreams as Illustrations of Involuntary Cerebration," Cobbe confronts mythmaking not as a primitive and obstructive faculty "specially belonging to the early stages of growth of society and of the individual," but as a mighty universal endowment that welds all cultures in sleep. "The instant that day-light and common sense are excluded, the fairy-work begins. At the very least half our dreams (unless I greatly err) are nothing else than myths framed by unconscious cerebration on the same approved principles, whereby Greece and India and Scandinavia gave to us the stories which we were once pleased to set apart as 'mythology' proper. Have we not here, then, evidence that there is a real law of the human mind causing us constantly to compose ingenious fables explanatory of the phenomena around us,—a law which only sinks into abeyance in the waking hours of persons in whom the reason has been highly cultivated, but which resumes its sway even over their well-tutored brains when they sleep?"[5]

Like feminist critics of the 1970s, Cobbe moves from the laws of society to those of mind. She goes on to assert that the moral will, "the noblest element of our nature," is absent from our common nocturnal excursions into mythmaking, but her awe before the powers of creatively dreaming humanity is central to an age that moved with unpredictable facility between iconoclastic reason and wonder. The exposure of social absurdity that evolves into a paean to myth links Cobbe to the great Victorian fantasists, to Freud as he created his mythically based science of dreams, and to the Joyce who imagined *Finnegans Wake.* Cobbe as representative Victorian perceives the twofold power of myth: although it is a dangerous citizen of our progressive daylight world, it is also humanity's binding mode of perception, endowing us with a grander society than those we fabricate with laws.

Frances Power Cobbe's nonliberal wonder at the centrality of mythic perception aligns her with a contemporary who may seem a strange bedfellow: the great Oxonian critic Andrew C. Bradley. Nine years after Cobbe's essay appeared, Bradley published an appreciation of mythic poetry, questioning whether it could animate his own seemingly irreligious age.[6] In his search for new varieties of spiritual apprehension Bradley brings Cobbe's fundamental mythmaking faculty out of the hidden community of sleep and into the world we know: "Is it not the case that every day, without knowing it, we are making new mythological modes of thought and speech? Is not the popularisation of that science which is the most active dissolvent of old mythology, itself thoroughly mythological?" (p. 29). In his hope for religious commonality, Bradley proposes a new definition of the sacred that will rouse the religious imagination by including much of what had once been "profane."

Bradley's exuberant sacramental claims are free of Cobbe's reformist wariness in the face of the nonunderstood. But this momentary convergence of a progressive feminist and an Oxonian celebrant of tradition exemplifies the widespread Victorian awareness of myth, the eagerness with which it was embraced even, or especially, in the "profane" vehicles of social and historical life. Such exhortations as Carlyle's in *Sartor Resartus* (1834), with its urgent insistence on a "new mythos" to replace the "Hebrew old clothes" that had lost their spiritual body, find joyful response in Cobbe's and Bradley's wonder at common modes of thought. Carlyle's exhortation is not a final despairing symptom of the disappearance of God, but the demand for a new belief which found one fulfillment in a belief in womanhood. Myth's glorifying legacy should remind us that Victorian culture did more than lament the death of faith: it also celebrated faith's manifold reincarnations, in whatever unconventional, grotesque, or profane new vehicles.

If womanhood was mythicized, so was much of profane life. The impulse to erect neurasthenic prisoners of the home into goddesses of the hearth was not a special plot against women, but part of a larger, complex and transfigured perception of Victorian dailiness. I cannot reweave the entire tapestry of Victorian mythologies here, but my final chapters do trace one larger configuration to which the myth of womanhood belongs: a belief in the transcendent, transfigured life of characters in fiction. As an essentially metaphysical creature, one whose very presence brings eternity into time, woman enlarged by myth has more in common with fictional creations than she does with living men; her fictionality is one source of the energy that aggrandizes her.

Before seeing her at her most exalted, though, we should examine her in the role that has been most obvious to many of us recently: that of victim. In a key tableau from the 1890s an apparently slain and supine heroine seems helpless before the controlling male who would dismember her; but, like the myth of womanhood itself, our slain heroine restores herself to appropriate the powers of the destroying male. In this myth of transformations the victim changes into the demon, popular documents of romance into the romance of psychoanalytic science, which appear to dissolve the myth of womanhood only to resurrect its patterns in the modern world. Finally, a cultural myth of a slain and self-restoring heroine merges imperceptibly with the lives of those who believe in it and thereby into the history they make.

Victorian Mythmakers

The myth I want to examine here flourishes most obviously in popular literature of the 1890s. Yet its roots extend before and beyond that eccentric decade: the deliberate freakishness of nineties imagery illuminates earlier ideals of respectability and later conventions of advanced thought.[7] For example, the alluring conjunction of women and corpses has a resonance beyond the titillating sadomasochistic vogue Mario Praz perceives, and beyond Frank Kermode's Romantic metaphor of art's self-contained detachment.[8] The female life-in-death figure may be a metaphor for higher, or at least other, concerns, but if we look at her simply as a literal woman, her recurrent fits of vampirism, somnambulism, mesmerism, or hysterical paralysis illuminate powers that were somewhat fancifully, somewhat wistfully, and somewhat fearfully imagined in women throughout the century; the passage of our own century has not entirely dispelled them. Let us look at three of her best-known incarnations, both for the shapes they take on in the nineties and for their revelations about imagined womanhood in general.

As is often the case, we first see not women, but men. In a key tableau three men lean hungrily over three mesmerized and apparently characterless women whose wills are suspended by those of the magus/master. The looming men are Svengali, Dracula, and Freud; the lushly helpless women are Trilby O'Ferrall, Lucy Westenra, and (as Freud calls her) "Frau Emmy von N., age 40, from Livonia." It seems as if no men could be more culturally and inherently potent, no women more powerless to resist. Svengali is not only a master mesmerist and musician—the vocal genius with which he endows Trilby is his alone, her mouth its mere monumental repository—but he brings with him incalculable inherited lore from his birthplace in "the mysterious East! The poisonous East—birthplace and home of an ill wind that blows nobody good."[9]

The master-mesmerist Dracula seems a derivation from Svengali, with his powers still further extended over time and space. The spell he casts on women—we never see him mesmerizing a man, though he captures several—includes the animal kingdom, whose power he draws to himself at will, and at times the elements as well. As he tells his relentlessly up-to-date antagonists, who destroy him with the modern weapons of committee meetings and shorthand minutes, his monstrous immortality aligns his power with time's: his memory encompasses not only the primeval lore of the vampire, but the military and political strategies of Hungarian nationalism through the centuries. Svengali and Dracula are endowed with a magic beyond their own: they possess the secret traditions of their culture, while the women they captivate seem not just enfeebled but culturally naked.

As a mere mortal and historical figure, Sigmund Freud might seem out of place in this preternatural company, but in his case history of "Frau Emmy von N.," his first contribution to *Studies on Hysteria* (1893–1895), there is delicious magic in the hypnosis he had not yet abandoned. After boasting that he can regulate Frau Emmy's periods under hypnosis, he revels in a psychic appropriation that is quite Svengali-like: "I made it impossible for her to see any of those melancholy things again, not only by wiping out her memories of them in their *plastic* form but by removing her whole recollection of them, as though they had never been present in her mind. I promised her that this would lead to her being freed from the expectation of misfortune which perpetually tormented her and from the pains all over the body, of which she had been complaining precisely during her narrative, after we had heard nothing of them for several days."[10] In the event, Freud's promise was too sanguine, but the virtually limitless powers he arrogates to himself in this initial amalgam of science, myth, and magic give him access to our mythic pantheon in a manner Andrew C. Bradley had foreseen in his prescient remark: "Is not the popularisation of that science which is the most active dissolvent of old mythology, itself thoroughly mythological?"

In these two popular romances and the romantic beginnings of a modern science we see the image of prone womanhood at its most dispiriting. Personal and cultural disinheritance, we feel, could go no further than these tabulae rasae, all selfhood suspended as they are invaded by the hyperconscious and culturally fraught male/master/monster. But when we actually read *Trilby*, *Dracula*, or *Studies on Hysteria* we are struck by the kinds of powers that are granted to the women: the victim of paralysis possesses seemingly infinite capacities of regenerative being that turn on her triumphant mesmerizer and paralyze him in turn. Dispossessed and seemingly empty, the women reveal an infinitely unfolding magic that is quite different from the formulaic spells of the men.

The put-upon heroine of George du Maurier's *Trilby* is not fragile, as her role in the plot would lead one to assume, but a virtual giantess. Her size is so important in the novel that she can be parceled into fragments with a self-contained and totemistic value of their own, such as her majestic (but not Cinderella-like) foot, or the awesomely cavernous roof of her mouth. As with George Eliot's noble, outsize heroines, she seems cramped by the setting and action of her story; underlying her sacrificial destiny (like Dumas' Marguerite Gauthier, she repudiates her true love at the instigation of his snobbish parent and thus falls under Svengali's fatal power) is the hint that the novel's world is too small for her to live on in. Du Maurier's illustrations reinforce our sense of her stature: in all of them, Trilby towers helplessly like Lewis Carroll's Alice over her interlocutors. None reflects the paradigm of prone victim and omnipotent devourer outlined above, though this tableau does appear in the text. When under the spell of Svengali, the Trilby of the illustrations looms so monumentally over him that she seems about to swoop down and crush him (see Figure 2).

Reinforcing her size is her seemingly boundless capacity for mutability. The great singer she becomes when mesmerized is only an index of her endlessly changing nature. From the beginning her three adorers, Taffy, the Laird, and Little Billee, see that she is a different woman in English and in French—as she will later have a tone-deaf and a singing self—and from then on they await with awe each "new incarnation of Trilbyness." Falling in love is yet another metamorphosis, leading her to renounce all three men with the odd declaration: "You have changed me into another person—you [Taffy] and Sandy and Little Billee" (p. 156). Trilby does not need Svengali to incite her to new incarnations; her power of metamorphosis defines her character.

When she becomes a great singer under Svengali's spell, her metamorphic power enervates her master (who dies of a heart attack while trying to mesmerize her to new heights of genius), but takes possession of the novel. The essence of her singing lies in its seemingly endless variations. What dazzles is her "slight, subtle changes in the quality of the sound—too quick and elusive to be taken count of, but to be felt with, oh what poignant sympathy!" (p. 250). These perpetual changes are not Svengali's endowment, but Trilby's maddening essence. As simultaneous siren and angel, she haunts Little Billee as an image of infinite change: "And little innocent, pathetic, ineffable, well-remembered sweetness of her changing face kept painting themselves on his retina; and incomparable tones of this new thing, her voice, her infinite voice, went ringing in his head, till he all but shrieked aloud in his agony" (p. 264). Even before this most dramatic of metamorphoses, however, Trilby's love for Little Billee was only one component of a comradely marriage à quatre that included Taffy and the Laird. Her endowed voice is an accidental index of the multiplicity which allows her always to be a new incarnation of herself.

2. *George du Maurier, Svengali and Trilby.*

Finally the role of magus and mythmaker passes to her. Her ability under hypnosis to ring endless variations upon familiar tunes is the power of her character to transform itself endlessly, and in so doing, to endlessly renew the world around her. Her exquisitely lingering death licenses her to marry all three of the artists who love her: she bequeathes to each a wedding ring for his future wife. The myth at the heart of the novel comes not from Svengali's lore, but from the capacious regenerating mystery of its heroine, which awes and destroys both hero and villain: though Little Billee is supposed to be a great artist and Svengali, a great musician, their artistry loses all meaning before the transforming bounty of Trilby's familiar presence. In drawing on ideals of the alluring vacuum of uncultured womanhood waiting for the artist-male to fill her, du Maurier imagines powers that dwarf male gestures toward redemption and damnation.

The potent essence of each "incarnation of Trilbyness," counterpointing her passive and stupefied role in the plot, is repeated in the characteristic patterns of du Maurier's drawings.

3. *Little Billee among women.*

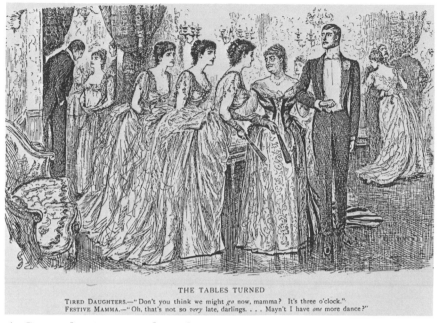

THE TABLES TURNED

TIRED DAUGHTERS.—"Don't you think we might *go* now, mamma? It's three o'clock."
FESTIVE MAMMA.—"Oh, that's not so *very* late, darlings. . . . Mayn't I have *one* more dance?"

4. George du Maurier, "The Tables Turned."

In an illustration of one of the few episodes in which Trilby does not figure, captioned "Darlings, Old or Young," the composition is such that she might as well be present: two giant be-decked women tower over a huddled-up Little Billee, suggesting that the overpowering Trilby is not an anomaly but the quintessence of womanhood (see Figure 3). The same pattern governs du Maurier's society cartoons in *Punch.* Typically a bevy of large-bustled society women sweeps up and down the plane of the picture's composition, taking to itself all available motion while a few rigid young men stand immobilized and iso-lated. In the configurations of "The Tables Turned" (Figure 4), while the women are saying stupid and trivial things, the force of their numbers and their costumes, the dynamic and multitu-dinous lines with which they are drawn, make them the genera-tors of the picture's activity. Du Maurier's women observe the proprieties with more demure compliance, less swelling fierce-ness, than those of his contemporary Aubrey Beardsley, but like Beardsley's women, du Maurier's appropriate all available vital-ity, whatever the demands of the ostensible context.

Moreover, du Maurier uses the contemporary fashion of

tight lacing and bustle for a significant reversal of physical fact. In actuality corsets and bustles transformed a woman's body to a construction of rigid, almost Japanese angularity, as any fashion plate from the 1880s illustrates, but du Maurier's women are creatures of active, curving lines. Their characteristic motion is a ceaseless, elegant swoop, while the men in their freer attire seem mysteriously hampered and inhibited. Du Maurier reverses the physical reality of a Victorian ballroom to accord with the sexual dynamics we have seen in his novel: in both, despite the demands of probability and the plot, the women are free, mobile, and flexible, while the men appear by nature becorseted and strangulated.

Despite the dominance of the wicked old Count in the popular folklore Bram Stoker's novel inspired, in *Dracula* itself women secretively take the novel away from him.[11] Early in his traumatic visit to Dracula's castle Jonathan Harker realizes that the sinister Count is less terrifying than his three hungry brides—"If I be sane, then surely it is maddening to think that of all the foul things that lurk in this hateful place, the Count is the least dreadful to me"[12]—and once the novel reaches England, it focuses on the vampiristic mutations Mina and Lucy undergo, of which the Count is reduced to an increasingly immobilized catalyst.

Like Trilby, Lucy Westenra has two selves. She is all silly sweetness in the daylight, but as Dracula's powers invade her, she becomes a florid predator at night. Like Trilby, too, she longs to marry three men but accepts only one of them until death grants her wish: as Trilby bequeathed a wedding ring to each suitor, so the blood transfusions, through which each suitor pours himself into the dying Lucy, provide the most convincing epithalamiums in the novel (p. 158). Lucy does not meet the usual fate of English belles; still, she is not an aberration in the 1890s. Not only do her fluctuations between virginal purity and bloody attacks link her to Hardy's dual-natured Tess Durbeyfield as well as to Trilby, but even before Dracula's arrival, her penchant for somnambulism, trance, and strange physical and mental alterations would find her a place either in a romantic sonnet by Wilde or in Freud and Breuer's garland of female hysterics.

Stoker might conceivably have known of Freud's work. In 1893 F. W. H. Myers reported enthusiastically on Breuer and

Freud's "Preliminary Communication" to *Studies on Hysteria* at a general meeting of the Society for Psychical Research in London. Stoker's alienist, Dr. Seward, indefatigably recording bizarre manifestations of vampirism, mentions the mesmerist Charcot, Freud's early teacher; Dr. Seward's relentless attempt to make sense of his patient Renfield's "zoöphagy" is a weird forecast of the later Freud rationalizing the obsessions of his Wolf Man and Rat Man. Seward's meticulous case histories of Renfield, Lucy, and Dracula's other victims introduce into the Gothic genre a form that Freud would raise to a novelistic art; his anguished clinician's record makes of Lucy both the early heroine of a case history and an ineffable romantic image of fin-de-siècle womanhood.

The word "change," sometimes modified by "strange" and "terrible," almost always accompanies Lucy in the text; along with "beloved" it is her epithet. After her first transfusion, "she looked a different being from what she had been before the operation" (p. 119), and in her fluctuations between passivity and prowling, consciousness and dream, innocence and experience, pallor and ruddiness, she can be said to be "a different being" every time she appears. Dracula supposedly instigates her capacity for perpetual self-incarnation; yet he appears only in shadowy glimpses as Lucy passes into life-in-death. In fact, as women gain primacy Dracula withdraws increasingly except for intermittent stagy boasts; though he is the object of pursuit, Lucy, and then the vampirized Mina, are the objects of attention. His threat to turn London into a city of vampires is never as real as Van Helsing's ominous confidence to Dr. Seward: "Madam Mina, our poor, dear Madam Mina, is changing" (p. 285).

By this time we have learned that Dracula's powers of change are limited to noon, sunrise, and sunset; he is denied the unpredictable changes of Mina and Lucy. As Mina's mind expands to meet his under hypnosis, his world contracts further into the box of earth within which he is paralyzed. As the novel draws to a close, its "good brave men" become more aimless and confused than ever. Heroes and villains recede as the metamorphosed Mina appropriates the qualities of all groups. As Van Helsing says of her: "we want all her great brain which is trained like man's brain, but is of sweet woman and have a special power which the Count give her, and which he may not take away altogether" (p. 298). In Stoker's influential literary myth the apparently helpless woman assumes male, female, and preternatural powers, taking away from the now-paralyzed Dracula the magus' potency.

It is fashionable to perceive and portray Dracula as an emanation of Victorian sexual repression. Despite Mina's pious disclaimer that she has anything in common with the New Woman, it seems more plausible to read the novel as a fin-de-siècle myth of newly empowered womanhood, whose two heroines are violently transformed from victims to instigators of their story. Aggrandized by her ambiguous transformations, Mina, and by implication womanhood itself, grows into the incarnation of irresistible Truth: "And I have read your diary that you have so goodly written for me, and which breathes out truth in every line . . . Oh, Madam Mina, good women tell all their lives, and by day and by hour and by minute, such things that angels can read" (p. 167). In her many incarnations Trilby also embodied Truth to her audience of reverent men: "Truth looked out of her eyes, as it had always done—truth was in every line of her face" (p. 309).[13] By the end, these seemingly supine women assume the authority of personifications, the guiding spirits of their novels' action. The power of Dracula himself narrows to the dimensions of his vulnerable coffin, for despite his ambitious designs on the human race, he seems to be the world's last surviving male vampire. Neither Renfield nor the Russian sailors Dracula attacked at sea are transformed after death: only his three thirsty brides, Lucy, and Mina rise into the Undead. Had Dracula survived the end of the novel, this army of women might indeed have devoured the human race under his generalship, for as far as we see, his greatest power lies in his ability to catalyze the awesome changes dormant in womanhood, those modest personifications of divine and human truth.

The implicit primacy of women in *Dracula* becomes explicit in Stoker's later romances: *The Lady of the Shroud* (1909), *The Lair of the White Worm* (1911), and *The Jewel of Seven Stars* (1912). These are sketchy and desultory repetitions of the myth that in *Dracula* was painstakingly and elaborately documented, but in all of them, the Dracula-figure is missing: like a vestigial organ of waning patriarchal divinities, he is displaced in centrality by a larger-than-life woman of a "strange dual nature." In *The Lady of the Shroud*, Stoker's one Radcliffian denial of the supernatural, the brave daughter of a Voivode nationalist disguises herself as an Undead. Before she reveals her mortal nature the hero, obsessed with her as a lamialike vision, marries her in a secret ceremony. In this slight story a woman takes over Dracula's role as Voivode nationalist with the powers of the Undead to transform and possess, but the rationalistic political context alchemizes male demonism into female heroism.

In contrast, *The Lair of the White Worm* is Stoker's darkest myth of womanhood. The book's Dracula-figure, Lady Arabella March of Diana's Grove, is in her true self a giant white worm older than mankind, living at the bottom of a deep and fetid well that crawls with the repulsive vitality of vermin, insects, and worms. From the mythic associations of her estate to the vaginal potency of her true lair, Lady Arabella's metamorphic power seems darkly intrinsic to womanhood itself. Lilla, the pure heroine, is so passive and susceptible as to be virtually nonexistent. She is recurrently mesmerized, but she has no capacity for transformation, suggesting that Lucy and Mina's powers are being divided: here, the acceptable womanly woman has renounced access to the powers of womanhood. *Dracula*'s women were poised between angelic service and vampiristic mutation; here, the lovable domestic woman loses her strength, while the dark outcast woman alone is equated with primal, self transforming truth.

The Jewel of Seven Stars is a still more blatantly unresolved allegory of female power. Its Dracula-figure is the ancient Egyptian Queen Tera, passionate and intellectual as Rider Haggard's mighty She-Who-Must-Be-Obeyed (1887). We see Queen Tera only through mysterious signs indicating that she is about to be reincarnated in our strapping heroine, Margaret Trelawny. The story builds ominously toward Margaret's amalgamation with her potent and ancient double, but at the designated moment the Queen fails to appear: Stoker can no longer accommodate his noble Victorian wives-to-be with his vision of primordial transfigured womanhood. Reigning without need of Dracula's catalyzing powers, Stoker's later magi-women hover without the gates, but they are blocked from invading modern London. Efficient contemporaneity may defeat an immortal foreign Count, but it could not withstand the assault of these dark and brilliant women.

The maimed females of Freud and Breuer's *Studies on Hysteria* seem incapable of asserting power over their age. Like Dr. Seward's possessed inamorata, they are presented to us through that new medium of portraiture, the case history; like that of Dr. Seward himself, the documentary rationalism of Freud's new science will be insufficient to conquer Dracula, a Dracula sleeping in himself as well as in his patients.

Freud knew himself to be a believer in the myth of womanhood; Rider Haggard's *She* haunted his dreams as "the eternal feminine, the immortality of our emotions." For Freud, however, myths bestow timeless order on the confusions of the present; as Philip Rieff perceives, "[h]is notion of myth is . . . basically anti-historical," giving glimpses of a deeper truth than history's.[14] Unlike Stoker's, his female hysterics are not directly associated with the assaults on family life that were current in the nineties; he seems to have insulated his turbulent consulting room from its adjacent, ordered domestic kingdom. Freud allows no topical authority to his female hysterics; yet he accepts as wholeheartedly as du Maurier did the absolute authority of performing womanhood. He wrote of Sarah Bernhardt in the 1880s: "But how that Sarah plays! After the first words of her vibrant lovely voice I felt I had known her for years. Nothing she said could have surprised me; I believed at once everything she said."[15] This faith in "Sarah" is a surprising reversal of Freud's skepticism toward virtually all the assertions of his female patients; his characteristic professional stance is to translate their helpless deceit into his own impregnable truth. It seems that only the controlled self-transformation of performance, rather than the involuntary mutations of illness, could move him to believe, as novelists did, that women and truth were one.

Freud's patients lack the immediate authority of du Maurier and Stoker's creations, but they, too, are vehicles of incessant metamorphosis. Their symptoms twist them into bizarre shapes; like Mina and Lucy, they are prone to somnambulism, inability to eat or to stay awake through the day; like Trilby, they divide into magnified totemistic parts of themselves, as with "Miss Lucy R., age 30," who is troubled by a smell of burnt pudding so overwhelming that she begins to disappear into her own nasal cavity, or "Katharina," whose anxiety attacks throw each part of her body into vivid relief:

"It comes over me all at once. First of all it's like something pressing on my eyes. My head gets so heavy, there's a dreadful buzzing, and I feel so giddy that I almost fall over. Then there's something crushing my chest so that I can't get my breath."

"And you don't notice anything in your throat?"

"My throat's squeezed together as though I were going to choke."

"Does anything else happen in your head?"

"Yes, there's a hammering, enough to burst it." (p. 126)

Freud's prompting forces our awareness to the hallucinatory consciousness that invades parts of her body in turn. He shows the same anatomical fascination with the hysterical pains of "Fraulein Elisabeth Von R.," which he locates precisely in a "fairly large, ill-defined area of the anterior surface of the right thigh" (p. 135). Like the discovery of Lucy's newly prominent teeth, these revelations that parts of a woman's body can become thus preternaturally animated make the reader uneasily aware of undiscovered powers.

Freud may present himself as a stabilizing presence, but his actual task resembles that of Svengali, Dracula, and Van Helsing, in that he strives to effect a further metamorphosis in his mobile victim. "Katharina's" cure is apparent in her speaking transformation, of which his interpretation is only a shadow: "At the end of these two sets of memories she came to a stop. She was like someone transformed. The sulky, unhappy face had grown lively, her eyes were bright, she was lightened and exalted. Meanwhile, the understanding of her case had become clear to me" (p. 131). Changing womanhood is the vessel of scientific, as she was of supernatural, power.

Freud reminds us with some pride of the similarity of his case histories to short stories, and as with so much contemporary fiction, the true theme of *Studies on Hysteria* is woman's capacity for amazing and empowering transformations. Here, though, Freud as narrator/healer/magus/master is always in control, as if to galvanize in anticipation the feeble magic of Svengali and Little Billee, Dracula and Van Helsing. Freud's own amalgam of mythic art and science, religion and iconoclasm, austerity and eroticism, combines the tools of all the men in romances who want to save and subdue mutable womanhood. The popularity of *The Seven Per Cent Solution* has allowed us to pair Freud and Sherlock Holmes instinctively when

we imagine the 1890s. It may be more difficult for some to associate him with this darker, more complex literary myth of womanhood. Freud himself, however, might not have repudiated the
role of hero/villain in a quintessentially British romance. Like
our other mystic foreigners, he was deeply drawn to the apparent rationalism of Victorian British civilization; in the last
months of his life he played out Dracula's role of exiled foreign
wizard in his imaginative homeland. Freud's affinity with British romantic mythology was one of the staunchest loves in his
life, but in his role as dark magician, evoking and controlling
the secrets of womanhood, creation sometimes battled human
reality. When a patient, now famous as Dora, wanted to take
her life from the master's possession, the result was Freud's anguished account of a failed myth that also became a failed case
history.

Unfortunately, "Dora" cannot be separated in our imagination from the resonant name Freud gave her, from her ever-
changing repertoire of hysterical illnesses, from the verdict of
one anonymous doctor that she was "one of the most repulsive
hysterics" he had ever met, and from her stiff-necked persistence in saying "no" to Freud. Despite his attempt to orchestrate her unconscious into an agreement with his consciousness—at one difficult point, he invents a consoling aphorism of
her infinite, if inaudible, acquiescence: "there is no such thing
at all as an unconscious 'No' "—Dora responded to Freud's interpretations with a perfect symphony of "nos" until, on the last
day of the year, she abruptly terminated treatment altogether.[16]
For me at least, the facts of Dora's life and Freud's construc-
tions explain her resistance perfectly: hedged by the pressure of
authoritative men, she was fighting for her life.

Dora's parents were unhappily married. In writing of the
family, Freud stresses the mother's "housewife's psychosis," or
compulsive domesticity, a disease he diagnoses more porten-
tously than he does the syphilis Dora's father brought with him
to the marriage. The father soon began a long-standing affair
with one "Frau K.," who had befriended Dora as well; when
Dora was fourteen "Herr K." began to make violent sexual
lunges at her. Her father insisted that she had imagined these
attacks, but her protests continued: as Dora saw the situation,
her acceptance of Herr K. was meant to sanction her father's
liaison with Frau K. It was then that her self-mortifying series of

symptoms and depressions began and her father "handed her over" to Freud.

Freud overrode Dora's father by accepting the truth of his patient's story. Incredibly, however, he insisted that a healthy young woman would become the sexual pawn her elders were trying to make of her. For Freud her illness and her resistance were one; by his definition, her unconscious could not but respond to Herr K. Dora's resistance to a coercive father and a loathsome suitor was that of the pattern British heroine Freud might have admired; her model could have been Richardson's Clarissa. Instead, he insisted that Herr K. was "prepossessing" and her feelings, aberrant: "This was surely just the situation to call up a distinct feeling of sexual excitement in a girl of fourteen who had never before been approached. But Dora had at that moment [of Herr K.'s sudden embrace] a violent feeling of disgust, tore herself free from the man, and hurried past him to the staircase and from there to the street door" (p. 43). Surely not only Victorian morality but the psychology and physiology of fourteen-year-old girls everywhere explain Dora's revulsion and fear. Yet Freud was so relentless in hammering at her her repressed desire for Herr K. that even his most sympathetic commentators grow uneasy.[17]

As Freud writes about it, the case is reduced to a series of skirmishes in which Dora, refusing to transform herself under his touch as had "Frau Emmy," "Katharina," and the others, meets his interpretative assaults as she did Herr K.'s—with a recurrent "no." The integrity of Freud's account lies not in his interpretations, but in his fidelity to the intransigence of his experience with Dora and the *Bartleby*-like drama of her recurrent refusals. Freud's pained definition of the case as "a fragment of an analysis" makes it for Steven Marcus a quintessentially modern document, great in its dogged awareness of the impossibility of solution. For Marcus, Dora's desertion of the great man is sufficiently punished by the fact that all her psychiatrists found her "an unlikeable person," though he does implicate Freud in a telling, though unexplored, insight: "Above all, he doesn't like her inability to surrender herself to him" (p. 309). But the loss of Dora seems to have inflicted on Freud a pain beyond modern malaise and personal dislike. What is lost, one feels, is the female capacity for metamorphosis without which male magic has no meaning.

The interpretations he thrusts at Dora are a pageant of symbolic transformations she will not enact. Not only are the objects and events in her dreams amenable to a boundless process of becoming something else, but in his vision, her emotions are constantly mutating. He begins with her suppressed love for Herr K., then goes on to insist that she is in love with (of course) her father, with Freud himself, with the suitor disguised in her second dream, and, finally and fundamentally, with Frau K.—in short, it seems, with everybody but her mother. Not only is Dora's inner life capable of seemingly limitless expansion, but her very costume is alive with significant transformations. Her commonplace reticule becomes a speaking symbolic narrative: "The reproaches against her father for having made her ill, together with the self-reproach underlying them, the leucorrhoea, the playing with the reticule, the bed-wetting after her sixth year, the secret which she would not allow the physicians to tear from her—the circumstantial evidence of her having masturbated in childhood seems to me complete and without a flaw" (p. 97). Freud's gratingly censorious tone here is typical, but, as with Svengali and Dracula, his disdain for the woman he has captured wars with his need for the gifts she brings.

Of all the predatory men in this story it is Freud whose lust for Dora is fiercest, but despite the pyrotechnical transformation of her reticule into a vagina, her sexuality is incidental to him. The sexual connotations of a woman's reticule, which Freud was not needed to translate, were familiar comic staples of Victorian art and pornography;[18] the metamorphosis of the reticule is as commonplace as the linguistic metamorphoses scattered throughout the German text, in which household objects translate themselves into crude symbols of female genitalia. A more valuable attribute than Dora's reticule or her "jewel-case" is her capacity for boundlessly suggestive dreams, the essence of her transforming power which she withholds from Freud by leaving. The case, which was originally to be called *Dreams and Hysteria* and to be published as an outgrowth of Freud's *Interpretation of Dreams* (1900), is organized around two central visitations: "The First Dream" and "The Second Dream." Like Trilby's voice, like Lucy and Mina's telepathic perceptions, Dora's dreams function in this case history as a token of a transforming power that enervates her increasingly paralyzed master. The note of frustration, of radical incompletion, pervading Freud's story seems less Marcus' ache of modernism than the ache caused by the loss of Dora and the powers she inadvertently brings. The central emotion of the case history is not Dora's "penis envy," as a vulgarizer of Freud might have it, nor, in Karen Horney's feminist inversion, Freud's "womb envy," but the teller's affliction, like that of an emotionally eroded Jamesian narrator, with what might be called "dream envy."[19]

Because in this case an imaginative myth played itself out in a real consulting room, Dora's story could not end satisfactorily. Freud makes several tentative and contradictory suggestions that she married, but these do not provide closure so much as further stabs in the dark. Later Freudians assert that she lived an appropriately miserable life, but in fact "Dora" seems to have died querulously at a ripe age without any violent emotional or psychic upheavals.[20] Life does not usually round things out: there was no last cry of "Svengali . . . Svengali . . . Svengali," nor did anybody need to drive a stake through her heart. But in reading the transcript of her case history, where Freud explains her obsessively but where she is never allowed to explain herself, she seems as much a product of the mythmaking mind as were the popular romance heroines I have discussed, though as a real woman she was reluctant to the end. Insofar as Dora "refused to be a character in the story that Freud was composing for her, and wanted to finish it herself" (Marcus, p. 306), she both repudiated his projection and attempted to exercise the powers it allowed her. She escaped Freud as she had her father and Herr K.; yet she never wrested the role of magus from her possessive master. For us at least she is inextricably entangled in the myth Freud wanted to make of her; his mythmaking imagination took its final revenge when he imposed upon his recreant patient the name of Dickens' most suicidally pliable and infantilized heroine. As with a character in a novel whose fate is muddied, we wonder how Dora would have named herself.

Freud's mythic and literary affinities are usually applauded, but their complex impact on his treatment of actual women has not yet been analyzed. From the beginning of his life to the end, his clinical work with women was intensely affected by an essentially literary mythology. As a young man studying with Charcot he was so profoundly moved by a lithograph of the master in his clinic that he kept a copy all his life. The lithograph depicts a rigidly upright Charcot explicating the bosom of a seductively supine patient; the woman is supported by a bearded assistant, peering solicitously into her dress, who looks suspiciously like the young Freud (see Figure 5). This prone, pliable woman psychically disrobed and recreated by the piercing eyes of men is the focus of a tableau closer in spirit to the popular image of Svengali and Trilby than du Maurier's actual illustrations are. One suspects that the constant presence of this picture told more to and about Freud than he realized.

Even in his treatment of women, Freud's powerful mythic urge fueled professional triumph with a woman who shared it. Late in life he analyzed the American poet Hilda Doolittle. The analysis must have been successful, for H. D. wrote a rhapsodically affectionate tribute to her master, though his art collection seems to have impressed her more vividly than his interpretations. Because H. D. was not a desperate young girl, but a successful poet in lifelong pursuit of her transfigured self, she approached Freud in the right occult spirit: " 'By chance or intention,' I started these notes on September 19th. Consulting my 'Mysteries of the Ancients' calendar, I find Dr. W. B. Crow has assigned this date to Thoth, Egyptian form of Mercury. Bearer of the Scales of Justice. *St. Januarius*. And we know of *Janus* the old Roman guardian of gates and doors, patron of the month of January which was sacred to him, with all 'beginnings.' "[21] Most Freudian analysts today would sternly untangle these exuberant oracular connections, but Freud apparently let them stand. Whether or not he feared that Jungianism had tainted H. D.'s correspondences, they seem to have been at one in their central aim: to metamorphose the woman's selfhood into an infinitely shifting myth. In his foreword to *Tribute to Freud* Norman Holmes Pearson quotes H. D.'s mythic creed: " 'For me, it was so important,' she wrote, repeating, 'it was so important, my own LEGEND. Yes, my own LEGEND. Then, to get well and re-create it.' She used 'legend' multiply—as a story, a history, an account, a thing for reading, her own myth" (p. vii). By the time of H. D.'s visit Freud was as surrounded by artifacts of old religions as "a curator in a museum" (p. 116), living as far as possible in a timeless atmosphere, yet one suspects that his central if unacknowledged faith belonged to the age that bred him. Long before he had accepted with resigna-

5. *Charcot explaining an anonymous woman.*

tion that "one still remains a child of one's own age, even with something one had thought was one's very own."[22] As a child of his own age, he apparently approached H. D. with the same mixture of awe, horror, and reverence that infused Van Helsing's words: "Madam Mina, our poor, dear Madam Mina, is changing." In Freud's imagination as in the fiction written during his life, the power of the magus is less than the self-creations of his prey.[23]

Realizing this dream in our own century, H. D. translated her analysis into an instrument of mythic self-creation. Her long autobiographical parable, *Helen in Egypt,* casts Freud in the ancillary role of the nurturing Theseus who enables the fleeing Helen to embrace her own grandeur. At first she shuns her transfigured self, asserting "I am not nor mean to be / the Daemon they made of me." Finally, Helen is soothed into embracing her demon by Theseus' "solution": "All myth, the one reality dwells here." H. D.'s narrative gloss makes it plain that the postanalytic Helen is reborn into magic, not mere adjusted humanity: "Was Helen stronger than Achilles even 'as the arrows fell'? That could not be, but he recognised in her some power other than her legendary beauty."[24] Like du Maurier's Trilby, like Stoker's Lucy and Mina, H. D. in her mythic awakening as Helen accepts possession by the magus as the crucible for her mighty self-apotheosis. Passing from Victorian romances through psychoanalytic documents to a modern poet's spiritual autobiography, the myth of the entranced victim is as covertly inspiring as it seems superficially enfeebling.

This myth is in its essence a dream of transfiguration whose power over lives as well as literature has lasted well into our own century. The self-transforming power surging beneath apparent victimization lies at the heart of this study; the subjection of women is a defensive response to this vision. As we have seen in its passage from Trilby through Freud to H. D.'s epic self-creation in our own day, our mobile literary myth shapes cultural reality. The mythmaking that was so intrinsic in the Victorian vision is not a fiction imposed on history, but part of history's self-creating energy. Making himself the vehicle of his age's imagination, Freud translated this myth into the idiom of our own culture. When the myth converged with the lives of his female patients, it was a radical insult to the already violated Dora, but it galvanized H. D.'s grand imagination of herself. In the same way, our cultural myth galvanized the fight of strong women against that very culture's oppressive impulses. Victorian women were an essential part of a complex and capacious milieu, not a separate and beleagured class or nation. As such, like all citizens, women were fortified by the dreams of their culture as much as their lives were mutilated by its fears.

II

The Myth
of Womanhood:
Queens

VICTORIAN WOMANHOOD is most delectable as a victim, but the victim consecrates herself into a queen with disturbing alacrity. In one of the nineteenth century's most powerfully suggestive new myths, Lewis Carroll's Alice must submerge her power as dreamer/creator/destroyer of the worlds she invades within the frightened and deferential politeness of the helpless child. Her progress through these extremities in *Through the Looking-Glass* epitomizes one fundamental metamorphosis of the Victorian woman. Alice cannot enter the giant chess game that is her story until she assumes the frail identity of Lily, the white pawn. The silent girl is hectored and threatened by the arrogant creatures she encounters until she reaches the eighth square, translated into queen and giantess, inflicting ruin on the rituals of her tormenters. In the same way, such pale victims as Trilby and Lucy Westenra enlarge themselves almost unconsciously into queens. Behind the victim's silence lurk mystic powers of control.

We cannot imagine the powerful corporate life of Victorian England without the pivotal image of its angry little queen. As the century wore on, many patriarchs similarly could not imagine themselves and their own power without Victoria's magically creating presence, whose ramifications in the social mythology Carroll's dream tale reflects are potent and subtle. Actual queens and queenly women proliferate in literature and art; so do ordinary women, such as George Eliot's typical but strangely mighty and enlarged heroines, who swell suddenly into regality. This chapter begins with two lavish queens of late Victorian romance, in whose image womanhood shakes off the victim's mask. Then I shall bring Ayesha and Lilith back into the homely world of mid-Victorian domesticity. As we move from the exotic to the apparently familiar, we shall move as well from the genres of romance to those of representational painting and nonfictional prose. Encompassing fantasy and facticity, these disparate genres concur in their mythic apprehension of woman's special powers, which declare themselves most memorably when they erupt in sudden, magical transformations.

Visible Queens

H. Rider Haggard's *She* and George MacDonald's *Lilith* are late Victorian crystallizations of the myth of ruling womanhood which in subtler form pervades the century's iconography. Haggard's Ayesha and MacDonald's Lilith need not pass through Trilby's chrysalis of victimization; like Stoker's post-*Dracula* landscapes as well as Carroll's Wonderland and Looking-Glass worlds, their magic empires lack even the token presence of a ruling male magus. Intellectual and volatile as well as dangerously beautiful, these divine-demonic women possess absolute power. At the last minute each is prevented from extending her reign beyond the looking-glass into the reader's reality; nevertheless, the womanhood these glamorous and strapping queens embody is associated with magical metamorphoses beyond the capacities of the strongest male.

Known to her enthralled subjects as She-Who-Must-Be-Obeyed, Haggard's Ayesha is a sorceress whose magic never palls. Unlike her successor, the vulnerable and hunted Dracula, Ayesha has preserved herself in unstinting glory for over two thousand years, awaiting the reincarnation of her faithless lover. Dracula incites changes in his victims while becoming increasingly immobilized himself, but Ayesha's power finds its essence in her own mutability and that of the world she rules and half-creates: "I tell thee that naught dies. There is no such thing as Death, although there be a thing called Change."[1] In a romance permeated with evolutionary intimations of endless flux, Ayesha rules because she shares the vital metamorphoses of an unfixed world. She survives empires ruled by men because her magic allows her to control and to embody Change.

When her lover returns at last, reincarnated as a muscular, somewhat cloddish Victorian adventurer, Ayesha mesmerizes him into sharing her dream of love and universal empire. Unlike Dracula, she never recedes before the awakened powers of her mesmerized lover: love neither subdues nor immobilizes her, but takes shape in an imperial blueprint for the invasion of England. Once she is fitted with a consort, Ayesha will become a suprahuman absolute monarch, a galvanized and transfigured Victoria, aligning Haggard's magic country alarmingly with his reader's expanding national reality. In Haggard's version of a national myth love does not tranquilize womanhood into domestic confinement, but fuels her latent powers into political life.

Stoker's Dracula invades England only to be isolated and defeated by the counterspell of indomitable British committee-men. Ayesha's greater power can be subdued by no team of good fellows: no magic but her own is sufficiently effective to annihilate her. Her conquest of the world beyond the looking glass is prevented only by her lover's cowardice and her own metamorphic glory. To soothe his fears, she bathes a second time in the magic fire of immortal life, only to find its effect reversed: in a great set piece, she evolves backward in a single dazzling moment to a baby, a mummy, and finally, a monkey. Haggard's prophetess of Change dies (if she does) in an appropriate symphony of incarnations.

Freud's were not the only Victorian dreams to be haunted by Haggard's best-selling vision of "the eternal feminine" unleashed. His popular romance embodied intimations about national and domestic reality, giving local habitation to fears that the learned and crusading "new woman" may incarnate as well the awakened powers of the old, adored woman. While our male magi governed by learned and transmitted lore, Ayesha's power is hers alone: she is a magus/queen not by virtue of an inherited cultural tradition, but by virtue of the mobile magic within her womanhood, drawing on the secrets of a Nature consistently personified as female. For all its florid exoticism, *She* is a parable of female typicality. Stoker's Dracula is dwarfed by women and alone among men, but his grand predecessor Ayesha is representative of a womanhood fully awakened to her powers in their magic congruence with an evolving universe.

The same is true of George MacDonald's Lilith. Lilith is a more conventionally malevolent divinity of a lunar, and always feminine, landscape, which (like that of George MacDonald's friend Lewis Carroll) the narrator can reach only by a magic journey through a mirror. Unlike the volatile and complex Ayesha, whose own magic is the sole agent of her triumph and defeat, Lilith seems too large and suggestive a figure for MacDonald's religious allegory to encompass; his declamatory female overreacher stalks about without being given much to do until she is chastened by an abruptly introduced and not very convincing male Adam. MacDonald further dilutes his queen by counterbalancing her ambition against the benevolent wisdom of Eve, Mara, and Lona, three "good" ruling women who preside over the House of Death, soothing its inhabitants into a mesmeric trance to await a vague universal awakening. Lilith's unalloyed hunger for power is nullified by these contrasting associations of ruling women with the soothing anodynes of maternity, religion, and death.

MacDonald softens his ruling woman by splitting her into several more palatable variations on herself; still, these women in malign or benevolent form retain their central power of metamorphosis. At various times women change identities with each other, with the moon, with "creatures," corpses, animals, and worms. The wicked Lilith changes most incessantly, but Eve's benevolence is also manifest in metamorphosis: "What a change had passed upon her! It was as if the splendor of her eyes had grown too much for them to hold, and, sinking into her countenance, made it flash with a loveliness like that of Beatrice in the white rose of the redeemed. Life itself, life eternal, immortal, streamed from it, an unbroken lightning. Even her hands shone with a white radiance, gleaming like a moonstone.

Her beauty was overpowering; I was glad when she turned it away from me."[2]

Once again the spiritual essence of the universe is incarnate in a woman's changing nature. Like Lilith, her anti-self, as well as Haggard's Ayesha, MacDonald's Eve is the transforming spirit of the endlessly self-transforming universe she rules. As overweening in her tender way as is Lilith, Eve becomes here her own creating Pygmalion, her own mage translating herself to heavenliness. The reference to Beatrice recalls that hypnotic Victorian icon, Dante Gabriel Rossetti's "Beata Beatrix" (1864), whose monumental entranced subject rehearses the changes preparatory to her coming death (Figure 6). Like our other mesmerized, somnambulistic, vampirized, or variously transfigured women, Rossetti's Beatrice has not yet died but has miraculously taken into herself life and death simultaneously. The women in this chapter, however, have shaken off the idiom of victimization along with the cover of the looming male magus who makes of their self-transforming power the instrument of his own virtuosity; these queens are the mesmeric subjects of their own magic possession. Even Rossetti, the quintessential Victorian artist/magus, creates a woman in the process of becoming her own creator. His Elizabeth Siddal/Beata Beatrix breaks free of creating male divinity to orchestrate her own beatitude. Rossetti's painting parallels Haggard's and MacDonald's romances in that it presents a grand woman as both object and source of worship, a Beatrice in the act of consecrating herself with no need of a controlling Dante, of Rossetti, or of God.

In this iconography the queen is not only magic, but the holy source of her own magic. Tennyson's King Arthur rules under the controlling instrumentality of God's instrument, Merlin; Ayesha is God, Merlin, and ruler in one, consecrating her own reign with no need of external possession. Such paradigmatic female victims as Trilby, Lucy, and Mina throw off their male makers to manifest their own self-transforming glory in their secret doubles, the demi-goddesses Ayesha, Lilith, Eve, and Mara. Princess Irene's great-great-grandmother, the omnipotent moon spirit of MacDonald's children's books *The Princess and the Goblin* and *The Princess and Curdie,* crowns this visionary company. The Victorian queen is not the anti-type of the Victorian victim, but the release of the victim into the full use of her powers.[3]

6. *Dante Gabriel Rossetti's "Beata Beatrix" envisioning her own death.*

The entranced woman with whom we began, seemingly helpless in the grip of her hyperconscious male oppressor, is fully understood only in her translation to majesty. Her trance is not passivity but an ominous gathering of power as she transfigures herself from humanity to beatitude. Like Rossetti's Beata

Beatrix, Lewis Carroll's Alice presides in sleep over a magic creation which is also a self-creation. It is no wonder that the Red Queen and White Queen in *Through the Looking-Glass* parody her dreaming might, commemorating their communal reign by falling asleep and consecrating themselves in snores. In *At the Back of the North Wind* (1871) George MacDonald presents a sleeping queen more solemnly: the violent and omnipotent, incessantly changing, personification of the North Wind, whose entranced form is the translucent gateway between life and death, humanity and magic. In all these works a woman's trance is the single medium of radical, and magical, change.

In an underplot, *At the Back of the North Wind* tells the story of Princess Daylight, MacDonald's variation on the Sleeping Beauty tale. A popular subject throughout the Victorian age, the Sleeping Beauty typifies all the sleeping queens we have surveyed, finding her most ornate apotheosis with the completion of Burne-Jones's monumental Briar Rose panels at Buscot Park in 1890; in these grand paintings, personified sleep exerts an hypnotic power over the dwarfed waking viewer. As a type of female power, both dormant and revealed, the Sleeping Beauty seems to contain in herself both victim and queen, the apparent passivity of the one modulating imperceptibly into the potency of the other.

Trilby, Lucy, Mina, Freud's early analysands, Ayesha frozen in time waiting for her redemptive lover, MacDonald's somnambulistic keepers of the House of Death, Rossetti's Beata Beatrix—all release their self-transforming powers in trance, death, or actual sleep. Victorian culture abounds in icons of beautiful corpselike women and in women—such as Dickens' Little Nell Trent, George Eliot's Maggie Tulliver, Tennyson's Mariana and the Lady of Shalott, Millais' Ophelia—who are transfigured in trance, sleep, lifelike death, or embalmed life. These figures came as close as possible to palpable realization in the animated Sleeping Beauty which drew unprecedented crowds to Madame Tussaud's waxworks exhibition. In 1851 Benjamin Silliman evoked the fascination of her seemingly living death: "She breathes, and her bust, with her dress, rises and falls so naturally with the respiration, that you instinctively move softly, lest she should be disturbed in her slumber."[4] In this erotic icon of Victorian womanhood, Rossetti's Beatrix approaches flesh. Life and death, the transcendent and the inorganic, the timelessness of myth and the contemporaneity of technology, converge in an embodiment of womanhood whose supine stillness contains the powers of her age.

This fascination with the Sleeping Beauty may seem at first merely cautionary and repressive, suppressing woman's energy and activity in favor of a desirability that emerges only in passive, semiconscious states. Bruno Bettelheim seems reassured in this way by the Sleeping Beauty when he endorses her as "the incarnation of perfect femininity."[5] But at one point in *She,* Rider Haggard offers a more sophisticated political analysis of the "perfect femininity" of the Sleeping Beauty's sleep as an antidote to her revolutionary potential when awake: "Ayesha locked up in her living tomb, waiting from age to age for the coming of her lover, worked but a small change in the order of the World. But Ayesha strong and happy in her love, clothed with immortal youth, godlike beauty and power, and the wisdom of the centuries, would have revolutionised society, and even perchance have changed the destinies of Mankind" (p. 309).

While our contemporary Bettelheim envisions an interminable sleep which awakes (if it does) only into propriety, the Victorian activist Haggard imagines sleep less complacently as something that ends: perfect femininity gives way before woman's power of arousal. Burne-Jones may have had this unnerving consummation in mind when he eliminated the kiss and awakening from his Briar Rose series, explaining, "I wanted to stop with the princess asleep and to tell them no more."[6] But the familiar story insists upon telling itself, and to rapt Victorians its essence seems to have been implicitly revolutionary. The Sleeping Beauty's meaning lies in her destined awakening and her attendant power to awake her world. True, only the Prince can wake her, but his power, like that of Svengali, Dracula, and Freud in his mythic projection of himself, is a limited catalyst for her broader and more disruptive powers: she alone can galvanize an entire society of which, like Ayesha, Lilith, and Eve, she is both the mesmerizing and the animating spirit. Embodying the victim who consecrates herself into a queen, the Sleeping Beauty who fascinated the age was a troubled and revolutionary intimation of her own power when awake.

As a traditional legend adapted itself to popular mythology, it told of terror as well as safety in sleeping womanhood, who as a vehicle of violent change implies her own explosive arousal. The apparent escapism of legend and romance transmitted the religious, sexual, and social tensions that animated actual Victorian life, wherein woman was both an incipient threat to be subdued and, by virtue of that very threat, a commanding source of metamorphic energy conserving human magic in a dark future. Extravagant as they may seem, these dangerous queens of romance are the subdued centers of Victorian realism as well.

In comparison with the works of the eighties and nineties, Victorian art at mid-century employs a rhetoric of seriousness and a veneer of realism. In the fifties Matthew Arnold legislated that the poet's mission was to wrestle with contemporaneity while transcending its doubts and contradictions; in fiction, Dickens subdued his inventive frenzy to write his most somber anatomies of contemporary life. The fantastic countries of the fifties do not lure the reader with the extravagance of Haggard's Africa and Stoker's Transylvania. When art penetrates remote places, such as Browning's Italy, Holman Hunt's Palestine, or even Rossetti's Heaven, its delineations are thick with detailed facticity, emphasizing the research rather than the magic involved in imaginative voyaging. The foreign is domesticated by study, as in 1851 the Great Exhibition had domesticated the very idea of foreignness; while in *Dracula, Trilby,* and the fin-de-siècle Never-Never-Lands of Robert Louis Stevenson, James Barrie, and Oscar Wilde, even the domestic is made foreign through the power of transformation that infuses it.

Women, too, were largely domesticated in mid-century life as well as art. The New Woman had not yet evolved as a powerful evolutionary type, harbinger of new worlds, new futures, and, in her most radical implications, new forms of the human species. Mid-century feminist policy worked toward greater equity for women within existing institutions of education, marriage, and law, but the fundamental equivalence of woman and home was scarcely questioned. Even Charlotte Brontë's Bertha Mason, that paradigm of incendiary womanhood who sprang out of the revolutionary forties, is in her mad confinement the spirit of home, not, like Stoker's Lucy Westenra, a solitary nocturnal prowler out-of-doors. Our queenly types, like Victoria herself, are exalted only as queens of home, not yet of empire.

7. *Ford Madox Brown, "The Last of England."*

Traveling backward to mid-century, we move from the foreign to the domestic and from the primacy of romance to the primacy of fact. But just as our florid victims of popular romance assumed historical substance in the clinical records of Freud's consulting room, which was one shadow of his adjacent domestic sanctuary, so we find queenly shadows within the homely realism of the 1850s.

The powers of the mobile queen animate the virtues of the wife in Ford Madox Brown's painting "The Last of England"

(1855; Figure 7). In this picture of solid and sustaining domestic womanhood, the representations of art hint at the evocations of fiction. Among the Pre-Raphaelites, Brown seems initially aloof from our myth of womanhood, indifferent to the monumental "stunners" who obsess Millais, Rossetti, Morris, and Burne-Jones. His historical and biblical epics "Chaucer at the Court of Edward III" or "Jesus Washing Peter's Feet" glorify powerful, Michaelangelesque men; "Work," his best-known painting, is a contemporary epic highlighting the knotty arms of working-class males. Yet, at significant moments women take unexpected possession of Brown's paintings. When he paints the Shakespearian characters who had become part of popular British mythology, men drift away from the center: Brown's King Lear series revolves not around the grand old king but around Cordelia, who for Brown was the pivotal figure in the tragedy.[7] Victorian exaltations of England's national bard were inextricably associated with a powerful national mythography of womanhood. For all his glorification of strong men, Brown's apprehension of the powers of women infused his paintings with the most intense faith of their age.

"The Last of England" is a documentary of contemporary life whose mythic content seems initially obscure. It records an actual event, the emigration of the Pre-Raphaelite sculptor Thomas Woolner to Australia, while evoking in its large-scale specificity the colonial departures, with their mingling of hope and defeat, that were a common occurrence in the 1850s. Its crowded contemporaneity seems to deny it the archetypal suggestiveness of, for example, Millais' "Ophelia," but in its spare documentary way Brown's painting is a sign of the voyaging consciousness that fascinated a domestic culture. In Brown's painting as well as Millais', the spirit of the voyage is female.

Brown's friend Wollner is the ostensible subject, yet all elements in the composition subordinate him to his determined wife, just as Brown's Lear fades before Cordelia. Because Woolner is taller than his wife, the peak of his hat should form the apex of the triangle their figures compose, but both are caught up in the great umbrella which crowns her—and which in the versions I have seen exactly reproduces the shape of Brown's canvas. Her upper arm further duplicates the circular sweep of umbrella and canvas; the circular movement of Woolner's arm provides obedient echo and closure of hers.

8. *John Everett Millais, "The Blind Girl."*

Thus, her homely umbrella allows the wife to govern the painting's structure and to become the primum mobile of its world, with all the dominant shapes being taken up in hers.

As she creates the composition, her huddled husband recedes. The series of jagged circles in which she is the center protect while they engulf and reduce him. Moreover, in the version now hanging in Birmingham, the wife's windblown ribbon is a warm pink, galvanizing the dim tones of the rest of the painting. Its sharp straight line is reinforced by her horizontal lower arm and by the echoing rope below, a movement in which all conspires to push the husband further into the background, reinforcing the wife's emergence as figurehead and mover. She is not the subject of this moment of change, but she makes of herself its motive energy. This pillar of domestic support becomes a transforming spirit as potent in her domestic virtue as Haggard's Ayesha will be in her autocratic power to embody in her changes a vibrantly fluid world.

Within the domestic triangle all motion belongs to the wife. While the husband is still and monochromatic, the swirl of her drapery reinforces the whip of her vivid ribbon. As she takes the child's disembodied hand on our right and her husband's on our left, her grasp alone unites these shrunken figures, making her the painting's literal as well as compositional mover. In the engulfing power of her umbrella/crown, her creation of the painting's composition, the mobility she alone claims, and her potency as a spirit of change, this powerfully good woman, guardian of the British home, shares vital characteristics with home's enemies: the possessed sleepwalkers who intoxicated the nineties and with the overweening rulers of its undiscovered countries. She is also aligned with the mobile old maids we shall meet in Chapter 4, whose voyages were a troubling counterpoint to domestic peace.

Brown's documentary includes a representation of its age's animating myth. His use of the intricate motions of a woman's hands as the vital center of his painting is a particularly suggestive motif common to the Pre-Raphaelites both in their realistic and in their overtly mythic paintings. In Millais' "The Blind Girl" (1856), for example, the clasped hands of the blind and the seeing girl are the heart of the painting, blending like the double rainbow the sightless figure and the visible world (see Figure 8). The left hand of the blind girl tentatively fingers a blade of grass; the hand of her companion grasps the blind girl's cloak, simulating blindness as she simultaneously leads us into the vivid landscape. Thus, in three different ways, for viewer and figures together, the hands alone interfuse sightlessness with sight, knitting into communion womanhood, nature, and vision.

This mystic movement of hands reminds us of the totemistic aura parts of a woman's body acquire in disjunction from the woman herself. It evokes the potency in Little Billee's sketch of Trilby's grand foot, and of du Maurier's illustration of the mesmerized and seemingly helpless Trilby whose giant hands are suggestively hidden from us behind her back; while in Freud's iconography of female hysteria, portions of his patients' bodies acquire a preternatural life of their own, assuming, like Stoker's wounded Lucy and Mina as well as Millais' blind girl, an eerie potency in dissociation. In *At the Back of the North Wind* we hear of North Wind's "gigantic, powerful, but most lovely arm—with a hand whose fingers were nothing the less ladylike that they could have strangled a boa-constrictor, or choked a tigress off its prey."[8] The independent power of a woman's binding hands is more than a compositional motif: through it, realistic representations acquire the resonance of icons.

In Dante Gabriel Rossetti's paintings of explicitly mythic subjects these twining female hands move to the center of the composition, often giving the still paintings their only movement. But the serpentine interfusion they create is more sinister and less loving than those of Brown's and Millais' grandly "good" women. Rossetti's "Proserpine" (1874) would be a virtual still life of woman with fruit were it not for the serpentine grasp of wrist with hand, then fruit with hand, that creates a gyre along which we move up to the face and hair (see Figure 9). Similarly, in his "Pandora" (1878) the crawl of fingers on box alone redeems the figure from stasis (see Figure 10). The slow circularity of this movement reminds us that Pandora's strong curled hand has the power to effect a dark transformation that injects an innocent world with evil. The hands of Rossetti's women are so vital that in one curious chalk drawing, "La Donna della Fiamma" (1870), a flame leaps from the palm of an otherwise inert woman (Figure 11), an experiment in mythmak-

---

9. 10. 11. *Three of Dante Gabriel Rossetti's anomalous divinities, whose mobility and magic coil in their hands.* Opposite: *"Proserpine."*

10. *"Pandora."*

11. "La Donna della Fiamma."

ing that crystallizes the metamorphic vitality of female hands as it was perceived by Rossetti and his circle. Belief in these spiritually ambiguous powers brings into collusion the conventional members of the Royal Academy with the experimental and unregenerate Pre-Raphaelite Brotherhood, Victorian realists with Victorian seers.

Fantastic as it seems, this iconography of womanhood tells us more about the Victorian experience than does the flattering literal-mindedness of much conventional portraiture. The binding, moving female hands that animate and unify so many Pre-Raphaelite compositions are a suggestive image of one central scientific vision of the age: that of the vital, infinitely connected, ever-changing universe of Darwin's and his colleagues' "entangled bank." Loren Eiseley defines the evolutionists' new universe as a world transformed into a strange likeness of Victorian womanhood in its radical interconnectedness and its incessant change: "[what] finally arose, in the eighteenth and the nineteenth centuries, [was] one of the greatest scientific achievements of all time: the recovery of the lost history of life, and the demonstration of its total interrelatedness. This achievement, however, waited upon the transformation of a static conception of nature into a dynamic one."[9]

The seeming stillness of Darwin's nature, which in fact crawls with interrelated life and generates magic metamorphoses, shares fundamental characteristics with such giant Rossetti women as Pandora. Like the early, pioneering Freud, Darwin incorporates his century's myth into his own scientific creation when in *The Origin of the Species* he consistently personifies his mystic interwoven Nature as "She."[10] For in the ambiguous webs they weave, binding the other characters and the reader/viewer to them, in their magic as embodiment and source of mutation and transformation, the women we have looked at share the characteristics of the tangled, changing, and awesomely new/old world of an age of evolution. As they mutate from queens of the hearth to queens of irresistibly spreading empires, they easily extend their reign over the new earth of an evolutionary age, whose capacity for divinely unsanctioned self-transformations echoes that of woman, its new embodiment and lord.

Science, realism, romance, and magic collaborate in a vision of ruling Victorian womanhood, presiding over a world amenable to her magic transformations. As a spontaneous belief, though one that was never formulated, the myth of woman pervades virtually all Victorian genres, creating a stratum of unifying faith underlying the age's official pieties. Our exploration began with magic and it will end with the closest equivalence of reality we can find: we shall move from the vivid colors of romance and of painting to the sober generalizations of nonfictional prose. Here, too, however, linguistic structures invest women with the fantastic mobility and presiding power that we have seen crystallize in late Victorian romance heroines. The essays of George Eliot, John Stuart Mill, and John Ruskin claim to eschew mythic kingdoms for reportorial descriptions of men and women in actual social existence, but we can still trace in the contours of their prose the queens and queenly victims who flourished in more extravagant Victorian genres.

Hidden Queens

In my brief survey of representative specimens of nonfictional prose in relation to the visions of realism and romance, of science and of art, I want to raise an issue this book cannot answer adequately: whether there is a stylistic of Victorian womanhood. To the degree that women were regarded as mysterious, boundlessly metamorphic creatures, the shift in perception woman generates may require stylistic modulations we can isolate; in keeping with her changing nature, for example, verbs appear to be the medium of woman, nouns of man. In the hope that the reader will pursue this contrast beyond the limits established here, I have placed passages about women side by side with analogous passages about men.

Written for the most part in the 1850s before she herself became a novelist, George Eliot's essays and review articles emulate Matthew Arnold's in their taxonomic purport: each author or genre pinioned or praised represents a wholesome or unwholesome social type. Two more or less contemporaneous essays, written just before and just after *Scenes of Clerical Life*—just when Eliot's own literary voice was defining itself—dissect female and male varieties of literary cant. "Silly Novels by Lady Novelists" mocks female cultural pretentions, postulating a yardstick of true womanly cultivation. "Worldliness and Other-Worldiness: The Poet Young" exposes egomania posing as religion in contrast to the instinctively altruistic and reverent heart. Both essays provide cautionary examples, for the reader and, one suspects, for George Eliot herself as well, but they anatomize female and male egoism in suggestively different terms:

A really cultured woman, like a really cultured man, is all the simpler and the less obtrusive in her knowledge; it has made her see herself and her opinions in something like just proportions; she does not make it a pedestal from which she flatters herself that she commands a complete view of men and things, but makes it a point of observation from which to form a right estimate of herself. She neither spouts poetry nor quotes Cicero on slight provocation; not because she thinks that a sacrifice must be made to the prejudices of men, but because that mode of exhibiting her memory and Latinity does not present itself to her as edifying or graceful. She does not write books to confound philosophers, perhaps because she is able to write books that delight them. In conversation, she is the least formidable of women, because she understands you, without wanting to make you aware that you *can't* understand her. She does not give you information, which is the raw material of culture,—she gives you sympathy, which is its subtlest essence.

"Silly Novels by Lady Novelists"

The adherence to abstractions, or to the personification of abstractions, is closely allied in Young to the *want of genuine emotion.* He sees Virtue sitting on a mount serene, far above the mists and storms of earth: he sees Religion coming down from the skies, with the world in her left hand and the other world in her right: but we never find him dwelling on virtue and religion as it really exists— in the emotions of a man dressed in an ordinary coat, and seated by his fire-side of an evening, with his hand resting on the head of his little daughter; in courageous effort for unselfish ends, in the internal triumph of justice and pity over personal resentment, in all the sublime self-renunciation and sweet charities which are found in the details of ordinary life.[11]

"Worldliness and Other-Worldliness"

These twin indictments crystallize fundamental contrasts between types of Victorian womanhood and manhood. To begin with, these passages utilize a pervasive nineteenth-century stereotype: while silly women are exhorted to rise to generalities, sublime men are encouraged to descend to particulars. Women were seen as by nature deficient in the capacity for abstraction; even John Stuart Mill's radical *The Subjection of*

Women concedes that woman's bent may be for "the practical" rather than for "general principles."[12] Barred from abstraction, woman seems by definition disqualified from the realm of the nobly human. Accordingly, one comic stereotype in the nineteenth century sets up a female character defined by a cascade of incoherent talk. Jane Austen's Miss Bates, Dickens' Mrs. Nickleby and Flora Finching, Gaskell's Cranford ladies, Gilbert's Yum-Yum, and Wilde's Gwendolen and Cecily join hands with George Eliot's silly woman novelist to flood themselves and others regularly in a torrent of shapeless and pre-rational particularity. But underlying stereotypical womanhood's uncontrolled silliness lies the myth of her disruptive capacity for boundless transformation. The totemistic portions of the body of the victim/queen, Ayesha's manifold incarnations, the mobile, magically charged hands of Pre-Raphaelite women, the interwoven multitudinousness of the personified female Nature of the Darwinists, all provide an animating undercurrent to this stereotype of feeblemindedness, galvanizing even silly women with an energy beyond the stasis of "masculine" abstractions.

Clearly male and female egos are prone to different sorts of diseases. Despite what may have been George Eliot's conscious intention, the shadow of female power determines the linguistic structure of her two contrasting denunciations in a manner we shall see if we look at the different sorts of verbs in each passage. The female type is always active: she is what she does or does not do. She is the subject of all but one of the positive or negative verbs, persistently being, making, spouting, quoting, thinking, writing, wanting, and giving. Whether she acts or refrains from action in the name of what is "edifying or graceful"—the degree to which George Eliot, a compelling talker, followed her own self-effacing prescription is questionable— this woman lives in verbs, according to degrees of mobility. Her essence is activity; her choice lies among varieties of activity. Never in the syntax of these sentences is she passive, never is she the object of others' activities.

In contrast, Young, the type of male religious egoism, virtually never acts. His passage begins with a cumbersome passive construction in which he hovers awkwardly as the object of two subjects. Thereafter he simply observes or fails to observe the activities of personified Virtue, Religion, or pious ordinariness. Young's syntactical role as adjunct rather than actor is not limited to this paragraph, but persists throughout the essay to the point of stylistic ungainliness: "*That*, in Young's conception, is what God delights in." "Young has no conception of religion as anything else than egoism turned inward; and he does not merely imply this, he insists on it. Religion, he tells us, in argumentative passages too long to quote, is 'ambition, pleasure, and the love of gain', directed toward the joys of the future life instead of the present. And his ethics correspond to his religion." "Virtue, with Young, must always squint—must never look straight toward the immediate object of its emotion and effort" (Pinney, p. 378).

In all these sentences Young is the static appendage of the primary activities of others. The single sentence of which he is the main subject—"he does not merely imply this, he insists on it"—is muffled by the dominant active impact of religion, and then of ethics, in the surrounding context. One wonders whether this pattern persists in George Eliot's prose; whether throughout the novels woman's syntactic activity is juxtaposed against a male stasis that verges on paralysis. These early moral types, at any rate, provide subtle verbal equivalences of, for example, Ford Madox Brown's "The Last of England," in which the husband is virtually immobilized while the activity and shaping power of the wife align her with mobility, direction, and the voyaging consciousness. In Ford Madox Brown's exemplary family and in George Eliot's cautionary egoistic types, woman rules her own perpetual activity while man recedes into a passive watcher.

The prose of John Stuart Mill, barer and more abstract, less flexible and self-aware than that of George Eliot, implies a similar contrast. Parallel passages from *On Liberty* and *The Subjection of Women,* the first anatomizing the normative citizen who is by definition male and the second analyzing woman's response to institutionalized subjection, embody stylistic distinctions all the more significant in that the passages amplify a common metaphor: in each, human nature is analyzed in Coleridgian terms as a tree, whose laws of organic development follow natural processes of growth.

> He who lets the world, or his own portion of it, choose his plan of life for him, has no need of any other faculty than the ape-like one of imitation. He who chooses his plan for himself, employs all his faculties. . . . Human nature is not a machine to be built after

a model, and set to do exactly the work prescribed for it, but a tree, which requires to grow and develop itself on all sides, according to the tendency of the inward forces which make it a living thing.

On Liberty[13]

in the case of women, a hot-house and stove cultivation has always been carried on of some of the capabilities of their nature, for the benefit and pleasure of their masters. Then, because certain products of the general vital force sprout luxuriantly and reach a great development in this heated atmosphere and under this active nurture and watering, while other shoots from the same root, which are left outside in the wintry air, with ice purposely heaped all round them, have a stunted growth, and some are burnt off with fire and disappear; men, with that inability to recognize their own work which distinguishes the unanalytic mind, indolently believe that the tree grows of itself in the way they have made it grow, and that it would die if one half of it were not kept in a vapour bath and the other half in the snow.

The Subjection of Women, pp. 22–23

Like George Eliot, Mill ascribes to men and women complementary powers. The passage from *On Liberty* ostensibly includes both sexes, yet it focuses inevitably on men, not merely because of its initial insistent repetition of the masculine pronoun but in its emphasis on the rights of citizens, for *The Subjection of Women* can insist only on the right of women to *become* citizens. At first the sense of *On Liberty* seems simply to reinforce stereotypical notions of male initiative and aggression, for the dominance of the tree is a law unto itself, while *The Subjection of Women* inverts the metaphor to emphasize the tree's vulnerability, its sensitivity to deflection and distortion. As a metaphor of manhood, then, the tree seems inspirational: it is dominant and must prevail. As a metaphor of womanhood, it appears malleable, grotesquely shapable. Mill's contrasting uses of the tree recall that tableau of apparent power with which we began, in which a predatory male looms over a prone female and wills her into unprecedented incarnations.

But as with our tableau from the 1890s of the dominant male and his prey, if we scrutinize Mill's language carefully, subtle counterpoints emerge in these two passages. Once again, let us look at the verbs. With two exceptions ("is" and "make"), the first passage contains verbs that are not active but infinitive: to be built, to do, to grow, (to) develop. Syntactically male nature is less the instigator of the action than the participant in an inevitable process beyond his control; despite the ostensible meaning, human nature of the male variety does not move so much as it is moved. Furthermore, it is removed from action both by the two metaphors, the machine and the tree, and then by the verb + infinitive construction. It does not grow and develop, but requires to do so, turning the ostensible subject from actor to adjunct; the fact that it is *made* "a living thing" by "inward forces" deprives it of initiative once again.

By contrast, in the second passage, though apparently passive and malleable, womanhood is the subject of every sentence in which it figures: it spouts, reaches, has growth, if stunted growth. Men, the apparently active manipulators of that growth, are relegated to the passive voice (shoots "are left" or "are burnt off," ice "is heaped," by them) except in their "unanalytic" or "indolent" beliefs about women. The syntax of this passage runs counter to its overt meaning: woman is the active instigator and man the passive attendant of her growth. As with Trilby and her kin, her capacity for involuntary self-creation surpasses man's will and skill at creating her. In the descriptive language of sober social analysis, while rationalistically dissecting one self-serving male myth about woman's nature, Mill aligns himself with a more fundamental, pervasive, and many-sided myth of woman's mobility and power.

Thus, even when their prescriptive social anatomies seem to diminish woman, chastising her belligerent ignorance or bemoaning her enforced compliance, the prose of George Eliot and John Stuart Mill runs counter to its own intention, creating a dominant woman, active and in motion. While the proliferation of verbs lends a potential explosiveness to her activity, in her undifferentiated energy and mobility, woman becomes more the instigator of her own actions than is man, that alleged monopolizer of noble initiative. She has the potential to be as mad a queen as those in Lewis Carroll's dreams, but in the structure of nonfictional prose as in fiction and art, she rules while man is ruled. The language of two proto-sociologists converges with the opulent visions of painters and romantic novelists to create an image of ruling womanhood its culture, like these essays, both created and suppressed.

In John Ruskin's *Sesame and Lilies* the piercing social anatomist and the visionary mythmaker cannot be disentangled as they combine to create a queen. Unlike George Eliot and John Stuart Mill, Ruskin writes as a celebrant, not a reformer, of womanhood. At first glance his hymned "Queens' Gardens" seem to be our most offensive example of Victorian paternalism; in fact Kate Millett has subjected this paean to womanhood to so withering an attack on the cant of Victorian patriarchal mythology that any later discussion of it carries the aroma of special pleading.[14] Yet we have seen that immuring women is an awed acknowledgment of special powers, and if we examine the capacities that take root in queens' gardens against the impotence lurking in kings' treasuries, we shall complete our portrait of a haunting Victorian paradigm.

> What have we publicly done for science? We are obliged to know what o'clock it is, for the safety of our ships, and therefore we pay for an observatory; and we allow ourselves, in the person of our Parliament, to be annually tormented into doing something, in a slovenly way, for the British Museum, sullenly apprehending that to be a place for keeping stuffed birds in, to amuse our children.
>
> "Of Kings' Treasuries"

> And wherever a true wife comes, this home is always round her. The stars only may be over her head, the glow-worm in the night-cold grass may be the only fire at her foot, but home is yet wherever she is; and for a noble woman it stretches far round her, better than ceiled with cedar or painted with vermilion, shedding its quiet light far, for those who else were homeless.
>
> "Of Queens' Gardens"[15]

Here in undiluted form are the Victorian stereotypes we love to hate: men and women inhabit separate spheres, with men appropriating the varied business of society, women the quietude of home. Yet there is a bold inversion of another pervasive stereotype: Ruskin's "kings" are accompanied by a flood of incoherent particularities, while his "queens" raise themselves to the level of personifications and abstractions. Woman claims all generalizing power; man is engulfed by the fragments of his world.

The male "we" of the first passage instigates no activity at all. The only verbs he claims express his acquiescence in institutional coercion, as he allows himself to be buffeted by demands that make willessly automatic the actions (limited to payments) he does perform. Like the immobilized man of George Eliot and Mill, Ruskin's institutional man lacks agency for either evil or good. His inner and outer worlds elude him. The format of Ruskin's lecture recreates in its auditors the helplessness of assault by society's alien incoherence through its barrage of quotations from contemporary newspapers: the audience becomes the "kings," subjected to the montage of disjointed attacks social life has become. In confronting these "kings" with newspaper accounts of paupered victims Ruskin may mean to call them to accountability, but the effect of his prose is to thrust them into the dimly incoherent wilderness of fragments into which they have already thrust the dispossessed.

No newspapers assault his queens' gardens. As free from the fragments of clamoring dailiness as is the nightworld of the vampire, the garden adjusts itself to the grand dimensions of its queen. Like a Pre-Raphaelite painting, it abounds in details, but these details group themselves to set off the large woman at its center who functions as the composition's source: the visible world is the world she emanates.

Like Alice's, the queen's garden is not a domestic enclosure but a large visionary world. The "home" Ruskin glorifies has cast off four walls for a nocturnal landscape with the contours of a grand woman. Purified of the encumbrance of house and the institution of family, "home" metamorphoses into an activity of solitary self-creation. Ruskin may want to hymn domesticity, but his language evokes omnipotence, with his queen supplanting God as the sole source of light in a darkness she inhabits. "Kings" are innundated by reality; "queens" are its source. In her agency, her activity of self-creation, her alliance with art, fairy-tale, and myth, Ruskin's queen appropriates the coherence-giving endowment not of the domestic appendage but of the mage.

Ruskin insists that man is "eminently the doer, the creator, the discoverer, the defender" (p. 135), but his own language contradicts him. His assertion that "the woman's power is for rule" (p. 135) runs away with his argument, though he tries to defuse this benediction by his denial to her of social power, the ground of rule, and by his nervous insistence that her native bent for self-sacrificial service neutralizes her commanding magic. This alternate evocation and exorcism of mythic womanhood embodies Victorian self-division in its pristine form; Ruskin's is the perfect specimen of the self-canceling simultaneity that both bows to power and mutilates it, allowing critics of our day to read "Of Queens' Gardens" as an anti-feminist and a feminist document alike, with equal plausibility. Yet when we see it in its proper context of a pervasive iconography of ruling womanhood, Ruskin's essay reminds us of how shallow the roots of patriarchal precepts were in contrast to their rich foundation of mythic perception. For Ruskin, domesticity is the veneer of apocalypse. Like Haggard's She-Who-Must-Be-Obeyed, his queen has the power not merely to create the walls of home, but to dissolve them along with all the boundaries masculine civilization calls immutable.

This grand woman who is so incessantly evoked and denied, moving to the foreground of literature and art while providing one hidden structural principle for nonfictional prose, is one unifying faith in a liberal culture that feared its own fragmentation into classes, sects, and sexes. She has a life beyond her incarnation as the madwoman in the attic, crushed into subterranean life in a female literary tradition, for she shapes the perceptions of men as well as women, scientists as well as artists, social anatomists as well as romantic adventurers. Her rule is not limited to an attic or a house; she is the source of a common cultural iconography of womanhood. In the nineteenth century her field was as broad and as wide as her culture's imagination.

In Victorian fiction these central, interdependent paradigms of victim and queen are further narrowed into three character types specific to the needs and institutions of their age: the angel/demon, the old maid, and the fallen woman. The angel/demon is the composite creation of a peculiarly Victorian theology. The old maid and the fallen woman are peculiarly Victorian social types; in complementary ways both are artificial creations of the tyranny of the patriarchal family, evading that tyranny as it shapes their mutilated lives. Startlingly, though they are responsive to cultural needs, these three central paradigms have virtually nothing to do with Victorian pieties about womanliness: women were exhorted to live in and through patriarchal family roles and exalted above all as mothers, but the three paradigms that animate the fictional imagination are outcasts from domesticity, self-creating rather than selflessly nurturing, regal but never maternal. Solitaries by nature and essence, they transcend the culture that creates them.

In my two final chapters I shall define their kinship to beings with no pretense of roots in family: those masters of self-creating autonomy, characters in literature, the only vehicles of immortality in whom many sophisticated Victorians could unreservedly believe. The essence of womanhood as a Victorian idea sprang free of family life to participate in a theology peculiar to its doubting but credulous age, wherein the literary imagination became the final available vehicle of transcendence. Attached only marginally to the daily business of her society, torn between the poles of victim and queen, woman was so powerful an imaginative abstraction that she assumed the status of literature-in-life, leading humanity beyond the limits of mortality to the transfigured freedom of the literary character.

The chapters to come will emphasize the life of this idea in the community of popular Victorian fiction. They will remind us as well of the extent to which womanhood was an idea made flesh, influencing the shapes of actual lives. Popular fiction embedded itself in world views, secretly influencing the choices of anonymous and forgotten readers. To dramatize the subtle convergences between literature and lives I shall move freely between fiction and letters, memoirs, and biographies, suggesting ways in which myths of woman influenced and empowered the lives of actual women. In a century whose women's lives were exalted to the status of fictions, fiction bestowed in return motive power to many lives. In its flowering, womanhood was a literary idea in perpetual incarnation, unifying a society at war with itself by spanning the gulf between its fictions and its acts.

III

Angels and Demons: Woman's Marriage of Heaven and Hell

THE TOWERING WOMAN who in so many guises possessed the Victorian imagination appears in art and literature as four central types: the angel, the demon, the old maid, and the fallen woman. The first two appear to be emanations of eternity; the latter two rise from within Victorian society. Yet there is incessant interfusion among these four categories: none is undiluted by the others. In this chapter we shall see the ease with which the Victorian angel becomes demonic, unaided by a Faustian pact or florid metamorphosis. With identities unsanctioned by marriage, the old maid and the fallen woman seem cast out of traditional theological definition, but they become angels and demons with equal facility. The old maid seems an innocent butt of comedy; the fallen woman is experienced and tragic; but in their exclusion from domesticity they amalgamate with each other at crucial moments. Discussing each type separately falsifies the fluid boundaries among them, for together they place woman at the junction between the social and the spiritual, the humanly perishable and the transcendently potent.

Angels Alone

We no longer adore angels; we do not even like them, dismissing them impatiently as soggy dilutions of human complexity. Our present revulsion against angels as anything more than smirking inhabitants of Christmas trees may take inspiration from Victorian England, whose prevailing popular angelology cast angels as irrefutably female and by definition domestic, rather than as the striding martial and potentially bisexual males they had been. Official religions of all sects may have been relentlessly patriarchal, but literary iconography gave womanhood virtually exclusive access to spiritual depths and heights. A casually muttered generalization by Tennyson's Merlin defines this new centrality: "For men at most differ as heaven and earth, / But women, worst and best, as heaven and hell" (*Idylls of the King*, "Merlin and Vivien," ll. 812–813).

Merlin is wrong about Victorian manhood: literature and art swarm with male demons but, while would-be heroes abound, there are virtually no male angels. Paragons like Tennyson's King Arthur and George Eliot's Daniel Deronda are at best ineffectual angels, full of vaporously right intentions but lacking the actual power to save. But Merlin is most interested in defining womanhood, and here, though he may not speak for King Arthur's age, he does for Tennyson's own. According to its governing imaginative convention, women exist only as spiritual extremes: there is no human norm of womanhood, for she has no home on earth, but only among divine and demonic essences. This imaginative scheme does not believe in a human woman. The "normal" or pattern Victorian woman is an angel, immune from the human condition and, unlike her feebly well-intentioned male counterparts, endowed by definition with suprahuman powers. No doubt this exclusion from her human birthright is a social insult, but imaginatively it promises the freedom of the spheres.

The nineteenth-century woman's angelic and demonic identities are not as exclusive as they may seem: her being extends as well through the magical and monstrous realm of more-than-human earthly life. The imaginative association of women with monstrosity, or with that which is conscious but not human, is both a stigma, as Ellen Moers insisted first in *Literary Women,* and a celebration of female powers of metamorphosis: Victorian fantasy art finds constant wonder in the juxtaposition of women with outlandish sorts of creatures. Lewis Carroll's *Alice* books and Christina Rossetti's *Goblin Market* are the most famous examples of works whose comedy and terror depend upon the potential interchangeability between woman and creature: to the grotesques of her dreams, Alice seems a still more curious monster, while Laura's thirst for goblin fruit reveals her own potential to become a goblin, squeaking and biting in her hunger.

Victorian iconography abounds in less canonical alliances between women and fairies, goblins, mermaids, vampires, and all varieties of creation's mutants; the Victorian universe crawls with anomalies from whose weird energy only man is excluded. Four illustrations, chosen almost at random, take their life from the taut affinities between woman and creature. Walter Crane's illustration (Figure 12) contains witty hints of an alliance between Beauty and Beast. For one thing, they wear complementary colors, the red slashes in Beauty's dress, her hair, and her fan seeming to beckon toward the Beast's blatant red waistcoat and hooves. Moreover, though her diminutive red feet are tucked demurely under her dress, Beauty's skirt extends out to meet the Beast's cloven hooves and to echo their shape. Crane's whisper of animality suggests a covert, affectionate complicity between the female's decorum and the monster's assault.

Like the half-somnolent little girl in Richard Doyle's *Fairy Book* (Figure 13), Aubrey Beardsley's Salomé eyes an imp familiarly (see Figure 14), as if his grotesquerie might as easily be shared as shunned. The little girl in Christina Rossetti's *Speaking Likenesses*, illustrated here by Arthur Hughes (Figure 15), is more suggestive still. This angry child dreams of a birthday party invaded by monstrous, anarchic creatures, over which she herself presides in the guise of a furious Queen. The central dreamer seems pliant and pure, yet monsters form themselves from the planes and contours of her body, her very grace giving shape to weird personifications of misrule. Like the mad Queens in the *Alices*, Hughes's doppelgänger Queen suggests an alliance between dream, monstrosity, and the magic yet institutionalized powers of womanhood; the creatures formed by the little girl's attitudes lead in a sinuous S-curve to a solitary Queen, ruling and unifying girl and mutants.

Today angels and demons may have disappeared from our horizon, but this titillating alliance between Beauty and Beast, the powers of monsters and of women, animates the hidden partnerships in such popular movies as *King Kong* and *Alien,* where women and creature are dynamically isolated by a male-controlled world over which they gain ascendancy. Excluded as woman is from "normative" maleness, she seems less an alien than man in the nonhuman range of the universe. Men are less her brothers than is the spectrum of creation's mutants.

It may seem blasphemous to link woman's association with fairies, mermaids, and other grotesques to her domestic incarnation as an angel, but popular Victorian angelology was itself a radical theological modification that flirted with blasphemy. The Victorian angel we know best is Coventry Patmore's "Angel in the House," his long poetic celebration of married love (1855–1856) whose title is so much more resonant than its content. Not all Victorian angels lived in houses—Dickens' Lit-

12. 13. Pure womanhood and undiluted monsterhood, as Walter Crane (above) *and Richard Doyle* (opposite) *combine them.*

13. Illustration from The Doyle Fairy Book.

tle Nell is an inveterate pilgrim, for whom "home" is only a place in which to learn to die—but according to literary convention, many did, making Patmore's title a convenient shorthand for the selfless paragon all women were exhorted to be,

14. 15. In these illustrations by Beardsley (above) and Hughes (opposite), woman and child gaze knowingly at monstrosity as a prelude to reign.

enveloped in family life and seeking no identity beyond the roles of daughter, wife, and mother. "Angel" and "house" become virtual synonyms. The social corollary of this identification is an equally implacable association between womanhood and domestic purity, a bond many women have been so eager to break that we forget the radical iconographic shift inherent in

Patmore's original phrase, together with its fascinating connotations when examined in the context of its culture.

In traditional Christian angelology, angels and women are only tangentially allied. Initially angels were by definition masculine; art historians find no unmistakably female angels until the fifteenth century.[1] Not only are angels masculine, but they are typically martial, armored figures. Above all, they are distinguished by their dazzling mobility as they conquer space, moving, according to Roland Frye, "with the grace and beauty of supernal athletes" (p. 173). In Shakespeare's *i Henry IV*, Prince Hal blazes into this exciting warrior angel, displaying his angelic attributes above all in his uncanny freedom of motion: "I saw young Harry with his beaver on, / His cushes on his thighs, gallantly armed, / Rise from the ground like feathered Mercury, / And vaulted with such ease into his seat / As if an angel had dropped down from the clouds / To turn and wind a fiery Pegasus / And witch the world with noble horsemanship" (IV, i, 104–110). Prince Hal as angel is Prince Hal in motion, with powers mightier and more ambiguous than those of the

16. *Detail, plate 21, William Blake,* The Marriage of Heaven and Hell.

static, decorative, drooping angel who survived into the twentieth century.

Milton's *Paradise Lost*, a text with which devout Victorian readers were as familiar as they were with the Bible and the Book of Common Prayer, is a still more explicit guide to traditional angelology. Though both angels and demons are said to be bisexual—"For Spirits when they please / Can either Sex assume, or both" (I, 423–424)—the angels we see are martial and commanding males, lords of vast spaces as Raphael is in his flight to Earth: "Down thither prone in flight / He speeds, and through the vast Etereal Skie / Sails between worlds and worlds, with steddie wing / Now on the polar winds, then with quick Fann / Winnows the buxon Air; till within soar / of Towring Eagles, to all the Fowls he seems / A *Phoenix*, gaz'd by all, as that sole Bird / When to enshrine his reliques in the Sun's / Bright Temple, to *Egyptian Thebes* he flies" (V, 226–274). Bisexuality in *Paradise Lost* is a largely disregarded manifestation of infinite angelic mobility. The armored seraph Raphael, cynosure of birds, scarcely evokes angelic femininity, nor does his pride of flight suggest affinities with home or house.

Even so radical a reviser of Milton as William Blake follows Milton's angelology in *The Marriage of Heaven and Hell* (1790). Some of Blake's illustrations suggest that his spirits, like Milton's, become bisexual at will, but angels as well as demons are designated by masculine pronouns throughout. They, too, sweep through chasms of space at will, in an implied association of spiritual with physical prowess. Moreover, the one angel we see clearly (Figure 16) extends his thighs and displays his maleness with traditional pride in his body's span, though he only gazes longingly toward the open spaces of which Milton's Raphael was in peerless possession. Blake's is a satirical illustration of a smug Swedenborgian angel who may be less insistently a man when he is able to become a devil. In teasing and mocking the pride behind the conventional equation of the angelic and the masculine, Blake prophesies the new angelic iconography his poem calls demonic.

To be an angel, then, is to be masculine and breathtakingly mobile: traditional angels take possession of infinite space with an enviable freedom that later Romantic poets dare attribute only to such birds as albatrosses, skylarks, and invisible nightingales. As heir of this tradition, the Victorian angel in the house

seems a bizarre object of worship, both in her virtuous femininity with its inherent limitations—she can exist only within families, while masculine angels existed everywhere—and in the
immobilization the phrase suggests. In contrast to her swooping
ancestors, the angel in the house is a violent paradox with over-
tones of benediction and captivity. Angelic motion had once
known no boundaries; the Victorian angel is defined by her
boundaries. Yet the stillness of this new icon is invested with
powers that earlier athletic angels did not possess, for as masculinity is superseded by her presence, so is creative divinity. This
new angel takes orders from no father-creator, but become herself the source of order.

Two Victorian poems explore the tension within this new
religious image. Dante Gabriel Rossetti's "The Blessed Damozel" (1847) translates the angel's house to Heaven, but its spare
dimensions remain unchanged. Women are granted unprecedented power in its prisonlike space. The Blessed Damozel does
make a climactic appeal to a nebulous Christ, but she need not
stay for an answer: hers is a Heaven purged of male control, a
community of women with the sole power to sanctify their
lovers. Its presiding genius is the Virgin Mary, but she stands
alone among female attendants like Tennyson's Princess Ida,
free from the burden of Christ Child and creating Father. But
these theologically unprecedented powers are gained at the cost
of flight. Spiritually minded readers have been shocked at this
angel's physical substance that makes "the bar she leaned on
warm" (l. 46), but the true emphasis falls on the bar, banning
the angel from space: like home, Heaven is woman's prison as
well as her sphere. When embodied in a woman, beatitude is
defined not by its mobility, but by its limits. This new angel
blesses a shrunken world.

The constricted posture of the angel in the house, immobilized possessor of unprecedented spiritual power, elicits a dying
cry of protest from Pompilia, Robert Browning's angel in *The
Ring and the Book* (1869). Sold into marriage by her foster parents, murdered by the hirelings of her sadistic though respectable husband, victim of all earthly families, Pompilia dies pro-
testing the equation of Heaven with family life: "Marriage on
earth seems such a counterfeit, / Mere imitation of the inimita-
ble: / In heaven we have the real and true and sure. / 'Tis there
they neither marry nor are given / In marriage, but are as the

angels" ("Pompilia," ll. 1807–1811). This angel dies repudiating all houses, but she owes a debt to them, for only her ordeal as daughter, wife, and mother has qualified her to become the poem's saint. Vehemently decrying the human and spiritual plight of the angel in the house while Rossetti's Blessed Damozel wistfully peers beyond the bar, the martyred Pompilia becomes Victorian literature's most convincing exemplum of this new angel's religious power.

In her own time the tragic and grotesque implications of the angel in the house did not go unexplored. Today she provides a convenient scapegoat for Victorian deficiencies. Walter E. Houghton sees her as little more than a ludicrous placebo for the religious doubts of floundering men: "Carlyle did not find his salvation in love. But many Victorians, consciously or otherwise, were able to quiet their anxious doubts by finding an angel in the house."[2] While they empathize with the angel's imprisonment, feminist critics have preferred loathing her to looking at her carefully. Beginning with Virginia Woolf, our characteristic response to her has been homicidal; some critics diffuse this impulse by regarding the angel herself as homicidal, undermining "masculine" energy and activity.[3] But in enshrining her as a symbol of cultural retrenchment, we dilute her iconoclastic power. This apparently quiescent figure is an implicit revolt against the patriarchal imagery of official Christianity, suggesting less a passive withdrawal from life than an active displacement by female of male religious icons. In their elevation of this female angel, men we dismiss too easily as reactionary were part of a broader surge toward the establishment of a new mythos.

In the Anglican Book of Common Prayer, angels barely ruffle the stern concentration on God. When they do appear, as in Collect 3: Of the Holy Angels (*Preface of Trinity Sunday*), they are anonymous manifestations of omnipotent divinity, held rigorously to their subordinate place: "Everlasting God, you have ordained and constituted in a wonderful order the ministries of angels and mortals: Mercifully grant that, as your holy angels always serve and worship in heaven, so by your appointment they may help and defend us here on earth through Jesus Christ our Lord, who lives and reigns with you and the Holy Spirit, for ever and ever."

In contrast to official precept, the domestic angel Leslie Stephen persisted in worshiping is pressed into no hierarchical order, but rises alone, free from any reigning divine "appointment." Her isolated being is its own sanction, whose theological implications that agnostic idolator Stephen appreciated as he transmitted for his children his epistolary prayer to his adored wife Julia: " 'And,' I said, 'you must let me tell you that I do and always shall feel for you something which I can only call reverence as well as love . . . You see I have not got any saints and you must not be angry if I put you in the place where my Saints ought to be.' She was for very sound reasons a better Saint for me than the Blessed Virgin."[4] These "very sound reasons" must include the fact that Stephen's "Saint" is not in the technical sense a saint at all, interceding for man with a higher Creator, but a solitary self-referential divinity who takes all saving power to herself. Julia's lone independence of God unites her reverential husband with a powerful community of heretical Victorian acolytes. However irritating this reverence must have made him as a husband and father, Stephen's religious allegiance is staunch and real, replacing decadent and masculine theological imagery with the freestanding if fenced-in image of a female God. The outworn love and agony of Christ on the Cross are translated into the vividly contemporary love and agony of the Angel in the House.

This shift of gender animates Victorian demonism as well. In medieval and Renaissance iconography, demons are so commonly masculine that Roland Frye includes "female-breasted demons with Medusa heads" among the sixteenth-century painter Alessandro Allori's iconographic distortions.[5] Like their angels, the devils of Milton and Blake are males with bisexual potential. But, like that of the angels, when conventional imagery lost authority, demonic iconography became predominantly female. Thus, in 1831 Sir Walter Scott's *Letters on Demonology and Witchcraft* sternly banish demonology from scriptural history. Because its lore can only embarrass a rationalistic modern civilization, Scott insists on the "connexion of modern demonology with the mythology of the ancients."[6] Later on, he further discredits demonology and witchcraft by associating them with older fairy lore. Purged of scriptural authority, demons find their proper home in a remote, half-imagined, pre-Christian world. Somewhat surprisingly, Scott welcomes them to imaginative literature as well: in "Maturin's Fatal Revenge" he praises Maturin's allegiance to real demons at the expense of Ann Radcliffe's rationalistic "machinery," and in "Remarks on *Frankenstein*" he offers the first wholehearted appreciation of the novel's pioneering exploration of the modern demonic.[7] For Scott—and here he speaks as a representative and cultivated man of his time—as demonology is stripped of scriptural authority it gains new imaginative life. The female demons who possess so much nineteenth-century art, the Liliths, Viviens, Faustines, Salomés, Lady Audleys, and the rest, suggest once again that when religious beings lose official credibility, they become women and flourish in the unsanctioned privacy of the general imagination.

It may not be surprising that female demons bear an eerie resemblance to their angelic counterparts, though characteristics that are suggestively implicit in the angel come to the fore in the demon. Their covert identification is motivated by their common cause: both are illicit invaders of traditional Anglican symbolism, announcing a new dispensation that is of pre-Christian antiquity. In the Socratic usage cited in the OED, "demon" need not designate an evil spirit alone but may incorporate divinity into its supernatural power: "[thing] of divine or demonic nature or character." The Soothsayer in Shakespeare's *Antony and Cleopatra* uses "demon" interchangeably with "angel": "Thy demon, that's thy spirit which keeps thee, is / Noble, courageous, high, unmatchable, / Where Caesar's is not. But near him, thy angel / Becomes afeard" (II, iii, 18–21).

In Victorian literature female demons often assume this broader identity, while male demons limit themselves to single-minded opposition to good. The female invasion of religious iconography is not a pallid surrogate for the real thing, but one agent of the radically new sort of terror, conflating divinity with demonism, that Peter Brooks locates in Matthew Lewis' *The Monk:* "at the dead end of the Age of Reason, the Sacred has reasserted its claim to attention, but in the most primitive possible manifestations, as taboo and interdiction, and ethics has implicitly come to be founded on terror rather than virtue."

In Victorian England, an age possessed by faith but deprived of dogma, any incursion of the supernatural into the natural became ambiguously awful because unclassifiable. As the primary agent of supernatural activity, woman hides within her virtue Brooks's divine-demonic terror, a nondenominational terror

René Girard defines as the source of all sacred experience: "For it is the violence whose very presence establishes the essential function of all myths and rituals: to disguise, to divert, and to banish disorder from the community."[8] The historical and sacred violence of our divine-demonic invader legitimizes her supernatural stature, explaining in part the homicidal feelings she has always inspired, in characters, authors, and readers alike, when she assumes her purely angelic guise.

Assiduous students of their own cultural symptoms, Victorian writers knew about the spiritual revolution their work furthered. Writing in 1834 but safely backdating his story to the era of another religious upheaval and transition, Bulwer-Lytton sketches the process wherein bizarre and violent female personifications inherit the religious credibility that has become detached from traditional forms. In *The Last Days of Pompeii* a doubting priest of Isis grinds his teeth and mutters the following unorthodox prayer: "O gods protect—hush! *are* there gods? Yes, there is one goddess, at least, whose voice I can command; and that is—Vengeance!"[9] Dante Gabriel Rossetti, who claimed not to consider himself a Christian, evoked with similar relief the goddesses of his outsize and spiritually ambiguous pantheon. For David Sonstroem, Rossetti's animating vision was religious, though its intensity was neither dogmatic nor aesthetic: "Rossetti's worship was genuine, and he worshiped, not Art, but the ladies he depicted."[10] John Ruskin, as devoutly non-Christian as Rossetti, wrote the following plaintive inscription on the flyleaf of the copy of *Queen of the Air* he gave to Rose La Touche, the fanatically pious young girl he loved hopelessly: "If she could but understand it, and if it was not quite so heathenish!" In Ruskin's opinion, Rosie was destroying herself by her allegiance to a life-devouring Christianity. *The Queen of the Air* (1869), which explicates and restores the omnipotence of "the great goddess Athena" in her many guises, is Ruskin's radical antidote to the deathgrip of conventional religion. In place of the old gods, he presents to a Rosie doomed not to understand, a giant pre-Christian goddess with the power to restore breath and substance to the religious impulse. As with other female icons, the salvation offered by Ruskin's Athena is not an insipid benediction of the status quo, but the afflatus of a revolutionary new-old force that liberates the sacred from convention while restoring its power of terror.

At various points in their writing such Victorians as Dickens, Thackeray, John Henry Newman, and Charlotte Brontë align this ambiguous woman-worship with an attraction toward the forbidden fruit of Catholic Mariolatry.[11] But at its most intense, the vision transcends Catholic iconography as well as Anglican, for despite her ostensible identity as wife and mother, woman is worshiped as a solitary, freestanding figure, released from her role as intermediary between Father and Son. For William Holman Hunt, the most formally devout of the Pre-Raphaelites, a woman hovers behind the iconic figure of Christ himself, not as mother or inspiration but as hidden alter-ego. There is a complex series of relationships among Hunt's "The Light of the World," "The Awakening Conscience," and "The Shadow of Death." "The Light of the World," probably the most widely known and beloved religious painting Victorian England produced, allegorically represents Christ's invitation to the darkened and suffocating soul. Hunt painted it in three different versions, each more famous and, in the opinion of some critics, each cruder than the next.[12] The delicate and suggestive work in Keble College, Oxford (1851–1853), was overwhelmed by a larger replica now hanging in Manchester, and finally by the painting's grandiose apotheosis in St. Paul's Cathedral. What is most striking about this adored image of Christ, painted by a devout Protestant though condemned as "papistical," is that its original models were two women, Elizabeth Siddal and Christina Rossetti. In the original version at Oxford (Figure 17) we can easily see a girlishness of form, even perhaps a certain amused archness of expression, beneath the traditional beard and robes of this eminently Victorian light of the world.

"The Light of the World" is generally seen as a companion piece to "The Awakening Conscience" (1853), whose fallen woman leaps to her feet as her sin and potential redemption are suddenly illuminated (Figure 18). She seems to be the fallen soul at whose door Christ is knocking.[13] In origin, at least, a female Christ offers illumination to a fallen woman. If we remember an earlier Protestant visitation, that of Milton's archangel Michael to a newly fallen Eden, where he blessed Adam with a vision of future history and redemption from which Eve was excluded, we begin to appreciate Hunt's inversion: in these companion pieces it is the oblivious singing man who is excluded from heavenly confidence. Both Hunt's Savior seeking entrance to the house and his fallen angel seeking a way out of it transmute traditional Christian iconography into a peculiarly Victorian typology of domestic female divinity.

The sudden epiphany of "The Awakening Conscience" is repeated in Hunt's later representation of Christ in "The Shadow of Death" (1870–1873). Conceived during Hunt's pilgrimage to the Holy Land, the painting represents a series of prefigurations in the life of Christ the carpenter of his coming ordeal and crucifixion. Like Hunt's fallen woman, his Christ springs suddenly to his feet at an apparent illumination that directs his gaze beyond the painting. (see Figure 19). He, too, springs away from a huddled and diminished figure behind him who appears oblivious of the thrilling portent. The wider spiritual vistas available to these large central figures are visible in the glimpse of a vernal landscape which frames them, but not their companions, alluringly. The environments of both are clotted with symbolic detail, alerting the viewer to their present or future perils.

The constricted position, gesture, and garments of the fallen woman remind us that she is a prisoner in her expensive house, while the expansive gesture with which Christ throws out his arms prefigures his crucifixion and the redemption that will ensue. Despite these and other differences, "The Shadow of Death" recapitulates key motifs from "The Awakening Conscience" so consistently that Hunt's fallen woman becomes a virtual type of his Christ. Once again, as in "The Light of the World," a woman lurks behind a reverent portrait of the Savior. Hunt's exactitude in reproducing traditional typological symbols did not preclude his appropriation of the female type that underlay so many Victorian incarnations of divinity. The shadowy female lurking within Hunt's traditional Christs may have guided Mary Braddon's seemingly perverse selection of him as the most demonic of the Pre-Raphaelites, the only one fitted to paint a portrait of her "Divinity of Hell," the plotting Lady Audley: "If Mr. Holman Hunt could have peeped into the pretty boudoir, I think the picture would have been photographed upon his brain to be reproduced by-and-by upon a bishop's half-length for the glorification of the Pre-Raphaelite brotherhood."[14] Braddon goes on to paint her demonic Lady in opulent purple prose, in a setting and attitude remote from the austerity of Hunt's strenuous Christ. Yet in seraphic or fallen

17. *William Holman Hunt, "The Light of the World."*

18. William Holman Hunt, "The Awakening Conscience."

19. William Holman Hunt, "The Shadow of Death."

guise, on bishop's half-length or in lurid sensationalism, Hunt's heroines as well as Braddon's energize the sacred for their age.

Victorian culture never quite domesticated its angels. In opposition to the startling eccentricities of Hunt and his fellow

Pre-Raphaelites, most Victorian genre painting limits woman's role to that of adored caretaker of a spreading family;[15] the plenitude of exhortations to potentially errant women, such as Sarah Lewis' *Woman's Mission,* Sarah Ellis' *Daughters, Wives,* and *Mothers of England,* Mrs. Octavius Frier Owen's *The Heroines of Domestic Life,* and Anna Jameson's *Characteristics of Women,* all equate her benevolent influence with her vicarious identity as family helpmate. Nevertheless, the most potent angels of Dickens and Thackeray, Victorian England's two most influential novelists, stand alone. In the alacrity with which they abandon or transcend all houses, they take strength from an older angelology which the Victorian age feminized but could never quite enclose.

Angels proliferate most freely in novels of the 1840s and 1850s. They collaborate in the shaping visions of Dickens and Thackeray, whose spectacular popularity at mid-century formulated and helped to create the mythologies of their culture. We have lost sympathy with those numinous elements of their novels the Victorians embraced, for among Dickens' early works the two angels into which the author pours his greatest romantic fervor have been received by the twentieth century with jeering distaste: Little Nell Trent in *The Old Curiosity Shop* and Agnes Wickfield in *David Copperfield.*[16] Little Nell and Agnes certainly seem displaced inhabitants of their novels, sentimentally overwrought abstractions in comparison to the denser human life that crowds around them. But if we consider them less as failed psychological portraiture than as emanations of an intensely felt and thoroughly non-Christian religion that Dickens shared with many of his most brilliant contemporaries, we might be able to revive their magnetism for their own time.[17]

We cannot doubt that Little Nell is an angel, but for roughly two-thirds of her novel she is also a houseless, doughty little pilgrim, leading her grandfather away from domesticity and temptation. When her exertions are finally rewarded by an idyllic Dickens cottage, she is more at home in the ancient and gloomy church adjoining it, where, like Browning's Bishop of St. Praxed's, she endlessly rehearses her own death. Influenced no doubt by Nell's own preference, we forget in focusing on her death that most of the novel is concerned with her life. In life Nell is not domestic, but solitary, stoical, and a leader: "The old man rose from his bed, his forehead bedewed with the cold sweat of fear, and, bending before the child as if she had been an angel messenger sent to lead him where she would, made ready to follow her. She took him by the hand and led him on."[18] Throughout the pilgrimage of Nell and her grandfather away from any home, the novel emphasizes both her loneliness—this angel is unaided and unimpeded by a superior divine creator; the religious rhetoric at the end assures us only of other angels waiting for her to join them—and her heroic persistence.

Until the end of her journey Nell is an angel not of death but of activity and strength of purpose: "Her momentary weakness past, the child again summoned the resolution which had until now sustained her, and endeavouring to keep steadily in view the one idea that they were flying from disgrace and crime, and that her grandfather's preservation must depend solely upon her firmness, unaided by one word of advice or any helping hand, urged him onward and looked back no more . . . There was no divided responsibility now; the whole burden of their two lives had fallen upon her, and henceforth she must think and act for both. " 'I have saved him,' she thought. 'In all dangers and distresses, I will remember that' " (p. 406). Here Nell is as energetic a leader as any Kingsleyan or Tennysonian hero crying "onward!" Her strength of will and sheer physical stamina align her with an older angelology than our own stereotype of the moribund Victorian maiden has acknowledged. Her possession of that most valuable angelic attribute, mobility, reminds us that in Renaissance iconography, guardian angels were habitually clad in robes that were girt up to allow rapid walking.[19] Those who have not read the novel recently may remember her death as a passive fading, like that of Paul Dombey, but in fact she seems to die of fatigue and perhaps infected feet. Her passivity in the final third of the novel is not her natural self, but a reaction to the transcendent activity of her earlier adventures.

Nell's characteristic attributes are mobility and power as a leader; these qualify her to fade into an angel's death. George Eliot seems to pay tribute to Little Nell's sturdiness in the following inspirational evocation of her own angel in *Silas Marner:* "In old days there were angels who came and took men by the hand and led them away from the city of destruction. We see no white-winged angels now. But yet men are led away from threatening destruction: a hand is put in theirs, which leads them forth gently towards a calm and bright land, so that they look no more backward; and the hand may be a little child's."[20] *Silas Marner* requires little active exertion of Eppie after her infantine toddle into Silas' house. In this gloss, more fitting for *The Old Curiosity Shop,* George Eliot emphasizes a journey rather than a domestic sanctuary, evoking, as Dickens did, an angel whose life is neither vicarious, domestic, nor passive. Here, too, to be an angel is to be mobile and a leader. George Eliot's characterization of her angel falters, as Dickens' does—perhaps an actual woman with the strength to do what they describe is too close to demonism for comfort—but Eliot, like her contemporaries, imagines an angelic force as an active shaping power.

*David Copperfield'*s Agnes is a more conventional angel in that she almost never ventures forth from the house she shares with her incompetent father and brightly transfigures for him. Agnes seems the paradigm of the immobilized angel defined above, though even she is scarcely dwelt on as a wife and mother, but as her stasis is greater than Little Nell's, so her power of transformation is more immediately magical. Early in the novel the adolescent David modulates with no transition from admiring her housekeeping to hymning her holy power: "The influence for all good, which she came to exercise over me at a later time, begins already to descend upon my breast. I love little Em'ly, and I don't love Agnes—no, not at all in that way—but I feel that there are goodness, peace, and truth, wherever Agnes is; and that the soft light of the coloured window in the church, seen long ago, falls on her always, and on me when I am near her, and on everything around."[21] With no more theological authority than the light that filters through the manmade church windows, Agnes is endowed with a virtually unlimited power of creation. From making tea she goes on to make order, to make abstractions (goodness, peace, and truth), and finally, to make David himself. On returning to her after many trials, he recognizes not only his true wife but the source of his being. Agnes' role in the novel makes sense only if we accept his tribute literally: "What I am, you have made me, Agnes. You should know best" (p. 916).

Admittedly Agnes has had some mundane help from the other women who embrace David in the novel, such as his actual mother, Peggotty, Aunt Betsey, and Dora, but it seems we are to see her as in some sense the creator of his soul. In moving at last from their embraces to Agnes', David moves from his mother (as she is refracted into various exaggerated facets of herself) to his Maker, a transition which explains the self-referential ardor of his marriage song: "Clasped in my embrace, I held the source of every worthy aspiration I had ever had; the centre of myself, the circle of my life, my own, my wife; the love of whom was founded on a rock!" (p. 938). One cannot believe that David clasps an actual woman as he pours out his gratitude to symbols and abstractions, but his last bride's unreality need not mean that he is clasping death. He seems rather to embrace the generative cause of his own perfection, revering in it a creative power that exceeds his own as novelist.

This sense of Agnes as the unmoved mover, pointing others upward though static herself, explains the somewhat unsettling conclusion in which David prayerfully imagines his own death. For as the novelist must painfully separate himself from the characters he has created, so the transcendent Agnes will let fall her own creation, the source of the novel whose source she is: "And now, as I close my task, subduing my desire to linger yet, these faces fade away. But one face, shining on me like a Heavenly light by which I see all other objects, is above them and beyond them all. And that remains . . . O Agnes, O my soul, so may thy face be by me when I close my life indeed; so may I, when realities are melting from me, like the shadows which I now dismiss, still find thee near me, pointing upward!" (p. 950). Agnes is to David as he is to his own novel. Her right to orchestrate his death comes from her magical role as maker and shaper of his life.

I emphasize the active strength of Little Nell and Agnes Wickfield, Dickens' two angel-women who are most disliked, to suggest their affinities with a larger literary myth of womanhood, whose angel is endowed with a force that supersedes traditional ideas of divinity. Lacking this broader context, such critics as Donald D. Stone have carelessly dismissed them as flaccid antidotes to the villains' dangerous vitality: "Where energy and willfulness seem to partake of evil, the Dickensian protagonists must gravitate toward figures and resolutions that resemble relaxation or atrophy of the will."[22] As women Nell and Agnes do seem curiously somnolent, defying all conventions of mimetic characterization, but as magic objects, they exude a power beyond the human. The active creating power they secrete can be defined by its absence in Quilp and Steerforth, their demonic antagonists, more dynamic than the angels but finally weaker and more willess than they.

Blazing with energy, the witty dwarf Daniel Quilp inhabits another sphere from shrinking Nell, who seems "to exist in a kind of allegory" (p. 56). Yet they die simultaneously, and their deaths define their respective powers.[23] Quilp drowns dramatically and pyrotechnically but alone, having barred his gate against possible rescuers. His death is a danse macabre in which all elements play wildly with his corpse; first the water

> toyed and sported with the ghastly freight, now bruising it against the slimy piles, now hiding it in mud or long rank grass, now dragging it heavily over rough stones and gravel, now feigning to yield it to its own element, and in the same action luring it away [until] it flung it on a swamp . . . And there it lay, alone. The sky was red with flame, and the water that bore it there had been tinged with the sullen light as it flowed along. The place the deserted carcase had left so recently, a living man, was now a blazing ruin. There was something of the glare upon its face. The hair, stirred by the damp breeze, played in a kind of mockery of death—such a mockery as the dead man himself would have revelled in when alive— about its head, and its dress fluttered idly in the night wind.   (p. 620)

Like Wordsworth's Lucy, or Emily Brontë's Heathcliff and A.G.A., Quilp dying is humanly alone while merging with a vital elemental company. His death is not separate and sacred: its passage through water, earth, fire, and air, the ironic motions of his corpse, all hark back to his life, whose uncontrolled demonic energy is subsumed into the "idle" vitality of mindlessness. As a corpse Quilp is an emblem of energy divested of will. His very activity becomes harmless when contrasted to Nell's steely determination.

The death of Little Nell, though it sent a greater shock through Victorian England than did the deaths of Wellington or Prince Albert, lacks the obligatory death scene. Kit and his rescuing company arrive to find her already a corpse; subsequently, her passing is narrated only in sketchy and muted flashback. Its impact comes not from any pathetic leave she takes of life, but from the fact that her corpse itself becomes a magic and magnetic object, pulling the travelers and villagers to it as she had once forced her grandfather "onward," becoming a totem not of peace, but of personal and divine power: "And still her former self lay there, unaltered in this change. Yes. The old fireside had smiled upon that same sweet face; it had passed like a dream through haunts of misery and care; at the door of the poor schoolmaster on the summer evening, before the furnace fire upon the cold wet night, at the still bedside of the dying boy, there had been the same mild lovely look. So shall we know the angels in their majesty, after death" (p. 654).

Like Agnes, Nell needs no violent transition between the mundane and the angelic: as with Quilp, Nell dead is Nell alive. But the dead Quilp's vitality remained in his insentient hair and his clothes; Nell's iconic force remains in her face, that part of our body most associated with consciousness and will.[24] Though Quilp's corpse has no audience but the reader, Nell's lives in the ambiguous personal-divine power it exudes upon awed beholders. Its burial is a spiritual event in the little village somewhat akin to the impact of another charismatic Victorian child, Bernadette of Lourdes. Legends spring up immediately over her grave: "A whisper went about among the oldest there, that she had seen and talked with angels; and when they called to mind how she had looked, and spoken, and her early death, some thought it might be so, indeed" (p. 658). This death differs from other sentimental deaths of Victorian children—Dick's in *Oliver Twist*, for example, or Beth's in *Little Women*—in that its emphasis is almost consistently impersonal. Nell's individuality matters less than does the impact of her death as a collective ceremony. Unlike Quilp's, her dying is a public, communally resonant activity in Dickens' novel, as it was in the real world of his readers. It has become impossible for us to weep at the death of a girl who was never alive, but we should not forget, as Nell's first audience could not, the determination which translated the privacy and passivity of dying into public history and ritual.

Like Little Nell, Agnes, David Copperfield's "good angel," has a demonic male opposite: David's "bad angel," that seducer of souls, James Steerforth. Like Quilp, Steerforth provides the novel's energy and wit, but his energy, too, is essentially in chaos: "As to fitfulness, I have never learnt the art of binding myself to any of the wheels on which the Ixions of these days are

turning round and round. I missed it somehow in a bad appren-
ticeship, and now don't care about it" (p. 382). For all his verve,
Steerforth beckons David toward his own indolence and passivity: "We'll drink . . . the lilies of the valley that toil not, neither
do they spin, in compliment to me—the more shame for me!"
(p. 353). Passivity rather than passion impels his flight with little
Em'ly: he yields in spite of himself rather than leading. Like
Quilp, he dies the appropriate death of drowning amid a storm's
mindless energy. His corpse, too, is an emblem of his essential
passivity, evoking most improbably his recurrent motif of placid
sleep: "I saw him lying with his head upon his arm, as I had
often seen him lie at school" (p. 866).

Steerforth's emblem is indolent sleep; Agnes has a single op-
posing motif. At key moments she smiles a sad, enigmatic smile
and shakes her head: "She smiled rather sadly, I thought, and
shook her head" (p. 426); "She only shook her head; through her
tears I saw the same sad and quiet smile" (p. 916). As a hu-
manizing device this is not much, but iconographically it does
indicate Agnes' self-contained power of will: her gesture is a
recurrent act of resistance. Detached from her impossibly
sanctimonious dialogue, it defines a certain solitary strength, a
disciplined and strenuous defiance we have not looked for in
Victorian angels. Like the earnest and resolute novelist David
becomes, Agnes reminds us that the divine as well as the human
creator's power is not a release but a rigorous discipline of will.
Here and throughout the novel the power of Agnes rests in her
face, recalling again (at least in theory) the union of her magic
with her consciousness and individuality. Steerforth, like the
manic Quilp, is our center of psychosexual interest, but his cozy
sleeping death defines his passivity as the other pole of Agnes'
active stillness. Like the corpse of Nell, Agnes is not a human
but a magnetic object, the angelic power that generates and
orders the novel's vital world.

Demonic Companies

Unlike those of Dickens, even the angelic heroines of
Thackeray belong in the section on demons. Dickens' angel heroines are the polar opposite of his male demons, but the interchange between Thackeray's female angels and demons is so
fluid that both lack definition apart from each other. In *Vanity*

Fair it is not until "the end of the third volume" that Amelia achieves her unenviable apotheosis as angel in the house; she gains it primarily through the prodding of the "demonic" Becky Sharp. Becky herself could achieve the demonic apotheosis her alleged murder of Jos Sedley creates only because Amelia angelically brought the two together in the first place. Without their interdependent friendship, their angelic and demonic essences could not come to flower; in Dickens' iconography the identities of Little Nell and Quilp, Agnes and Steerforth, were immune from contamination by their opposites.

Thackeray believed in female angels as fervently as Dickens did, but he avoided Dickens' problem of characterizing a superhuman agent as a psychologically nonexistent icon. In Thackeray's view, the very fact that angels possess female psychology as he observed it in his possessive mother, his insane wife, and the fiercely self-sacrificial Jane Brookfield makes their influence all the more irresistible, for in them Heaven's power is clothed in earth's psychic avarice. In 1852 he wrote of his mother: "When I was a boy at Larkbeare, I thought her an Angel and worshipped her. I see but a woman now, O so tender so loving so cruel."[25] As his subsequent relationship to his mother proves, his realization that she is "but a woman" does not strip her of angelic power, which is, traditionally, tender, loving, and (when denied) cruel. The excruciating duality of her identity is captured in *The History of Henry Esmond* when Henry, no longer a boy, experiences a similar impulse of iconoclasm upon returning to Rachel: "goddess no more, for he knew of her weaknesses; and by thought, by suffering, and that experience it brings, was older now than she; but more fondly cherished as woman perhaps than ever she had been adored as divinity."[26] But just a few pages later, as Thackeray himself did, Henry restores his angel, weak womanhood and all, to her rightful title: " 'I think the angels are not all in heaven,' Mr. Esmond said . . . so for a few moments Esmond's beloved mistress came to him and blessed him" (p. 156).

Thackeray's early faith in angels emerges in the topic he proposed to the Trinity College Debating Society, dated 27 November 1829: "Has woman, since the fall, been the cause of more good or evil to mankind?" Like many of his contemporaries, he seems to have displaced woman from Eden's blight, for his own answer was "Good." As well as illustrating the ambiguously theological terms in which early Victorian young men discussed womanhood, distinguishing her condition from that of indisputably fallen "mankind," Thackeray's topic illuminates the spiritual urgency within the apparent worldliness of his characterizations. From a more strictly aesthetic perspective, Joan Garrett-Goodyear defines his unique interfusion of psychological tension into traditional literary typology: "Thackeray sees very clearly how conceptions of character which are social and literary clichés serve as expressions of irrational psychological energy."[27] Thackeray's angelology brings Dickens' vision to earth without secularizing it. The power of his women comes not from their transcendence of human eccentricity, but from their more potent compound of the human, the angel, and the real woman as Thackeray understood her.

Blessed with the wit, intelligence, and acumen of their author, Becky Sharp, Blanche Amory, and Beatrix Castlewood are even more attractive demons than Quilp and Steerforth for, unlike the men, they forge lives in full realization of their humiliating dependency. Perhaps it is this social self-knowledge that makes these heroines demons, for that, in Thackeray's terms, is what they are. Thackeray is free with theological celebrations of his angels, but, unlike many of his contemporaries, he is shy about invoking the powers of hell directly. His stock euphemism for "demon" is "siren" or "mermaid." His best-known description of the mermaid comes toward the end of *Vanity Fair*, in which the showman exhibits Becky's secret life in decorative metaphor: "They look pretty enough when they sit upon a rock, twanging their harps and combing their hair, and sing, and beckon to you to come and hold the looking-glass; but when they sink into their native element, depend on it those mermaids are about no good, and we had best not examine the fiendish marine cannibals, revelling and feasting on their wretched pickled victims."[28]

The mermaid is a less fiendish apparition in Thackeray's illustrations to chapter titles from *Vanity Fair* and *Pendennis* (Figures 20, 21, 22), but here, too, she is "about no good." In Thackeray's best novels no character walks about "in a kind of allegory," as Little Nell does, but the illustrations often provide allegorical glosses on the import of his rich material. Whether he knew it or not, Thackeray's recurrent emblem of the mermaid has an iconographic history which reveals a great deal

20. 21. 22.
Three illustrations of the
mermaid who teases her way
into Thackeray's iconography.

21.

22.

about the mythology of womanhood as he and his unorthodox contemporaries understood it.

Traditional demons are generally male; however, an old and widespread tradition in Christian iconography makes a "serpent with a 'lady visage,' " as Roland Frye calls her, the agent of the fall. This hybrid creature is as close as we come to a Christian female demon. No doubt she was originally intended to point up woman's responsibility for the fall of the race, but over the years she moves beyond the garden, her hybrid form becoming the standard type of female demon, while her mixed allegiances to official Christianity, ancient legend, and modern monstrosity define woman's anomalous position in the spiritual hierarchy. Frye associates this creature with Frau Welt, a female figure of sin with an animal's lower torso, and with the serpent-woman who guards the gates of Hell in Book II of *Paradise Lost*. Thackeray's formal convictions exempted woman from the fall, but Becky Sharp and her Victorian sisters remind us that this "serpent with a lady visage" had a longer, stronger fictional life than did her male counterparts in heaven and hell.

In her origin, this serpent-woman from whom the mermaid derives has a life more triumphant than that of the female demon who crawls through Christian iconography. According to Merlin Stone, she begins as an oracle of the earliest universal divinity, a female God. For Stone the serpent is not originally phallic, but the emblem of a prophesying female divinity whom the archaeologist Stephen Langdon described in 1915: "He wrote that the Goddess known as Nina, another form of the name Ianna, perhaps an earlier one, was a serpent goddess in the most ancient Sumerian periods. He explained that, as Nina, She was esteemed as an oracular deity and an interpreter of dreams, recording this prayer from a Sumerian tablet: 'O Nina of priestly rites, Lady of precious decrees, Prophetess of Deities art Thou,' and commenting that, 'The evidence points to an original serpent goddess as the interpreter of dreams of the unrevealed future.' "[29]

It may be that the origin of this demon was divine. In Victorian iconography, which freely adapts traditional types to its own vision, the mermaid carries the broader spiritual resonance of her ancestor the serpent-woman. Her hybrid nature, her ambiguous status as creature, typify the mysterious, broadly and evocatively demonic powers of womanhood in general. As Burne-Jones imagines her (Figures 23 and 1), the mermaid arrests us because nonhumanity in human form looks out at us. In his verbal portrait of Leonardo's *La Gioconda* Pater achieves the same shocking effect in prose of a sea creature looking out of a woman's face. The painter need not show the tail for us to see that human moral categories are inadequate to her preternatural intensity.

Her powers underlie the intense popularity of Shakespeare's "mermaidlike" Ophelia in Victorian iconography. Dante Gabriel Rossetti, John Everett Millais, and Arthur Hughes painted Ophelia directly, and her presence infuses such unlikely prose contexts as the ending of George Eliot's *The Mill on the Floss*, transmuting into myth Eliot's obsession with the figure of the drowning Mary Wollstonecraft, and Thackeray's distraught let-

23. *Edward Burne-Jones, "The Depths of the Sea."*

ter to his mother describing his wife's attempt to drown herself (Ray, p. 256). All these visions emanate from the nineteenth century's attraction to the demonic, otherworldly mermaid. In her mysterious hybrid nature whose humanity is only an appearance the mermaid becomes an emblem of Victorian womanhood generally, promising human repose but exercising preterhuman powers. This emblem of womanhood tells us as much about our angels as it does about our demons. In the final illustration to *The Old Curiosity Shop* (Figure 24), Nell floating among the angels looks as mermaidlike as Thackeray's vixens. Even George Orwell's denunciation of Agnes as "the real legless angel of Victorian romance" touches on this kinship to hybrid monstrosity. While male demons in Victorian literature have a vibrant but limited existence, the female demon in her incarnation as a mermaid spreads her net more widely, taking to herself the anomalous life of the mysteriously distinct female species.

In Thackeray's *The History of Henry Esmond* the interaction between angel and demon is clearest because Rachel and Beatrix Castlewood are mother and daughter; as we are told several times, they appear to others like sisters as well. The rhetoric of Esmond the narrator as he shuttles between Rachel and Beatrix, kneeling reverentially to each in turn until his startling marriage to his foster mother Rachel, does everything to dissociate the nobly spiritual mother from her vain and worldly daughter. Actually, the affinities between them are fundamental, as Thackeray characterizes them and as they combine against the novel's larger historical framework.[30]

Mother and daughter spend a large part of the novel denying each other. Beatrix is possessed by a self-loathing that takes this form: "I am not good, Harry: my mother is gentle and good like an angel. I wonder how she should have had such a child" (p. 444). But, among other things, they share a feminist despair at their enforced dependency on little men. In thrall to her boorish husband, Rachel takes revenge upon young Henry: "The men who wrote your books . . . your Horaces, and Ovids, and Virgils, as far as I know of them, all thought ill of us, as all the heroes they wrote about used us basely. We were bred to be slaves always; and even of our own times, as you are still the only lawgivers, I think our sermons seem to say that the best woman is she who bears her master's chains most gracefully. 'Tis a pity there are no nunneries permitted by our church:

24. *Little Nell transported by angels.*

Beatrix and I would fly to one, and end our days in peace there away from you" (p. 134).

This desperate sisterhood never takes shape, but its impetus finds new form in the equally desperate mockery of the adult Beatrix, whose longing for power is as intense, and as frustrated, as was her mother's for seclusion: "Why am I not a man? I have ten times [my brother's] brains, and had I worn the—well, don't let your ladyship be frightened—had I worn a sword and periwig instead of this mantle and commode, to which nature has condemned me . . . I would have made our name talked about . . . I solemnly vow, own, and confess, that I want a good husband. Where's the harm of one? My face is my fortune. Who'll come?—buy, buy, buy!" (p. 386). Beatrix's quest for power and Rachel's for peace are accompanied by a common helpless scorn of the men who are their world's only providers.

This scorn finds one shared target in poor Tom Tusher, the sycophantic Bishop of Castlewood, to whom Rachel is rumored to be engaged after her husband's death but to whom Beatrix must subdue herself in the end. Like Esmond himself, Tusher is alternately despised and knelt to by both women, forging an implicit if reluctant bond between them. Moreover, the *Spectator* parody which Esmond writes under the name of Oedipus ostensibly mocks Beatrix's worldliness, but it conflates her identity with her mother's by making of the Beatrix-figure a "young widow" named Jocasta and garnishing the dialogue with a florid compliment associating her with an angel. Thus, in exposing the daughter, Henry slyly creates her as a composite figure with her mother, incriminating them both in a bitingly satiric counterpoint to his love. Their shared resentment against the men who mock, adore, and control them may fuel the intense jealousy which even Beatrix acknowledges brings them together: "[Mamma] is jealous; all women are. I sometimes think that is the only womanly quality I have" (p. 444).

Jealousy may be womanly, but in the Old Testament at least, it is also God's paramount attribute. While mother and daughter form a tacit sisterhood, knit as well as divided by jealous rage and helpless awareness of dispossession, Thackeray compensates for their social powerlessness by making them the central poles of power in the novel. From their domain at Castlewood, Rachel and Beatrix overwhelm not only Henry Esmond, the novel's narrator and ostensible hero, but also the great men who try to form him—and the unreliable pageant of history itself.

Thackeray dismissed his sanctimonious narrator by calling him a "prig," but compared to the two women who dominate his life, Henry's very identity seems as uncertain as his degree of nobility.[31] As a young orphan of dubious status, he complains that he has "a father and no father." He also has a self and no self, as we see in his convoluted autobiography, whose chapter titles in the first person introduce a narrative about himself in the third person which is dotted with occasional emotional outbursts breaking into the first person. With his fractured identity, which alternates between admitting himself as "I" and displacing it as "he," Henry finds an appropriate foster father, not in the beefy Lord Castlewood, but in the slippery Jesuit Father Holt, whom he refers to in moments of emotion simply as "Father." But once again, Henry has a father and no father: in his quixotic defense of the Pretender, Holt dissolves his identity into a ludicrous series of disguises and progressively incoherent intrigues. At his death, a disenchanted Henry gives the "Mr. Holt" he once worshiped a brutal epitaph: "Sure he was the most unlucky of men: he never played a game but he lost it; or engaged in a conspiracy but 'twas certain to end in defeat" (p. 511).

In his compulsive disguises, meaningless intrigue, and utter defeat, Father Holt stands for the futility of a history governed by fathers. The novel erects the great men of the age, possible Carlylean heroes and father-figures, only to expose their mean futility: Addison, Swift, Marlborough, and finally the Pretender himself, ascend the stage only to be hissed off.[32] The central section describing Henry's military experience in the War of the Spanish Succession is narrated in a deliberately undramatic, disjointed, incoherent style, made manifest by the intensity of his intermittent visits to Castlewood. The coherence of the woman's world exposes history's blunders and gives meaning as well to Henry's fractured selfhood.

Thackeray's novel cannot be divided as neatly as Tolstoy's can into the fragmentation of war and public life and the human, domestic continuity of peace. At the climax of the novel history invades the family: the Pretender, to whose succession the Castlewood family has devoted itself, hides his ineptly disguised self among them to sue for the Crown. In this episode, where Rachel and Beatrix seem most in conflict, they are in fact most in collusion as they bring down this Prince from history to his knees. Seeing in him her one remaining path to glory, Beatrix seductively distracts him from his great mission. Rachel turns bitterly against her former idol and, to save the family honor, sends Beatrix away. The Prince, as unstable of purpose as the other great men, lets his chance at the throne slip away as he awkwardly pursues the exiled Beatrix. The Cause is lost, but at Rachel's instigation and with Beatrix as lure the family has triumphed. Between them, with Henry as their agent, the demonically seductive Beatrix and the angelically censorious Rachel expel this royal interloper and, by implication, history itself. Our little colony migrates to a savage but pastless and partyless America where, conflict-ridden as they always were, the values of Castlewood preside in the new world.

The overpowering influence Rachel and Beatrix exert on Henry's stricken identity, and their final expulsion of History itself as the Pretender's great Cause embodies it, dramatize the transcendent power of angelic-demonic womanhood in the face of what Victorians like Carlyle saw as life's essence: history and its pageant of great men. Thackeray's social acuteness does not elide the dispossession of actual women—in fact, I can think of no mid-Victorian novel more incisively outspoken than *Esmond* is on this subject, perhaps because the material is safely backdated to the turn of the eighteenth century—but the novel's myth displaces generals, kings, and causes by placing motivating and shaping power in the hands of women. Jealous of each other, irritated by each other, ashamed of their complex kinship, Thackeray's angels and demons are neither sentimental nor abstract: in the power of their complicity they are truly angelic and demonic because as women they are real.

Chafing at the demands of both virtue and vice, Beatrix Castlewood is probably Thackeray's most impressive female character. With her undercurrent of self-torment, her bitterness at being a queen without a country, she strikes a more complicated note than does the infallibly high-spirited Becky Sharp. Since Thackeray never illustrated *Esmond,* we have no demure emblem of Beatrix as a mermaid to guide our responses. Instead, there is his famous prose portrait of her descending the stairs in all her glory; in case we miss the significance of this tableau, it is repeated three times at key moments in the novel. As one might expect, du Maurier's illustrations to *Esmond* (1868), which were used in most nineteenth-century editions, make the most of Beatrix's majestic descent. Dickens seems to have appropriated it to his own ends in *Hard Times* in Mrs. Sparsit's florid vision of Louisa descending a more starkly abstract and allegorical staircase: "She erected in her mind a mighty Staircase, with a dark pit of shame and ruin at the bottom; and down these stairs, from day to day and hour to hour, she saw Louisa coming."[33]

Louisa's staircase is an emblem of hopeless doom, but in Beatrix's brilliant descent her demonism is inseparable from triumphant power. Her covert alliance with her angel-mother, who must have seemed to du Maurier so pure that as illustrator he barely bothers with her, furthers this pervasive power. Like Beatrix, Victorian female demons generally provide the active momentum for the works in which they figure; and, like her, they keep dangerous if hidden company with their angelic counterparts. In fact, Thackeray's perpetually falling Beatrix seems a looking-glass image of Dante's celestial rising Beatrice whom Victorian mythography so devoutly reanimated. The pictorialism of Beatrix Castlewood's florid descent finds its holy counterpart in the self-inspired ascent of Rossetti's Beata Beatrix. Male demons lack this mobility, though they exude at least as much pyrotechnical bravado, and are thus more readily banished from the works in which they appear.

We have seen the relative willessness and dissociation of Quilp and Steerforth from the female angelic powers shaping their novels. The case of Heathcliff, who unquestionably dominates Emily Brontë's *Wuthering Heights* in absence as well as presence, is more complex, in part because he is the creation of a female author, leading some feminist critics to find autobiography in his outcast rage.[34] Yet, for all his symbolic resonance, in his attempts to transform the genealogies of the Earnshaws and the Lintons, Heathcliff is more ineffectual even than Dickens' demons. If we detach him from the eloquence with which the other characters talk *about* him, he becomes virtually amorphous. He has none of Beatrix's self-assertive and flamboyant drive; his essential reticence leads him to two feebly ironic denials of a demonism projected onto him entirely by women.

"Is Mr. Heathcliff a man?" asks silly Isabella Linton, who has become Mrs. Heathcliff to her doom. "If so, is he mad? And if not, is he a devil?"[35] As Heathcliff is dying, Nelly Dean plays variations upon Isabella's wondering question: "Is he a ghoul, or a vampire?" (p. 260). Not only does Heathcliff disdain to answer, but his avarice to possess Catherine makes the question irrelevant to him. His demonism is the creation and obsession of women, most explicitly of Nelly and Isabella, but, most memorably, of Catherine as well. Though she never uses the word, her great set piece, with its anti-heavenly elemental imagery of fire and rock, is the novel's most resonant creation of Heathcliff as a demon. Her resounding cry, "I *am* Heathcliff," suggests a Svengali-like possessive magic. But unlike Svengali, Heathcliff never corroborates this power. Nor does he agree that she is he or he her: he uses only the conventional idioms of romantic love which cast her as his "life," his "soul." In short, Heathcliff seems less a fully realized demon than a stricken Frankenstein monster, unable to live independently of the women who create him.

The choric power of the novel's women to half-create Heathcliff in their image was reinforced by the commentary of a real woman: in her Preface to the posthumous 1850 edition Charlotte Brontë insists that only his regard for Hareton and Nelly (which does not run very deep) redeems him from being "a man's shape animated by demon life—a Ghoul—an Afreet" (p. 12). Because neither the novel nor Heathcliff confirms this projection, and since such language is parodied by the fanatical Joseph, who calls everyone in sight a devil, we see Heathcliff's amorphousness shaped by a demonic creative force that is essentially female, operating free of Mr. Lockwood's nervous self-qualification: "I bestow my own attributes over-liberally on him" (p. 15).

Dickens' male demons are passive creatures compared to their opponents, female angels. In an ostensibly naturalistic historical context Thackeray ascribes angelic and demonic powers exclusively to subtly related women. Emily Brontë's Heathcliff barely exists without the demonic creative force of the women who imagine him. We have not yet seen how angelic and demonic powers work when they distribute themselves exclusively among men, as they do in Robert Louis Stevenson's popular parable, *Dr. Jekyll and Mr. Hyde.*

To begin with, like most Victorian men, Dr. Jekyll is no angel. The self he opposes to the monstrous Mr. Hyde is merely "the old Henry Jekyll, that incongruous compound of whose reformation and improvement I had already learned to despair."[36] Lacking angelic powers, he is no magic shaper of society, but can boast only his prominence within it: Dr. Jekyll's "was a name at least very well known and often printed" (p. 6), a useful credential in the gentleman's clubs of Stevenson's London, but a poor one against the devil.

Compared most often to an ape, a monkey, or a child, the dwarfish Mr. Hyde is less vividly present than was Dickens' Quilp, from whom he seems to have derived. Like Heathcliff, this monstrous creature is most alive as a compound of what others imagine him to be, but he lacks Heathcliff's suggestive intensity. Hyde's association, not only with apes and children but with criminality and the working-class district of Soho, detach him from demonism proper to equate him with those "elements" Victorian men feared would unravel the fabric of social life. Fears of apes, of workers, of criminals, were too palpably distinct for myth. Hyde's dwarfishness reduces his impact as Quilp's does, especially if we recall Milton's Satan in his initial Leviathan-like majesty, which in Victorian England seems the legacy only of such women as the statuesque Beatrix, Ruskin's Queen of the Air, the Amazonian personifications and goddesses of the Pre-Raphaelites and Watts, and even, perhaps, of George Eliot's large-souled outsize heroines. The equation of an exclusively male demonism with dwarfishness indicates the dimensions of its power.

Both Jekyll and Hyde are further diminished by their extraordinary disjunction from each other. Rachel and Beatrix were mother and daughter and, to discerning observers, "sisters." Jekyll and Hyde inhabit the same body, but there is no visible kinship between them: not only do their voices and statures differ, but the cultivated hand of Jekyll and the hairy one of Hyde associate them with different species. A woman's face is the source of her spiritual power, but the careful lawyer Mr. Utterson stares straight into Hyde's face but finds no trace of his friend Jekyll there. This fragmentation of divine/demonic man into two distinct faces represents a radical fragmentation of his spiritual power. As with the divorce between Oscar Wilde's beautiful Dorian Gray and his increasingly monstrous portrait, Jekyll is so helplessly disjoined from his demonic anti-self that both are fatally enfeebled. Indeed, Dr. Jekyll insists, the two have nothing in common but their memories and their handwriting. Demonic man does not include divinity in his nature, and is thus a poor stunted counterpart to grandly demonic womanhood.

The identities of Jekyll and Hyde are ultimately determined by the secular code of Stevenson's London, its gentleman's clubs and its thieves' dens. The gulf separating "Dr." from "Mr." is wider than that between Thackeray's Heaven and Hell: "A moment before I had been safe of all men's respect, wealthy, beloved—the cloth laying for me in the dining-room at home; and now I was the common quarry of mankind, hunted, homeless, a known murderer, thrall to the gallows" (p. 96). As identity here is social, Hyde's crimes are appropriately antisocial. He tramples a child, who emerges unhurt (a horrible act largely because of the shock it brings to decorous passersby), he strikes a woman (breaking another gentleman's taboo), and finally murders "an aged beautiful gentleman with white hair," who (most horrible) turns out to be a distinguished M.P. He is also guilty of unspecified but undignified "pleasures" and such "ape-like tricks" as destroying the letters and portrait of Jekyll's revered father and scrawling blasphemous graffiti in his Bible.

The novel's true temptation is not demonism, but the "pleasures" Jekyll wanted to indulge through the medium of Hyde (p. 86). Like Milton's Satan, Thackeray's Beatrix and her kin embark on an earnest quest for power. In contrast, these "pleasures," aligned with the forbidden boyish gaiety that animates both Mr. Hyde and Dorian Gray, equate demonism with a nostalgia for boyhood and a boy's escape. The female demonic knows no social boundaries and no fond regrets. Instead, in its purest form it is animated by a longing not for childhood but for transcendence.

In this context, Algernon Charles Swinburne's divine-demonic pantheon of goddesses and personifications is not a perverse departure but a crystallization of a myth central to the Victorian imagination. Like Rossetti's Astarte Syriaca and the rest, like Ruskin's Queen of the Air, like Thackeray's jealously controlling women, Swinburne's giantesses may originate in boyish memories of a mother's primacy, but they embody the adult's longing for a new theology. The sea, that "great sweet mother" who dominates Swinburne's canon and seems to provide the paradigm for his carnivorous goddesses,[37] has much in common with Thackeray's transcendentally equipped mother, "so tender so loving so cruel," though Swinburne's language is a more explicit blend of the erotic with the theological:

> Fair mother, fed with the lives of men,
>   Thou art subtle and cruel of heart, men say.
> Thou hast taken, and shalt not render again;
>   Thou art full of thy dead, and cold as they.
> But death is the worst that comes of thee;
> Thou art fed with our dead, O mother, O sea,
> But when hast thou fed on our hearts? or when,
>   Having given us love, hast thou taken away?
>
> "The Triumph of Time," ll. 289–296

It may be splitting hairs to find in this image of an inces-tuously biting, loving sea-mother a grandeur missing from the perverse "pleasures" of Mr. Hyde and Dorian Gray, but Swin-burne is too full of awe to cast his little self in the role of demon. That honor belongs to the female, embodiment of a transcen-dent new/old power reclaiming rule over the world. Though his Venus (in "Laus Veneris"), Proserpine, Faustine, and Dolores would suit the taste of Mr. Hyde at his silliest, their demonic assault on conventional male gods is more earnestly iconoclastic than Mr. Hyde's scribbled blasphemies. Dolores, or Notre-Dame des Sept Douleurs, swells from sadomasochistic reverie to ancient goddess newborn, ingesting heaven and hell to restore the true demonic:

> What ailed us, O gods, to desert you
>   For creeds that refuse and restrain?
> Come down and redeem us from virtue,
>   Our Lady of Pain.   (ll. 277–280)

Hertha, Swinburne's later and more austere world-goddess, is on an identical mission to reclaim the world from inadequate divinities: "before God was, I am." The pleasures these personi-fications inspire are ancillary to their divine-demonic ambitions. Nothing in the poems questions their demonic authenticity, nor are their powers dissipated in antisocial "tricks." Like Thack-eray, but more explicitly, Swinburne equates the loving pain his women inflict with the death of worn-out gods and the advent of a new dispensation superior in its authority because it is also an ancient one. Male demons in Victorian literature may be ex-emplary citizens or the bane of exemplary citizens, but they lack the theological urge to inaugurate a new mythos.

In short, when they are demons at all and not simply poor and angry, men are demonic in the narrow, or exclusively evil, sense, not in the broader usage that incorporates the divine. Mr. Hyde is an unrecognizable alien. The good citizen is too limited to know his equally limited double, while an angel-woman, free from the boundaries that determine the citizen, is also free to acknowledge her intimacy with demonism. The best Gothic and sensation novelists perceived these affinities intuitively: with no Swinburnian ado, their female demons appropriate characteris-tics such writers as Dickens had reserved for their angels. A well-known passage in *The Old Curiosity Shop* defines the magic accord among Nell, her mother, and her grandmother, implying that angelic power is deathless while it compounds the tragedy of Nell's early death: "If you have seen the picture-gallery of any one old family, you will remember how the same face and figure—often the fairest and slightest of them all—come upon you in different generations; and how you trace the same sweet girl through a long line of portraits—never growing old or changing—the Good Angel of the race—abiding by them in all reverses—redeeming all their sins—" (p. 627).

This portrait gallery reminds us that the angel is magically free from change; in *Bleak House*, too, Esther's scars vanish magically in the course of the novel, restoring her dear original face. Thackeray's Esmond insists similarly that Rachel Castlewood never ages or changes. These imaginary portraits also recall a point touched on before, which Alexander Welsh was the first to note, that the power of Dickens' angels is carried in their faces. An angel seems unlike the paradigmatic woman defined in my previous chapters in that she resists continual mutation: her face is her emblem of her kinship with eternity.

But this touchstone of angelic power belongs to demons as well. Dorian Gray's false possession of it reminds us how far he is from being either true angel or demon, since his unnaturally changeless face is as discrepant from his increasingly monstrous portrait as Dr. Jekyll was from Mr. Hyde. In contrast, J. S. LeFanu's tender vampire Carmilla, leaning over the bed of her child-victim, bears a purity of face as real as Nell's: "to my surprise, I saw a solemn, but very pretty face looking at me from the side of the bed. It was that of a young lady who was kneeling, with her hands under the coverlet. I looked at her with a kind of pleased wonder, and ceased whimpering."[38]

Carmilla's indelible face hovers over the sleeping child like those of Dickens' motherly angels as Welsh describes them (p. 172), except that this angel proceeds to bite the child sharply in the breast. Her behavior of course is more appropriate to Swinburne's than to Dickens' divinities, but the loving and cruel Carmilla absorbs the power of both. When the still-unsuspecting narrator is shown a seventeenth-century portrait of one Mircalla, Countess Karnstein, she cries: "It was quite beautiful; it was startling; it seemed to live. It was the effigy of Carmilla!" (p. 299). Like Nell and unlike Dorian Gray, Carmilla exemplifies the magic union of art and life, the speaking portrait and the living face. Here, though, the conceit of the Good Angel of the race has turned literal and become demonic, for Carmilla (or, as she calls herself in other incarnations, Millarca or Mircalla) has a vampire's power to survive generations, her cannibalistic loves keeping her face intact. Carmilla's literal transmutation of angelic attributes may have given Victorian readers a secret relief that Little Nell died so young.

The shared motif of the eternal face shows that the angel can modulate almost imperceptibly into a demon, while retaining her aura of changelessness. Even Beatrix Castlewood clings to the source of her mother's magic when she cries, "My face is my fortune." In his imaginary portrait of Leonardo's *La Gioconda* Walter Pater uncovers the experience of the vampire within the Madonna's placid face. In a less canonical work, Mary Elizabeth Braddon's sensation novel *Lady Audley's Secret*, to whose shrewd heroine the terms "demon" and "mermaid" are liberally applied, we find Lady Audley's magic power radiating out of her face: "Wherever she went she seemed to take joy and brightness with her. In the cottages of the poor her fair face shone like a sunbeam . . . For you see, Miss Lucy Graham [as she initially calls herself] was blessed with that magic power of fascination, by which a woman can charm with a word or intoxicate with a smile" (p. 4).

Braddon employs with scholarly precision angelic iconography for demonic purposes throughout the novel. Like Dickens and LeFanu, Pater and Wilde, she paints an imaginary portrait, one unlike Dickens' and LeFanu's in that it captures her heroine's demonic anger and rage for power—in other words, her soul—while unlike Wilde's, it stays true to an angel face: "It was so like, and yet so unlike. It was as if you had burned strange-colored fires before my lady's face, and by their influence brought out new lines and new expressions never seen in it before. The perfection of feature, the brilliancy of coloring, were there; but I suppose the painter had copied quaint medieval monstrosities until his brain had grown bewildered, for my lady, in his portrait of her, had something of the aspect of a beautiful fiend" (p. 47). "So like, and yet so unlike" are the female angel and the demon. It requires only the fire of an altered palette to bring out the contours of the one latent in the face of the other.[39] Lady Audley and her mermaidlike sisters need not show a tail or awaken to a suddenly hairy hand: their angelic faces and natures become demonic with a shift of the viewer's perspective. As sacred objects rather than human beings, they assault the sources of power, sexual, social, and divine, whose new vulnerability is woman's new life. Iconoclastic in her essence, the angel becomes a demon by realizing the implications of her being. In Harrison Ainsworth's historical novel *The Lancashire Witches* (1848) two upstanding Jacobeans debate a topic that unnerved many of Ainsworth's contemporaries, the affinity between womanhood and demonism:

> "But since you are so learned in the matter of witchcraft, resolve me, I pray you, how it is that women are so much more addicted to the practice of the black art than our own sex."
>
> "The answer to the inquiry hath been given by our British Solomon," replied Potts, "and I will deliver it to you in his own words. 'The reason is easy,' he saith; 'for as that sex is frailer than man is, so it is easier to be entrapped in those gross snares of the devil, as was over-well proved to be true by the serpent's deceiving of Eve at the beginning, which makes him the homelier with that sex sensine.' "[40]

King James's royal explanation proves tragically feeble even within Ainsworth's novel; by the nineteenth century Genesis had become as insufficient as the King. In Ainsworth's own day, woman's tacit association with "the black art" was a source of torture laced with hope, hinting at new sources of transfiguration that found final shape in the characters whose vitality lived beyond history. An answer to this resonant question that is truer to the Victorian vision of our artists might be: woman is not frailer than man is, but stronger and more powerful; her nature is broadly demonic rather than fallibly human; she must lead us out of history toward a new dispensation; in short, woman is "so much more addicted to the practice of the black art" because by definition, woman is an angel.

IV

Old Maids and the Wish for Wings

THE VICTORIAN OLD MAID, as commonly perceived, leads no armies to heaven or hell. Grotesque, out of nature, her very name reducing itself to a snicker, she is unwanted even by the devil. In fiction, we remember first the laughingstocks, hungrily and hopelessly swarming around lovable bachelor heroes who are pure in spirit: famished for marriage, they throw into relief the spiritual integrity of Dickens' Pickwickians or of George Eliot's saints of humanity, the clergymen Mr. Farebrother and Mr. Tryan. In her most familiar comic incarnation the old maid is by definition barred from the gates. But the superior smile this stereotype evokes is the symptom of a profound taboo attached to the potential powers of her life and their implication for humanity's future.

In Victorian England the steadily rising percentage of unmarried women made the old maid a familiar domestic appendage and a frightening social harbinger. But a culture gamely determined to tolerate the alien and to avoid acting upon its own

25. *Rejected and caricatured, Cruikshank's spinster nevertheless embodies the lure of voyage, which carried heroic and seditious associations to domestic Victorians.*

deepest fears had ceased to burn single women as witches.[1] Socially conscious Victorians averted their minds from the demonic contagion with which an earlier age had invested spinsterhood, comically expressed in the 1690s in the rampant similes of Daniel Defoe's *Appleby's Journal:* "Horrible! Frightful! Unsufferable! An OLD MAID! I had rather be metamorphosed into an *Humble Bee*, or a *Screech Owl*; the first, all the Boys run after to Buffet it with their Hats, and then pull it a Pieces for a poor dram of Honey in its Tail; and the last, the Terror and Aversion of all Mankind, the forerunner of Ill-luck, the foreboder of Diseases and Death."[2]

In theory, in an enlightened age old maids were no longer capable of such frightening transformations: their dark power of misrule became largely unmentionable. When written about sympathetically, the old maid generally moves from a Gothic to a gently pathetic figure, shedding her tokens of witchcraft to become a plaintive variant of the angel in the house. Margaret Oliphant's *Autobiography* affectionately recalls her first sentimental juvenilia, relying on an angelic stereotype that was hackneyed even then: "I wrote a little book in which the chief character was an angelic older sister, unmarried, who had the charge of a family of motherless brothers and sisters, and who had a shrine of sorrow in her life in the shape of the portrait and memory of her lover who had died young. It was all very innocent and guileless, and my audience—to wit, my mother and brother Frank—were highly pleased with it."[3]

The Victorian old maid is clearly diminished. Rarely allowed even to earn the death of a witch, she is assimilated most easily as a comic grotesque, forcing her hopeless needs on fastidious men, or as sacrificial angel to a surrogate family. But in the fervent vision of some less orthodox writers, she becomes a figure we do not expect: an authentic female hero, with angelic and demonic capacities shaping the proud uniqueness of her life. Charlotte Brontë's letters about her friend Mary Taylor, who emigrated to New Zealand to escape the domestic constrictions England forced on single women, imagine an awesome paragon of courage, intellect, and love, whose heroic stature is inseparable from her spinsterhood. In 1840 Brontë wrote: "God bless her—I never hope to see in this world a character more truly noble—she would *die* willingly for one she loved—her intellect and her attainments are of the very highest standard . . . yet I doubt whether Mary will every marry." Brontë's uncertain "yet" might just as well read "therefore": in this vision Mary's grand capacities, emotional as well as intellectual, insure her spinsterhood. In 1841 Brontë writes with more assurance: "Mary alone has more energy and power in her nature than any ten men you can pick out in the united parishes of

Birstall and Gomersal. It is vain to limit a character like hers within ordinary boundaries—she will overstep them. I am morally certain Mary will establish her own landmarks."

Mary's life offers its chronicler a law unto itself and a hero's inspiration. Her letter from Brussels, where she lived for a time before moving to New Zealand, awakens Brontë less to the intimacies of friendship than to the width and promise of the world: "I hardly knew what swelled to my throat as I read her letter— . . . Such a strong wish for wings—wings such as wealth can furnish—such an urgent thirst to see—to know—to learn— something internal seemed to expand unexercised—then all collapsed and I despaired."[4]

This stirring celebration of Mary Taylor as hero, her chosen life inspiring not pity but an envying "wish for wings," differs from other Victorian visions of unmarried women only in its clarity of faith. Limiting her hero worship to private letters, Charlotte Brontë need not insert the obligatory snicker of derision or sigh of pathos that undermine the old maid's stature even in her own novels *Shirley* and *Villette*. Charlotte Brontë's letters provide the outline of a general Victorian myth of the spinster as hero. Like all heroic myths, this one is fraught with unspoken doubts and terrors, and thus is repeatedly undermined by diffident self-qualification. But if we piece it together, often from little-known sources of women's biography, autobiography, and fiction, we recover glimpses of an animating myth that worked beneath the surface of its age and has not entirely faded in our own, in which the old maid transcends the laughter and tears with which cultural complacency endows her, to "establish her own landmarks" with the audacity and aplomb of an authentic hero.

The outlines seem at first unclear because few Victorian writers were as explicit in their presentations as Charlotte Brontë. Official reverence of the family was inescapable, and the implicit challenge represented by the growing numbers of unmarried women was so radical that even sympathetic portrayals are diluted with euphemisms. For example, Catherine Sinclair introduced her novel *Jane Bouverie; or Prosperity and Adversity* with this disclaimer of responsibility: "It was a favourite suggestion of the late much-lamented Basil Hall, frequently urged with characteristic eagerness on the Author's consideration, that, as crowds of excellent books have already been addressed to wives, mothers, and daughters, a useful and interesting volume might now be devoted to that hitherto neglected class, the single ladies, or, *par excellence*, 'The Sisters of England!' "[5] Jane Bouverie is so unadventurously miserable in her spinsterhood, so faithful to the paternal roof and to the memory of her one exemplary suitor who fulfilled his mission in her life by dying before the wedding, that one might think she could give no offense. Yet despite her estrangement from her worldly and ambitious siblings, the author must sanction her humble isolation by the title of "sister," the one familial role she detests, in order to keep her within the boundaries of a woman's known world. With its additional reminder of the convent, "sister" encloses the heroine's life still more securely than the novel does. Before writing about an old maid, the author must assure us from the first that she will never overstep boundaries to establish her own landmarks.

The establishment during the nineteenth century of actual Anglican sisterhoods depended on similar euphemistic tact. Despite the clear admission of unmarried women, who modeled themselves upon Florence Nightingale and welcomed the new communities as sources of the purposeful work family propriety forbade, advocates of Anglican sisterhoods were careful never to challenge the family directly, praising its separate but equal holiness or even arguing for sisterhoods as surrogate providers of family ties.[6] It is a delicate job to disentangle Victorian visions of old maids from the accompanying commentary intended to soothe the family-minded reader. At times the old maid reveals herself in negation alone: the more authorial commentary insists on her misery and emotional deprivation, the more strongly we may feel the unacknowledged challenge of her life to the boundaries in which the implied reader invests his faith.

One of her most powerful and indirect challenges was her incarnation in statistics. Studies of the Victorian spinster abound in stark statistical tables or ominously swelling percentage charts indicating her inexorable proliferation, a creature born less of feminist ideology than of the Malthusian march of numbers. In "Toilers and Spinsters" Anne Thackeray Ritchie meets these tabulations with the horror her age made obligatory: "Statistics are very much the fashion nowadays, and we can not take up a newspaper or a pamphlet without seeing in round number that so many people will do so and so in the course of the year . . . so many remain single to the end of their lives, of whom so many will be old maids in the course of time. This last number is such an alarming one, that I am afraid to write it down."[7] The pity and contempt that diminish so many Victorian portrayals of spinsterhood are talismans to dispel two central cultural fears: that of the female hero, and the starker, still less readily confronted spectacle of the defeat of the family and the mutation of the race forecast in impersonal, irrefutable tabulations.

The vision of a new race of old maids assuming power over the future seeps into some of our most beloved and familiar works of Victorian fiction. Even characters who remain faithful to family memories and houses, with none of Mary Taylor's determination to venture forth and forge unprecedented lives for themselves, are strangely potent in altering the histories the novels give us. Sally Mitchell locates a typical palliative in popular fiction—"Virtually the only old maids of Victorian fiction who are happy and fulfilled have nephews, nieces, or wards to raise"—but she ignores its accompanying threat.[8] In Elizabeth Gaskell's *Cranford*, for example, Miss Matty wins the reader's approving pity by parading her thwarted maternal feelings. By the end of the novel, however, she and Cranford's other Amazons find themselves "happy and fulfilled" with no child to raise; instead they rejoice in their collective creation, "our society" itself, which has defeated all patriarchal assaults to thrive as a model for societies to come.[9] Fictional spinsters who do raise children often cast a more sinister, if more oblique, shadow on the future. In Ellen Wood's *East Lynne* the formidable old maid Cornelia Carlyle refuses to relinquish her hold on the brother she has raised. She moves in with him and wrests domestic authority from his frail new wife, her unyielding grasp of power becoming the primary agent of the wife's fall and the family's collapse. In Dickens' *Great Expectations* Miss Havisham's withering power over her ward Estella's nature and destiny is more irresistible still: this demon mother has the power to lay waste the younger generation, remaking the future in her own deformed image.

Even when they remain true to their domestic roles, old maids are often granted a shaping power ordinary fictional mothers and fathers do not have. The ineffectual if passionate parents in Elizabeth Gaskell's *Mary Barton, North and South,* and *Wives and Daughters* can barely live in society, let alone create a purer one. The patriarchal power of Ellen Wood's Mr. Carlyle is nullified by his sister's control of his household. The foster parents of Dickens' Pip might be as impotently dead as are his actual parents in their powerlessness to counter Miss Havisham's grasp on the boy's imagination. Stronger than the family, these old maids of popular fiction reform it in their images, suggesting a perverse imaginative tribute to the new shapes of actual lives that had no basis in family.

Lives

Fictional old maids may unleash unexplained and unexpected powers, but the heroic texture of a spinster's experience is most dramatically apparent in the records of actual Victorian lives. Christina Rossetti seems initially impenetrable, a mute and homebound icon surrounded by reverent men conspiring to transform her into an angel. Early in her life we find her sanctified as the Virgin Mary in her brother Dante Gabriel's first two paintings (*The Girlhood of Mary Virgin* and *Ecce Ancilla Domini*); at its close, her brother William Michael altered her posthumous poems to make them more saintly still. Yet this atmosphere of fraternal reverence offered potential grandeur as well as inhibitions. In 1858, when Christina was twenty-eight, Thomas Dixon wrote a letter to William Michael that metamorphosed a superficial acquaintance into a transcendent presence. For Dixon, Christina was "full of that quiet peaceful piety and faith, such as I always remember in thinking over the few hours' conversation I have had the pleasure of having in her presence. I see now as I write this, in my mind's eye, the quiet face, and hear the calm quiet voice—so full of the spirit that one finds in the simple though expressive old Fathers—a reflection to me of a deep lover of Thomas à Kempis, and of one who had achieved that rare and arduous task in this life, the realization in actual life of the teachings of that beautiful book."[10] For the men who revere Christina, her silent singleness is its own apotheosis. Humanly implausible as her poems reveal this brooding placidity to be, she becomes here larger than the conventional pinched appendage to family life, scrutinizing it unmoved from her large and triumphant solitude.

Christina Rossetti complicates but never disentangles herself from attendant men's angelic dream of her: her own ironic, relatively laconic poetic voice never quite denies that she is an angel. The identity her art forges associates angelic powers with the piercing vision of spinsterhood. As Jerome McGann suggests, her poetry is not the moan of a woman amputated by disappointed love; it has the difficult self-completeness of a single woman's radical perspective on a betraying world.[11] Recreating her own spinsterhood in the complex narrative poem "The Lowest Room," Rossetti moves through conventional lament to visions of heroism and of ultimate, militant victory. The speaker begins by contemplating her graying hair and her grayer future of subordinate spinsterhood in an unheroic age. But like *Goblin Market*'s strong-willed, saving Lizzie, her noble sister rouses her by a ringing affirmation of their own dormant heroism:

> "But life is in our hands," she said:
>   "In our hands for gain or loss:
> Shall not the Sevenfold Sacred Fire
>   Suffice to purge our dross?
>
> "Too short a century of dreams,
>   One day of work sufficient length:
> Why should not you, why should not I
>   Attain heroic Strength?
>
> "Our life is given us as a blank;
>   Ourselves must make it blest or curst:
> Who dooms me I shall only be
>   The second, not the first?"[12]

This vision of heroic potential, so rare an intrusion into the modest rhetoric of womanhood, survives only in muted form in the rest of the poem. Prophetess of heroic self-creation, the sister evolves into "a stately wife," compared conventionally to "a vine . . . full of fruit" (l. 250). The unmarried speaker lives secretively and alone, having learned after all the inevitable lesson, "Not to be first" (l. 265). In her enforced humility she, too, seems to have renounced heroic ascendancy, but in the final stanza the vision of her sister returns, though postponed, qualified, and transmuted:

> Yea, sometimes still I lift my heart
>   To the Archangelic trumpet-burst,
> When all deep secrets shall be shown,
>   And many last be first.   (ll. 277–280)

The pagan immediacy of her early hope becomes the apocalyptic faith of her last: pious patience does not subdue heroic selfhood, but validates it. The poet's vision of self-transfiguration takes its authority from the violent reversals prophesied in the Book of Luke: "But when thou art bidden, go and sit down in the lowest room ... For whosoever exalteth himself shall be abased; and he that humbleth himself shall be exalted" (Luke 14:10–11). The social deprivations of spinsterhood become the stuff of intricate and inevitable transformations, as Rossetti implicitly endorses Thomas Dixon's awe at her affinity with angelic powers.

The poem's epic undercurrents make it unclear as to whether the "Archangelic trumpet-burst" must be deferred to Judgment Day or is imminent for the poet at some mystic, private time on earth; as heroic assertion twines itself into biblical prophecy, the speaker's triumph may as easily be secular as celestial. Rossetti's self-portrait as an angel mocks Dixon's paragon of detached serenity to embrace the humiliating disciplines of banked anger and enforced secrecy, masks of selflessness that qualify her for an archangelic summons dispelling the repressions of obedience for the revelations of achieved and transcendent ambition. Her very poem's confession of rage and mortification fulfills the Bible's promise of triumph: "For nothing is secret, that shall not be made manifest; neither *any thing* hid, that shall not be known and come abroad" (Luke 8:17).

As she gave artistic form to the complex and demanding condition of her own spinsterhood, Christina Rossetti fueled her own dream of self-apotheosis with the revolutionary proclamations of heroic epic and the Bible. This Victorian old maid claims her place among the angels, not in their self-negation, but in their militant and dangerous potential to reverse life's comfortably familiar order. In its essence, as in the final complaint of Robert Browning's martyred Pompilia in *The Ring and the Book*, Christina Rossetti associates angelic transformations with biblical visions of triumphant singleness: "But they which shall be accounted worthy to obtain that world, and the resurrection from the dead, neither marry, nor are given in marriage" (Luke 20:35). The quiet sister's devout, family-bounded existence contained its own divine potential for violent metamorphoses.

Unlike Christina Rossetti, the virtuous spinster who found salvation in her secrets, George Eliot associated her spinsterhood with an abandonment of family conceived in the language of demonism. The five years between her father's death in 1849 and her departure for Germany with George Henry Lewes in 1854 have been dubbed "the dire years" by her most recent biographer.[13] These are her years of seemingly random motion, of fluctuations between Warwickshire, Switzerland, and London, between ambition and clinging dependency, between uncontrollable half-fantasized love affairs and a new, breezy companionship with the men she worked with. In this inchoate interim between demanding father and protective lover, Eliot's germinating identity has no coherent tone: the rebellious girl had died and the compassionate wise woman was powerless to be born. Eliot never described these five experimenting years as a new birth into angelic triumph; for her, their very formlessness whispered of demonism. On the day her father died and she lost her life's formal purpose of caring for him, she wrote to the Brays: "What shall I be without my Father? It will seem as if a part of my moral nature were gone. I had a horrifying vision of myself last night becoming earthly sensual and devilish for want of that purifying restraining influence."[14] Provocatively she asks, not "what shall I do without my father?," which was the real dilemma she confronted, but the more radical "what shall I be" without fatherly definition. The spinsterhood inaugurated by loss of family repeats in little her renunciation of God, throwing her into a chaos of identity, demonic not merely in its potential sensuality but in its infinite potential of selves. For George Eliot, as for Christina Rossetti, becoming an old maid is an awesome activity, a baptism into transcendent new incarnations.

The grandiose self-presentations of Christina Rossetti, the angel who stayed home, and George Eliot, whose wandering demonic life defined its phases by its moves, may seem beyond the pale of typical Victorian womanhood. After all, those familiar types of the downtrodden, the poor seamstress, governess, and teacher, or the genteel spinster in her fragile dependency, have no artistic apotheosis, no divine/demonic powers, into which they might dream of being born. Yet the ambitions and fears of an age's artists may place for us the deprivations of its victims and may speak for its less eloquent survivors. In the biographies and memoirs of Victorian spinsters with no artistic vocation, there is a consistent heroic perspective. In all, the woman is a being apart, separated by nature and stature from the race of common humanity, her spinsterhood marking her as a finer, stronger being. It is a shorter journey than it seems from Christina Rossetti's complex archangelic invocation to a once-famous jingle about those two majestic pioneers of Victorian female education, Dorothea Beale and Frances Mary Buss:

> Miss Buss and Miss Beale
> Cupid's darts do not feel.
> How different from us,
> Miss Beale and Miss Buss!

Here of course we are relieved of access to the old maid's finer, striving consciousness; we are stolidly, complacently, comfortably "us." Our corporate ordinariness sees in her a being set apart, too remote for easy laughter or tears. How ambivalently "we" perceive her is evident in two opposed variants of the jingle. In the first, we hesitantly enter the charmed sphere of the special:

> Said Miss Beale to Miss Buss
> "There is no one like us."
> Said Miss Buss to Miss Beale,
> "That is just what *I* feel."

In the second, we shrink back from the chosenness of "us" into its cozy anonymity:

> They are not like us,
> Poor Beale and poor Buss![15]

If we may trust awed contemporary observers, this ambivalent tribute is a faint echo of the regal distinction of the actual Dorothea Beale and Frances Buss. As public presences, for all their austerity, they had no truck with Christina Rossetti's discipline of humility, but paraded through their schools and school boards with the solitary authority of queens. Both aged rapidly and both reminded observers of Queen Victoria.[16] The regality they so naturally adopted, the awed respect they so readily earned, remind us that in Victorian life as well as literature, spinsterhood generated an authority that was no less potent for being virtually unmentionable.

Ironically, Queen Victoria, that panoply of family happiness and stubborn adversary of female independence, could not help but shed her aura upon single women. Her long and early widowhood that drowned out the memory of her marriage, her relentlessly spreading figure and commensurately increasing empire, her obstinate longevity which engorged generations of men and the collective shocks of history, lent an epic quality to the lives of solitary women.[17] In the heroic life of Florence Nightingale and in the myth that life instantaneously generated, there is a symbolic rightness in the Queen's staunch and often solitary loyalty to Nightingale's fiercest crusades. Neither woman wanted to be a feminist, each saw herself as working for and through men, but their lives added transfiguring possibilities to the Victorian myth of womanhood, particularly of woman alone and in command.

In her continuing mythic commentary on her own activities Florence Nightingale did not hesitate in finding mystic correspondences between her own destiny and that of her Queen. When Sidney Herbert died, drained and exhausted, her own "widowhood" took definition from Victoria's; in 1887 Victoria's Jubilee conveniently commemorated her own "fifty years of service."[18] In contributing her own regal properties to Florence Nightingale's self-creation Queen Victoria was in good company: Jesus Christ and Joan of Arc were Nightingale's commonest models for her own inspiration. She wrote on her birthday, "To-day I am 30—the age Christ began his mission," and her still more resonant journal entry for New Year's Eve 1852 clothes her own destiny in an epic vocabulary commonly reserved for men: "all my admirers are married . . . and I stand with all the world before me . . . It has been a baptism of fire this year."[19] As George Eliot inaugurated her official spinsterhood in the language of demonism, Nightingale borrows Milton's description of a fortunate fall into new spaces. But if this metaphor of her heroic destiny is too strongly suggestive of Puritan punishment, she corrects it with a more contemporary heroic myth: that of Teufelsdroech's "baphometric fire-baptism" in Carlyle's *Sartor Resartus.* The resoundingly masculine epics of Milton and Carlyle are fearlessly plundered to create this female hero. There is no whiff of sentimental pathos in Florence Nightingale's spinsterhood, which sprang from her unyielding opposition to the tyrannical trivia of family. She scorned feminist collectivity, identifying herself instead with her chosen hordes of wounded soldiers, but her proclamation of spinsterhood is the most outspoken defiance we have of the Victorian family. The idioms of power she selects align her own self-portrait with Lytton Strachey's iconoclastic evocation in *Eminent Victorians* of an amoral and irresistible force driven by "her Demon," rather than with benevolent Victorian images of "the lady with the lamp." In the self-glorifying vocation of this old maid, whose state is both a liberating fall from protective grace and a radical new consecration, the female hero emerges most vividly in idioms wrested from men who could not have imagined her.

Biographers and autobiographers more obscure and soft-spoken than Florence Nightingale shared her vision of the heroic dimensions of a single woman's life. Elizabeth Missing Sewell wrote a privately printed autobiography that paid such reverent attention to her life in her family, so little to her independent achievements as author and founder of a school on the Isle of Wight, that a modern reader defines it only by the perplexed question: "Can an autobiographer be both self-effacing and vain?"[20] Sewell's autobiographical novel, *The Experience of Life,* suffers from the same tension between worship of family and exalted visions of independence, yet it finds its inspiration in the grand, controlling figure of Aunt Sarah as she guides the family toward her own elevated spiritual plane and initiates the young narrator, Sally, in a continuing tradition of heroic spinsterhood: "In pursuing her even course, [Aunt Sarah] had lived far more earnestly, and to a far higher purpose, than hundreds who have been held up to the world's admiration as heroines of fortitude and energy."[21] For both Sally and the author, Aunt Sarah is a being set apart, "such as one might imagine to inspire a soldier with courage" (p. 18), a figure of romance, a yearned-for transfigured self, and finally, though she barks orders of feminine submission—"Don't try to be a man when you are only a woman; and don't set up to preach when you are only called upon to practise" (p. 149)—the only consecrating divinity this novel allows. Sewell was immovably orthodox in religion and political theory. Yet her autobiographical imagination produced an old maid of a stature as heroic, of powers as holy, as the self-image Florence Nightingale forged from her rebellion.

For some autobiographers a spinster's life gains magnitude beyond its component activities because it is free to amalgamate with its age. The feminist Elizabeth S. Haldane defines, in writing about George Eliot, the central assumption of her own autobiography: "For women as a rule are much more under the influence of their time than men. They are—or were—brought up from infancy to respect it and all its implications."[22] Despite her self-depreciating idiom, Haldane exempts her subject from woman's traditionally private sphere, equating her life with the historic shape of its age. She is more assertive in her own memoirs, as she identifies her long single life with history's mutations: "[this book] shows from one special view point how the world goes on and how a woman passed from the restrictions of one century to the interests of another. It may also show she may have a perfectly happy and full life, though devoid of some of the ameliorations that novelists and psychologists tell us make life worth living."[23] This is a personal and historical apologia: setting aside the pious strictures of authorities, it finds the richness of a single life in its alliance with the spirit of its age. Haldane's autobiography takes its moods from the changing emotional colorations of decades and the excitement of historic identification. In its dramatic culmination it dares to quarrel with G. M. Young's magisterial *Victorian England: Portrait of an Age* in its insistence that the two unassailable Victorian institutions were "Representative Institutions and the Family." From the perspective of an ardent woman, insisting equally on the authority of her Victorian life, these institutions lose their sanctity: "I should be inclined to say that it was the development of the democratic spirit, that is the Spirit of Liberty, that was the predominant influence" (p. 308). In fact, she adds, the family was less an article of faith than a repressive impediment to civilization in the age in which she, too, came to consciousness. Her beloved brother became Lord Chancellor, but Haldane, unlike Florence Nightingale, moved no armies on her own account. Yet she, too, writes of her spinsterhood as a consecration into her age, endowing its authority upon her life.

Frances Power Cobbe's autobiography is cast in a similar epic and heroic mold. She need not borrow the vocabulary of *Sartor Resartus;* its spirit pervades her sense of her life's special import. This posthumous memoir is introduced by Blanche Atkinson in an appropriately heroic tribute to its subject: "One felt always on leaving her that every one else was dull, uninteresting and commonplace. One felt, too, that the whole conception of womanhood was raised. *This* was what a woman might be. Whatever her faults, they were the faults of a great-hearted, noble nature—faults which all generous persons would be quick to forget. Nothing small or mean could be tolerated by her."[24] Like Beale and Buss, like Sewell's Aunt Sarah, Cobbe is defined by her grand distinction: it is her triumph that she is "not like us." In writing of herself Cobbe, like Haldane, insists on the richness of a life convention insists must be miserable: "Perhaps if this book be found to have any value it will partly consist in the evidence it must afford of how pleasant and interesting and withal, I hope, not altogether useless a life is open to a woman, though no man has ever desired to share it, nor has she seen the man she would have wished to ask her to do so" (p. 8). The interest of her life derives from its singleness. Again like Haldane's, Cobbe's life as she perceives it takes resonance from her identification of her experience with history: "I have tried to make it the true and complete history of a woman's existence *as seen from within;* a real LIFE, which he who reads may take as representing fairly the joys, sorrows, and interests, the powers and limitations, of one of my sex and class in the era which is now drawing to a close. The world when I entered it was a very different place from the world I must shortly quit, most markedly so as regards the position in it of women and of persons like myself holding heterodox opinions, and my experience practically bridges the gulf which divides the English *ancien regime* from the new" (pp. xxviii-xxix).

"A real LIFE" is inseparable from its era. We accept this instinctive public identification in the autobiographies of John Stuart Mill and John Henry Newman, but it may shock our assumptions about the Victorian age to find single women assuming equal rights as historically defined lives. The century's wittiest feminist, Cobbe has no intention of waiting for her rights to be won. Her ego assumes its prerogatives as she traces the root of her name back to "head," finding in etymology an allegory of her heroic leadership, unabashedly quotes laudatory letters from the famous men of the age, and snubs Gladstone when he belittles her fierce anti-vivisection crusade. Cobbe bases her feminism on the refreshing assumption that legislation on behalf of women must measure up to the high standard her own life has already set.

Cobbe's writings bring to the fore a motif belonging to the

old maid as a Victorian type: that of heroic exile. We may think first of the housebound spinster Sewell seems to glorify, knitting on the margin of her brother's family or moldering alone in the old family house; yet mobility was the mark of many actual lives, as it was of Sewell's own. George Eliot consecrated her spinsterhood by sensing a new, demonic identity and moving to Geneva; Florence Nightingale embraced hers upon the marriage of her suitors and her thirtieth birthday, whereupon, to dramatize her heroic self-creation, she went to the Crimea. When Frances Power Cobbe's beloved father died, she made what seems a symbolic pilgrimage to the Holy Land and was baptised into a new relationship to money:

> After I had spent two or three weeks once again at my old home after my long journey to visit my eldest brother and his wife, and also had seen my two other dear brothers, then married and settled in England with their children; the time came for me to begin my independent life as I had long planned it. I had taken my year's pilgrimage as a sort of conclusion to my self-education, and also because, at the beginning of it, I was in no state of health or spirits to throw myself into new work of any kind. Now I was well and strong, and full of hope of being of some little use in the world; just thirty-six; and I had my little independence of £200 a year which, though small, was enough to allow me to work how and where I pleased without need to earn anything. I may boast that I never got into debt in my life; never borrowed money from anybody; never even asked my brother for the advance of a week on the interest of my patrimony.   (p. 275)

The descent of spinsterhood is the dawn of adulthood. Cobbe has no need to borrow Milton's voice as Florence Nightingale did; the world is all before her.

These journeys, literally out of England and figuratively out of the family, are as central to a Victorian spinster's sense of her life as they might be for an Oxford graduate embarking on his initiatory Grand Tour. In an earlier essay Cobbe locates them as the symbolic essence of spinsterhood: "The 'old maid' of 1861 is an exceedingly cheery personage, running about untrammeled by husband or children; now visiting at her relatives' country houses, now taking her month in town, now off to a favourite *pension* on Lake Geneva, now scaling Vesuvius or the Pyramids. And what is better, she has found, not only freedom of locomotion, but a sphere of action peculiarly congenial to her nature."[25] Students with a taste for Victorian victims might not expect such a buoyant presentation of spinsterhood in the early 1860s. Though this particular essay evades the central crusade surrounding the Victorian spinster—equal professional and financial opportunities with men—it celebrates mobility and rootlessness in cheery counterpoint to the more familiar cult of home. Grandly ignoring inhibiting social prejudice, Cobbe finds in the old maid a specially endowed being for whom the large and changing world is home. Her closest literary analogue is not the man-hungry grotesque audiences wanted to make of her, but such dangerously assertive heroes as Tennyson's experience-hungry Ulysses, scorning family ties to take his being from his world: "I am a part of all that I have met."

As with Tennyson's Ulysses, this mobility is not always as "cheery" as Cobbe's. As often, exile brings despair, but it is a despair that enriches and aggrandizes the sufferer, setting her still more profoundly apart from those who stayed home. Anna Jane Buckland's *Record of Ellen Watson* (1884) is a heroic eulogy to a gifted and consumptive young woman who traveled to Grahamstown, South Africa, for her health and for the elevation of the native women's intellects; she died there at twenty-four. Buckland is less interested in immortalizing Watson's fragmentary writings or missionary work than in celebrating the exaltation of spirit exile brought about: like many of her contemporaries, Watson was an unbeliever at home, but the anguish of separation restored her to faith and, ultimately, to a rapturously expectant death. Writing on board ship, Watson seizes on exile as the painful source of grandeur: "The old hope rises, only it seems a new one to-night, that this sorrow, which at this hour seems more than I can bear, may dwell with me always as greatness from which my life may take its tone."[26] In Buckland's eyes at least this wish was granted; Ellen Watson finds her apotheosis in exile, dying "a centre of life to those around her" (p. 276).

This vision of salvation through exile rarely sees itself as radical. Neither Florence Nightingale, George Eliot, Frances Power Cobbe, Anna Jane Buckland, nor Ellen Watson could be called a radical feminist, even in the Victorian sense of the term. Yet the aristocratic aplomb with which all five ignore family life, finding in exile the symbol of their grand and special destiny, aligns them with James Joyce's self-created, selfmythicizing hero Stephen Daedalus. Like him, but more despised, the Victorian old maid is forced to live a psychic life of "silence, exile, and cunning." For heroes of both sexes it is in such conditions that myths are born, giving rise to new selves and new lives.

Exile, temporary or complete, was not merely the grand symbolic choice of a spiritual elite: the growing promotion of female emigration to the colonies associated exile with one official definition of Victorian spinsterhood. The wildly contrasting visions of female emigration, rather than its relatively prosaic reality, crystallize the intensely paradoxical emotions that created the old maid as a Victorian type. Arguments for female emigration range from the greater availability in the colonies of husbands who could not afford to be too selective—a position of which W. R. Greg is the best-known and most outrageous exponent[27]—to Mary Taylor's strenuous ideal of work and independent self-realization. Ignoring Greg's stigma of the colonial marriage barter, which in any case was attached rather to Australia than New Zealand, Mary Taylor tried to rouse the vegetating Ellen Nussey to take the "desperate plunge, and you will come up in another world. The new world will be no Paradise, but still much better than the nightmare [of England]. Am I not right in all this? *and don't you know it* very well! Or am I shooting in the dark? I must say I judge rather by my own history than from any knowledge of yours . . . What in the world keeps you? . . . You could get your living here at any of the trades I have mentioned, which you would only die of in England. As to 'society' position in the world, you must have found out by this time it is all my eye seeking society without the means to enjoy it. Why not come here then and be happy?"[28]

For Greg, emigration was a means of ridding the country altogether of old maids and their inherent threat to the family and the race; for Mary Taylor, it enabled old maids to consolidate their position by earning their way to a new and stronger life. The same clash between social preservation and rebellion appears in the disparate missions attributed to female emigrants: on the one hand, they were hymned as agents of family and civilization, and, on the other, associated with the convicts, fallen women, and prostitutes who were transported to the colonies.[29] Thus, emigrating spinsters were society's agents and its outcasts, at once indispensable and seditious. *Great Expectations* is, among other things, a brilliant dark parable of this duality: in allowing the old maid Miss Havisham to share Pip's psychic parentage with the transported convict Magwitch, Dickens plays on the association of spinsterhood with exile and with enterprising criminality, though like the angel in the house turned rancid, Miss Havisham need never leave her room.

Exile is embedded not merely in the personal lives and imaginations of actual Victorian spinsters, but in their institutional definition. The myth of sedentary sadness is uneasily crossed with the more dashing myth of heroic voyage, messianic and subversive at once. We hear these two voices in two contrasting mid-century narratives of Charlotte Brontë's life: Charlotte Brontë's own autobiographical novel, *Villette* (1853), can be read like Elizabeth Missing Sewell's *The Experience of Life* (1852), as a novel about the making of a strong spinster,[30] while Elizabeth Gaskell's biography *The Life of Charlotte Brontë* (1857) commemorates the tragic virtue of a pattern Victorian woman. Gaskell elides Brontë's journeys to Brussels to concentrate on her heart-wrenching incarceration in her father's isolated parsonage at Haworth. Gaskell makes her as immobile as an enchanted princess, an anguished servant of and martyr to her doomed, demanding family. But in her own autobiographical fiction Charlotte herself had ignored all home, all family, on behalf of her life's single odyssey: the torment and discovery of her move to Brussels, which *Villette* transmutes into a lifetime exile. Lucy Snowe's passage out of England on the *Vivid* is surrounded by heroic portents; her discipline through despair as she evolves into independence is equated with her battle with an alien culture and her ultimate incorporation of the best of that culture into her new life; even her brief love story is presented as a dialectic between languages, religions, and countries. Gaskell's biography is structured around the omnipotence of home, while Brontë's autobiographical novel finds its structure in the odyssean myth of heroic growth. Brontë forged *Villette* as her greatest hero-worshiping tribute to Mary Taylor's Ulysses-like belief in a "desperate plunge, and you will come up in another world." In organizing her own experience around Mary Taylor's heroic pattern, Brontë may have come closer to the heart of her age's myth of spinsterhood than did Gaskell in depicting an equally heroic saint of family life.

When we observe actual Victorian spinsters imaginatively creating their lives, we do not see the broken ego and the lacerated heart of convention. Instead we find a heady faith from which most Victorian women were barred, founded on the heroic capacity of a chosen being, on pain transmuted into destiny, on the seemingly solitary life finding union not with one man but with an age of men, women, changes, and places. This myth seems to have been in many ways an underground phenomenon, sustaining itself in isolation from the mocking, pitying main culture. When we move from lives to literature the myth shapes itself in a broader context, suggesting a wider power over the imagination than individual citizens might have been willing to acknowledge.

Novels

Villette is one of the very few Victorian novels about spinsterhood to use the perilous journey as a shaping principle: perhaps to subdue the old maid's potential defiance and capacity for self-renewal, fiction rarely allows her mobility and exile. In this sense Gaskell's *Life* is closest to fictional visions of old maids, while Brontë's novel appropriates the shape of memoir and biography.

Despite her relatively static and domestic life, the old maid retains one salient heroic attribute in fiction: she is almost always a being chosen and set apart, ineffably distinguished by her "difference from us." As in Sewell's *The Experience of Life,* her superiority to common womanhood is generally emphasized by juxtaposition with a married or marriage-hungry sister. Christina Rossetti's "Commonplaces" ranks three sisters on a spiritual hierarchy. Catherine, the eldest, is a confirmed spinster and the most spiritual. Lucy, the next, approaches her crucial thirtieth birthday; the emotional heart of the story is her heroic struggle with conflicting visions of her destiny. Pretty young Jane is vapid and heartless, alienated from us at the very beginning: "A man might fall in love with Jane, but no one could make a friend of her; Catherine and Lucy were sure to have friends, however they might lack lovers."[31] Rossetti allows no doubts that friendship ranks higher on the spiritual scale than heterosexual love.

Jane's love reduces itself to social climbing: she marries a wealthy man she despises. Only Lucy, torn between Catherine's remote serenity and Jane's submergence in the marriage market, feels anything approximating passion, and the man she cares for drops her to marry someone richer. Though a tepid, true-hearted suitor does come along to redeem her from spinsterhood at the last moment, Lucy's finest moment is her transcendence of humiliation in accepting her singleness: "her birthday was just over, and it was gratifying to find herself not obsolete even at thirty. The birthday had loomed before her threateningly for months past, but now it was over; and it became a sensible relief to feel and look at thirty very much as she had felt and looked at twenty-nine. Her mirror bore witness to no glaring accession of age having come upon her in a single night. 'After all,' she mused, 'life isn't over at thirty'" (p. 128).

Compared to the proud self-affirmation of single women's memoirs, Lucy's step toward self-acceptance may seem a low level of heroism, but in terms of the choices Rossetti offers, her evolution from Jane's materialism toward Catherine's inner grandeur is a major leap. "Commonplaces" appears to be a slightly simplified fictional revision of Rossetti's poem "A Triad" (1862), which also juxtaposes the spiritual destinies of three sisters in terms of their contrasting attitudes to love:

One shamed herself in love; one temperately
    Grew gross in soulless love, a sluggish wife;
One famished died for love. Thus two of three
    Took death for love and won him after strife;
One droned in sweetness like a fattened bee:
    All on the threshold, yet all short of life.

(ll. 9–14; Crump, p. 29)

In its juxtaposition of three central types of Victorian womanhood—the fallen woman, the old maid, and the wife—"A Triad" achieves a finer balance than "Commonplaces," assigning spiritual pluses and minuses with less avidity. Yet here, too, there is no doubt that the "temperate" wife is lowest on the scale, nearest to matter and farthest from the consciousness born in struggle. As "fattened bee," she provides a negative gloss on the nobler married sister in Rossetti's "The Lowest Room," who is compared with greater apparent neutrality to "a vine . . . full of fruit." Though the fallen woman and the old maid win no spiritual triumphs, they are allies in heroic struggle against the soulless torpor of marriage. To "win" death "after strife" shows a capacity for heroic activity admirable in nineteenth-century terms, no matter what the prize. Abandoning the wife to the level of matter while partitioning the struggle that makes souls among the old maid and the fallen woman aligns the vision Rossetti achieved in privacy with the iconography of her age.

There is an almost identical triad in a later novel, Annie E. Holdsworth's *Joanna Trail, Spinster* (1894). When we meet the heroine, her spinsterhood manifests itself as a spiritual endowment distinguishing her from her gross married sisters: "Miss Joanna Trail was herself the most refined object in the room. Her hopeless face, with its colourless eyes and colourless hair, was not wanting in a certain charm of indefiniteness, strongly in contrast with the strident well-being of her sisters. Her sorrow set her on a higher pinnacle, and made her the superior of the two young and prospering women who were uttering their fiat on her life with well-intentioned, unemotional cruelty."[32] In this novel, which appeared at the height of the aesthetic movement, the spinster's soul has the fineness of a few brushstrokes by Whistler as opposed to the fat realism which was the boast of the Royal Academy.

Joanna is saved from her sisters' dominance when she takes in a fallen woman, Christine, and attempts to reclaim her. The novel is the story of their difficult emotional alliance: Joanna civilizes Christine, while Christine brings out Joanna's joy and beauty. The women effect a mutual salvation by teaching each other love and pride. "The Magdalen" and "Joanna Trail, Spinster," the ennobling titles of the final chapters, in which Christine marries and Joanna dies, heroically redeem each other less from men than from the coarse imposition of wives. Set in a plausible narrative framework, their corporate self-creation echoes the struggle and partial victory Christina Rossetti sketches in "A Triad."

Even in Catherine Sinclair's Jane Bouverie, our most conventionally self-sacrificial and lugubrious old maid, the spiritual paragon is distinguished from her worldly and selfish married sisters. The latter end as badly as they deserve, while Jane, like the speaker in Christina Rossetti's "The Lowest Room," ends her story with a vision of her apocalyptic triumph on Judgment Day, when she can break the silent anonymity of a suppressed life. Though she is as self-mortifyingly dutiful as Margaret Oliphant's angelic heroine with her "secret shrine of sorrow"—she cheers herself up with charitable visiting and Bible-reading—Jane Bouverie achieves an epic stature despite herself by virtue of her role as her family's sole survivor: "I have lived to be the last depository of their memories, the last on this visible earth who remembered their countenances, who had shared in their thoughts, or would drop a tear over their graves" (p. 20). The survivor's implicit power over the family which had abandoned her is a domestic replica of Queen Victoria's over her country: her longevity alone keeps alive past victories and betrayals. Jane Bouverie acknowledges the majesty and power of her lonely life in an apparently offhand remark: "An old fable relates that there is a paradise in which the spirits of departed men exist only so long as they are remembered and lamented on earth . . . in such a case, how many . . . would now have been indebted to my memory for their last lingering glimpse of existence" (pp. 99–100). The mind of the author becomes God's mind, withholding and bestowing eternal life, as the humble old maid swells into controlling consciousness. Within the domestic frame of her novel, even this paragon of renunciation assumes epic dimensions. In her awareness of the mighty powers of survivorship and authorship combined, Jane Bouverie's pious hope loses its last veneer of humility: "It may be perhaps that God has marked me for his own" (p. 135).

In these novels the common fictional iconography of sisterhood dramatizes the old maid's distinction as one of God's elect by revealing her superiority to an ordinary woman, her married sister. The old maid displays not merely superiority of soul but of heart as well: wives in these novels are loveless investors of themselves on the marriage market, while old maids are secret and passionate emotional gamblers, willing to forfeit security for the solitary intensity of hopeless love. Ellen Wood's *Mildred Arkell* (1865) is a vivid paean to the old maid as heroic saint of love, mocked by the shallow materialism of wives: " 'The old maids' they would be slightingly termed by those who knew little indeed of their inward history. And in their lonely hearts enshrined in its most hidden depths, the image that respectively filled each in early life, the father and son, William and Travis Arkell, never, never replaced by any other, but holding their own there so long as time should last."[33]

As well as making the old maid its only vehicle of untarnished and unwavering love, this little-known tearjerker by the author of *East Lynne* is more explicit than our other novels in celebrating her heroic capacities. Mildred's stature is indicated not only by the conventional juxtaposition with lesser women but, more subversively, by one with lesser men as well. Mildred Arkell, whose forte is suffering and enduring, is no Frances Power Cobbe, nor even a Lucy Snowe. She brings no associations of independence and adventure, challenges no male boasts of authority, elects no superb exile, only a dreary life as paid companion after William, her adored cousin, has broken her heart by marrying stylishly vicious Charlotte. Though she seems to have only one poor weapon against a progressively vulgar society—"and yet she was in mind and manners essentially a gentlewoman" (I, 12)—Mildred quietly gains control over the blundering man she professes to worship. In using resolute men as well as insipid women as yardsticks for the spinster's triumph *Mildred Arkell* shares the iconoclastic vision of another highly colored popular romance of the 1860s, Wilkie Collins' *The Woman in White*.

True, Wood's Mildred is more self-effacingly ladylike, though richer in innuendo, than is Collins' grand Marian Halcombe. In fact, although she gives her name to the entire canvas of this long and complex saga, Mildred herself appears only at the beginning and the end. After William marries a lesser woman, Mildred leaves the scene of the action, the small cathedral town of Westerbury, to amass a fortune in secrecy in order to return as a deus ex machina, buying William out of bankruptcy after his business has failed and his extravagant wife has run through his capital. Through her fortune Mildred becomes the novel's Destiny and molder of the future: her money enables William's son Travis to marry his modest, Mildred-like cousin rather than an enormous heiress, and thus saves the next generation from repeating the father's mistake. "Mildred's Recompense," the suggestive title of this final resolution, is the old maid's simultaneous apotheosis and revenge through her one legal source of power, that of property-owning. In becoming the novel's God, Mildred, like Jane Bouverie, never abandons the language of service: "If you knew what the happiness of serving you is, William! If you knew what a recompense this is for the bitter past!" (II, 325). This sort of rhetoric alone distinguishes Mildred from Dickens' wealthy figure of Destiny, the witchlike manipulator Miss Havisham.

Mildred's return as a capitalist Jane Eyre, propping up her broken lover and redeeming his title to the future, is appropriate to a novel dealing with the social and financial fluctuations that destroy the complex tapestry of Westerbury society. Concentrating on a broader and denser social canvas than does the claustrophobic domestic drama *East Lynne,* Wood focuses on the displacement by rude moneymakers of the town's time-honored gentility. The novel's true protagonist is the traumatic renewal of social change, of which the newly wealthy Mildred becomes at the end the embodiment. Its intrigues and love stories are subsumed into its central rhythm of social rise and fall, crystallizing in Charlotte's snobbish horror at the sudden wealth of her crude sister Betsey who has married a gauche if good-hearted businessman:

> Come to *this* fortune! While hers and her husband's was going down. How the tables were turned.
> Yes, Mrs. Arkell. Tables always are on the turn in this life.
> (II, 303)

The subtlest, strongest thread in the novel is the relation of women to these implacable reversals of power: as gentility is supplanted by the new money it scorned, so men are supplanted by women. Mildred's accession of power over William and his family is echoed in the novel's many subplots, the majority of which concern the unexpected eruption of strength in women as the men mysteriously decline. In the most dramatically suggestive of these, Betsey Dundyke and her capable husband travel to Geneva, in whose sinister climate Dundyke is abducted by a mysterious adventurer. After a long period he makes his way back to Westerbury with some undefined affliction of the brain; under Betsey's sturdy care he ekes out a clinging life as half-animal, half-child. William Arkell, his son Travis, and Mildred's brother Peter (an unworldly scholar) suffer at various times from similar inexplicable collapses of the brain, while, with the sole exception of Peter's consumptive wife, the women remain in unyielding good health.

The malady of Mrs. Peter Arkell pales in the face of the lingering decline of her gifted son Henry. The death of Henry Arkell, prize student and exemplary Christian youth, must surely be the most heavily orchestrated death of a youngster in Victorian fiction. Henry suffers under many debilities: he is in love with a spiteful, unworthy girl; his fellow students hate him because he is a paragon of learning; he has at great personal risk uncovered a hidden marriage and solved a knotty inheritance suit; and he has endured opprobrium because his father's destitution has forced him to pawn in secret his watch and his scholar's gold prize medal. The catastrophes that buffet his purity combine with the jealous spite of a fellow-pupil who trips him to cause a long death resulting from a vague "internal injury to the head."

Henry's long dying is no more a digression than that of little Hanno Buddenbrook will be for Thomas Mann. In Henry's brain disease is concentrated the malady that makes of all the novel's men stricken creatures; we are to mourn in the death of this young saint the death of Westerbury's waning aristocracy and the superiority of the male sex. The ceremonial relish of Henry's death owes much to Little Nell's, but his is of a far more nostalgic order. Nell's death was a final, consummate expression of her strong will, an act of angelic self-assertion by which an unworthy world was forced to take its own measure. Similarly, the death of little William in Ellen Wood's *East Lynne*, published four years before *Mildred Arkell*, was an equally lingering retribution on his fallen mother. Little Nell's death shamed the world; little William's shamed his mother. Henry Arkell's death does make everybody around him squirm with guilt, but here the guilt cannot be located and exorcised; so the death becomes an epitome of all the other deaths the novel chronicles, finally typifying the mortal illness of gentility and of the men who transmit or withhold it. Even as *Mildred Arkell* ends with Travis' marriage to the girl he loves, in its final sentence the strapping heiress who had good-heartedly released him from their engagement supplants his class and sex in an unconscious gesture: "Travis was taking [her wedding gift] from her, but awkwardly—he was one of the incapable ones, like poor Peter Arkell. Miss Fauntleroy rated him and pushed him away, and lifted it on the table herself, with her strong hands" (II, 344–345).

Mildred Arkell, tactfully offstage for most of the novel, presides over its reversals of power not merely in the authority of her name on each page and in her final dispensation of her money, but through the various avatars whose "strong hands" appropriate the burdens and the power of incapable males. *Mildred Arkell* chronicles an intricate revolution that moves beyond the inward-turning, male-worshiping masochism of *East Lynne*, as if Wood's determined old maid, a type of social change in a large, rapidly changing world, were created to redeem the self-flagellation which was the fallen woman's only allowable ambition. When the tables turn, the old maid's strong hands turn them.

Despite pockets of melodrama, *Mildred Arkell's* emphasis on the imperceptible revolutions within familiar provincial life distinguishes it from that flourishing genre of the 1860s, the sensation novel. Wilkie Collins' *The Woman in White* also has an old maid as its central figure, but Marian Halcombe does not direct the hidden economic currents that regulate daily life. Thriving among the strange explosions that constitute the novel's action, she stands out as that Victorian anomaly, the strong woman whose nature finds its substance in extremity. The atypical extravagance of the action allows the old maid an overt supremacy that in ordinary life must cover itself with self-effacing rhetoric. The form of sensation fiction, a series of revolutionary challenges to the expectations of conventional realism, and Collins' identity as a bohemian male writer, with connections through his Pre-Raphaelite brother to bohemian schools of art, allow him greater license than our other writers to celebrate his monumental old maid in her exposure of the little world around her.

The Woman in White opens with a pious invocation of personified sexual stereotypes that threatens to obliterate the dashingly intelligent Marian before she even appears: "This is the story of what a Woman's patience can endure, and what a Man's resolution can achieve."[34] These poles of conventional masculinity and femininity are reasonably good introductions to Laura Fairlie, the nebulous, incompetent heroine, and her colorless suitor, Walter Hartright. The initial hymn to this boring pair has led feminist critics to dismiss the entire novel as sexually "conventional."[35] But in his 1861 Preface to the second edition, Collins himself rescued the novel from Man and Woman by pointing to its success as "a narrative which interests [readers] about men and women—for the perfectly obvious reason that they are men and women themselves" (p. 32). The pluralism offered by lower-case men and women allows us to appreciate such unfeminine characters as Marian, as well as her dangerous double in wit, intelligence, and perception, that obese and effeminate schemer, Count Fosco.

Spinsters were frequently exalted as humanity's chosen spirits, great souls set apart from the mass of common, married humanity; in fiction they often became as well love's hidden saints in a world of mercenary marriages. Marian has no personal interest in love, but even in this grand context, our first introduction to her is startling. We greet her as a being familiar in life, but painfully rare in Victorian fiction—a truly sexy woman: "The instant my eyes rested on her, I was struck by the rare beauty of her form, and by the unaffected grace of her attitude. Her figure was tall, but not too tall; comely and well-developed, yet not fat; her head set on her shoulders with an easy, pliant firmness; her waist, perfection in the eyes of a man, for it occupied its natural place, it filled out its natural circle, it was visibly and delightfully undeformed by stays" (p. 58).

In this promising introduction Marian's physical presence acts on us as a Rossetti or a Whistler portrait, offering less a lure than the grace of self-possession. But on closer look, Walter (for only he and Count Fosco describe Marian) dissipates her power for the conventional reader: "The lady is ugly!" (p. 58). At a stroke, Walter transforms Marian's abandonment of stays from a defiant assertion of new space and scope for herself to a humble admission that her ugliness puts her beyond the pale of womanly accessories. In the same way, the novel never allows her to stray an inch from the old maid's prescribed self-sacrificial role as Laura's solicitous protector; but, like her figure, her character asserts claims beyond the boundaries of the plot. For one thing, we must ask, *is* Marian ugly? Walter's ensuing itemization characterizes himself as much as it does "the lady": "The lady's complexion was almost swarthy, and the dark down on her upper lip was almost a moustache. She had a large, firm, masculine mouth and jaw; prominent, piercing, resolute brown eyes; and thick, coal-black hair, growing unusually low down on her forehead. Her expression—bright, frank, and intelligent—appeared, while she was silent, to be altogether wanting in the feminine attractions of gentleness and pliability, without which the beauty of the handsomest woman alive is beauty incomplete" (pp. 58–59).

Had Robert Browning written this passage, we would have no trouble appreciating the speaker's complacent self-exposure in that last remark; Wilkie Collins' dramatic monologues display equal ironic deftness. For one thing, despite Walter's iteration that being intelligent Marian is thereby "masculine," in the context of the novel she is no such thing: with the exception of the villainous Fosco, none of the male characters is distinguished by intelligence, or by largeness or firmness of mouth and jaw. As a physical type Marian shows less kinship to a man than to a Pre-Raphaelite "stunner" whose image would possess the 1860s: the swarthy, Italianate Jane Morris (Figure 26). Marian's "coal-black hair, growing unusually low down on her forehead," her large mouth, and her prominent jaw, all evoke Jane Morris' un-English and unorthodox magnetism, though this similarly uncorseted Pre-Raphaelite idol would no doubt appal a drawing-master like Walter, who sees and works by the rules.

Marian's incipient moustache remains a problem for a depilatory-conscious age. No doubt most twentieth-century readers would accept Walter's fastidious view that it is a further "masculine" stigma on this ugly woman; cosmopolitan Victorians might, however, have linked it to Marian's swarthy complexion as a further sign of French or Italian womanly beauty. The Italian wizard Count Fosco, exile in a joyless land, adores Marian's flexible body as Walter does, studying "the poetry of motion, as embodied in her walk" (p. 622), but he has no Anglo-Saxon problem in loving her face as well. Her very moustache may be the real object of Count Fosco's love, which is sincere to the point of self-destruction. Unlike most of melodrama's dashing foreign villains, Count Fosco shows no sexual interest in the vapid Laura whose life he controls. If his passion for Marian somehow implicates her intelligence in his wickedness, it redeems her from facile associations with masculinity, highlighting the spinster's foreignness as well as her unwomanly sexuality.

As Collins controls our perspective, Marian is larger than her own compulsive self-depreciation and self-sacrifice would seem to sanction. The very form of the Victorian novel, and perhaps of the novel itself, forbids her the self-assertion of a Frances Power Cobbe, but within her prescribed role she, too, claims our attention as a superior, chosen being. She does so most visibly by her outstanding performances as detective and dreamer: she must be fiction's first female detective, and she is certainly the most versatile, for in addition to skill as acrobat and eavesdropper she gains salient information in oracular dreams and trances. In fact, Collins can prevent her physical and mystical prowess from ending the novel prematurely only by striking her down with a violent illness just as she is about to spoil the suspense. More subtly and pervasively, Marian's powers are intensified when Collins places her in juxtaposition with the other characters.

She gains obvious stature in comparison to her half-sister Laura, who for Walter is the image of womanhood. Like Fosco, Collins seems to question his hero's taste when Laura, infantine at best, is thoroughly infantilized by the plot against her. Knockout drops and trauma reduce her in the second half of the novel to a virtual replica of the half-witted Anne Catherick, her half-sister and double whose identity the villains have foisted on her, so that it is no wonder the other characters fail to tell the difference. Her pathetically inept attempts to fend for herself and earn some money align her with such fictional parodies of the Victorian child-wife as Dickens' Dora and Thackeray's Amelia. Collins never draws the line as to where her half-wittedness ends and her femininity begins, nor does his happy ending bother to note whether her sanity has returned: clearly Walter and those readers who share his taste don't know and don't care. As the novel progresses, the heroine's declining competence throws Marian's agility into greater relief.

If Laura is the ideal woman, Marian may indeed be masculine, for the novel drops several hints that a woman is by definition either child or man. Here is one of our clearest messages, from Marian's narrative:

> My tears do not flow so easily as they ought—they come almost like men's tears, with sobs that seem to tear me in pieces, and that frighten every one about me.
> "I have thought of this, love, for many days," [Laura] went on, twining and twisting my hair with that childish restlessness in her fingers, which poor Mrs. Vesey still tries so patiently and so vainly to cure her of. (p. 187)

If women are children, then the adult Marian must be a man, but this sort of Wonderland logic merely reminds us of one subject of this book: that Victorian culture had no firmly

26. *Dante Gabriel Rossetti's portrait of Jane Morris, stressing her powerful, un-English beauty.*

rooted imagination of adult womanhood and so envisioned a creature of almost infinite mobility. In fact, the novel's true paradigm of womanhood seems to be neither child nor man. In the spiritual ambiguity of her origins, her cryptic appeals and her mysterious powers as source and influence of action, Collins' true female image is the woman in white herself—the addled prophet and victim Anne Catherick, without whose oracular imaginations Collins' men and women could not exist. This evocative figure brings together Marian's enterprising and foreign magic with Laura's infantilism, a central Victorian symbol of woman's social incompetence and mysterious powers.

The uncertainty of the novel's language is the resonant uncertainty of its conception of womanhood and that of its age. In the novel's own terms, Marian Halcombe is no more a man than she is a child. More obviously than Ellen Wood's Mildred Arkell, she surpasses the men with whom the novel juxtaposes her. The hero Walter is as brave as she, but less intelligent; the villain Fosco is as intelligent, but betrays himself through fundamental cowardice and an indecision motivated by his protective adoration of her. While Collins' men repeat the double-edged praise that a superior woman is almost as good as an average man, Marian contrives with womanly dispatch to bring about the downfall of the villain through her sexuality and the marriage of the hero through her intelligence.

Apart from her superiority to the novel's men, we know that Marian is a woman because she moves easily between angel and demon. In comparison to Laura, she is more properly demon than man: "My father was a poor man, and Miss Fairlie's father was a rich man. I have got nothing, and she has a fortune. I am dark and ugly, and she is fair and pretty. Everybody thinks me crabbed and odd (with perfect justice); and everybody thinks her sweet-tempered and charming (with more justice still). In short, she is an angel; and I am— Try some of that marmelade, Mr. Hartright, and finish the sentence, in the name of female propriety, for yourself" (pp. 60–61). Much as she deplores it, the passion Marian inspires in Fosco springs from his thrilled recognition of "a person of similar sensibility," confirming her essential identity as demon. But when Walter crowns her at the end as "the good angel of our lives" (p. 646), this apotheosis does not cancel the demonism, but includes it, insuring her transcendence of the villain's arrogant machinations and the hero's arrogant bliss.

As Marian gains stature in conjunction with the novel's principal women and men, her spinsterhood gains authority from the only marriages that are described at length: Laura's nightmarish alliance to Sir Percival Glyde, and the more decorous though no less monstrous marriage of the Foscos. Laura's, and even Marian's, helpless pliability under Sir Percival's insane but legally authorized bullying, the vulnerability of Laura's fortune (from which she herself is virtually indistinguishable) to her husband's depradations, are highly colored dramatizations of any Victorian husband's authorized power over his attendant women and his wife's property. The ensuing florid plot against Laura's identity is a terrifying reminder of the jeopardy of any Victorian woman's selfhood once she has attained the socially approved but psychically and legally menacing position of wife.

In case we miss these parallels with domestic reality, the Foscos' marriage throws a thoroughly respectable shadow over Laura's lurid ordeal. As Laura becomes dissembling, cowed, and ultimately infantilized by marriage, her strong-willed aunt undergoes a still more startling metamorphosis: "For the common purpose of society the extraordinary change thus produced in her is, beyond all doubt, a change for the better, seeing that it has transformed her into a civil, silent, unobtrusive woman, who is never in the way. How far she is really reformed or deteriorated in her secret self, is another question. I have once or twice seen sudden changes of expression on her pinched lips, and heard sudden inflexions of tone in her calm voice, which have led me to suspect that her present state of suppression may have sealed up something dangerous in her nature, which used to evaporate harmlessly in the freedom of her former life" (p. 239).

Marian's unease leads the reader to anticipate an eruption of grand villainy in the Countess Fosco, but no such thing occurs. She remains a dutiful ancillary in her husband's plots; her ominous suppression shows her "reformed or deteriorated" into nothing more or less than a good English wife. In his witty final confession the Count is quite clear that, according to prevailing standards of marriage, his wife is neither victim nor villain but an ordinary domestic paragon:

First question. What is the secret of Madame Fosco's unhesitating devotion of herself to the fulfillment of my boldest wishes, to the furtherance of my deepest plans? I might answer this by simply referring to my own character, and by asking, in my turn, Where, in the history of the world, has a man of my order ever been found without a woman in the background self-immolated on the altar of his life? But I remember that I am writing in England, I remember that I was married in England, and I ask if a woman's marriage obligations in this country provide for her private opinion of her husband's principles? No! They charge her unreservedly to love, honour, and obey him. That is exactly what my wife has done. I stand her on a supreme moral elevation, and I loftily assert her accurate performance of her conjugal duties. Silence, Calumny! Your sympathy, Wives of England, for Madame Fosco! (p. 632)

Sensationalism becomes indistinguishable from domestic duty. The Countess' metamorphosis into a model of smouldering and suppressed wifehood is a chilling parallel to Laura's more flamboyant metamorphosis into addled and helpless child, for nothing in the novel denies that the Countess Fosco is an exemplary British woman. With this model of wifely submission before our eyes, it is no wonder that, like her husband, we aggrandize the "interesting" figure of the old maid, who, unencumbered by the stays that mutilate the other women, makes her own path with the integrity of visionary and detective.

The Woman in White is our most explicit exaltation of the old maid as a criticism of traditional wifehood. Generally she is glorified in a certain vacuum, as an escape from the ordinary rather than an overt challenge to its norms. Collins, bohemian writer of romances whose most articulate satiric character is his Napoleonic villain, is freed by the extravagance of sensationalism to let his old maid expose the deficiencies of common lives: when juxtaposed against pliable, lovable femininity, exemplary wifehood, male heroism and villainy, Marian reveals herself as one of nature's heroes, if not convention's or ideology's. In a last insistence that Marian is a hero but never a man, Collins juxtaposes her with one more social type: her bachelor uncle, the neurasthenic aesthete Frederick Fairlie.

Bachelors are cozily idealized figures in Victorian novels, adorned perforce with the cloistered spiritual authority of the Church, the university, and other revered communities of celibate men. But Uncle Fairlie shrinks in petulant selfishness to the dimensions of his room, his art reproductions, and his quivering nerves: "Why—I ask everybody—why worry *me?*" (p. 360). Fairlie's shrinking dependence on his seclusion and his valet throws into still greater relief Marian's grand venturousness; he could not exist without protective social rituals and prerogatives, while Marian establishes her own landmarks alone. Dickens' Miss Havisham, who appeared a year later, combines

Fairlie's appearance of helpless seclusion with the powers and determination of Marian. Like Fairlie, Miss Havisham hides from the sun and refuses to leave her room, but instead of shrinking from life she controls destinies from her magic spot; her lonely room becomes the novel's dark center, from which the lives of the other characters are shaped.

Wilkie Collins, remaining within conventional definitions of womanhood and apparently impervious to feminist causes, makes of his old maid the only true hero in his romance of "men and women" as they form themselves into representative social types. Marian's grandeur in relation to the novel's petty bachelor is a typical Victorian vision, for more likable, even lovable fictional bachelors are in comparison to our pageant of old maids as ineffectual as Mr. Fairlie, though less willfully so. Unlike Miss Havisham, Mr. Pickwick cannot transmit his magic aura beyond his own intimately appreciative circle, and while John Jarndyce in *Bleak House* provides orphans with a tender refuge, he fails sadly when he tries to become their Providence and shape their destinies. In George Eliot's *Adam Bede* the beloved clergyman Mr. Irwine diffidently withdraws his spiritual counsel at a crucial moment, thus manifesting his impotence to avert the novel's tragedy and reshape its action. Miss Havisham, Mildred Arkell, and Marian Halcombe do have the novelist's power to arrange destinies and form the future, but these bachelors manifest nothing stronger than the protective love which breeds no action.

Apart from the adorable frauds who sing Gilbert and Sullivan's patter songs, Victorian England's most famous bachelors are probably Charles Dickens' Ebenezer Scrooge and George Eliot's Silas Marner. The modestly domestic salvation of their similar conversions provides a striking contrast with the heroic, odyssean figure of the old maid. Scrooge's rejection of Christmas is in no way a grand Faustian rejection of its theology. Christmas in this tale means family, and society viewed as a family: Scrooge rejects not God incarnate but his own role as munificent father. He is redeemed not into awe but to jollity, in token of which he does not bow to a child but takes one on his shoulders. Similarly, George Eliot's wounded Silas crouches away from a familial society until a golden child redeems him into a broad if pseudo-fatherhood that encompasses both hearth and village. The isolation of Scrooge and Silas is a petty idolatry with no divine or demonic associations; both are reborn out of its subhuman misery into idealized family life through the magic touch of children.

What is remarkable about this redemption is that initially it seems more appropriate for women; contemporary as well as Victorian moralists have apotheosized family and children as woman's only salvation. Scrooge and Silas are saved by becoming in a sense conventional women, finding transfigured new identities in family life and roles; yet in the lives of the old maids considered here this rapturous consummation is barely considered. In fact, Miss Havisham becomes the future's bane when she takes in a child as Silas Marner does, just as in our own century Muriel Spark's divine-demonic spinster Jean Brodie finds betrayal rather than salvation of her powers through her appropriation of children. The salvation of men becomes the dark, damning power of women. This may be so because the excruciating isolation of Scrooge and Silas is a disease lacking heroic associations; thus they are cured by reassimilation into the ordinary. The old maid's isolation is her heroic mark, which the ordinary cannot engulf. Absorption into family would deny her splendid identity, while it is the only hope of growth for her stunted bachelor counterparts.

The endearing incapacity of literary bachelors, compared to the old maid's more fearful isolation and power of control, must have had some basis in social fact. No doubt the impact of feminism made heroic women more imaginable, for though none of the works considered in this chapter would have considered itself radical, there is no doubt that the messianic intensity of Victorian feminism infused lives and literary representations that were untouched by its ideology. Yet in all these works heroism is not a vision for women of a better age, but a stubborn fact within existing conditions and definitions. Considering the same anomaly seen in literature, the strength of single women as opposed to the incapacity of single men, Frances Power Cobbe offers a profoundly convincing, if essentially nonfeminist, explanation. Cobbe's essay "Celibacy V. Marriage," quoted earlier, suggests that it is precisely the conventional properties of womanhood—woman's greater emotional capacity and her instinct to make a home—that allow her to thrive without family definition as man cannot:

And further, if a woman have but strength to make up her mind to a single life, she is enabled by nature to be far more independently happy therein than a man in the same position. A man, be he rich or poor, who returns at night to a home adorned by no woman's presence and domestic cares, is at best dreary and uncomfortable. But a woman makes her home for herself, and surrounds herself with the atmosphere of taste and the little details of housewifely comforts. If she have no sister, she has yet inherited the blessed power of a woman to make true and tender friendships such as not one man's heart in a hundred can even imagine. And while he smiles scornfully at the idea of friendship meaning anything beyond acquaintance at a club or the intimacy of a barrack, she enjoys one of the purest of pleasures and the most unselfish of all affections. (p. 233)

In this devastating because thoroughly traditional statement, Cobbe turns Victorian celebrations of womanhood against the ideology of family they were intended to serve. It may be that woman's instinct for creating a home and her rich gift of intimacy equip her for the roles of daughter, wife, and mother; more significantly, these blessed additions to her heroic capacities equip her to become none of the above, but to love as well as thrive alone. The myth of the heroic old maid does not refute official Victorian definitions of womanhood; it is one of their strongest, if most subversive, creations.

Visions

The grand myth of spinsterhood, reconstructed from fragments of lives and of popular novels, had far-reaching implications for thoughtful Victorians. The old maid, tolerated most easily as society's piteous victim, is in her fullest incarnation its leader, endowed with ambiguously awesome powers that intimate the destined future of the race. Aware of her potential importance as a sign of the times and of times to come, essayists distinguish scrupulously between the authentic old maid and the accidentally unmarried woman, crippled by disappointment in love and centering her vicarious life around father, brother, or other omnipotent male. An essay in *Blackwood's* defines the true old maid as born, not made by circumstances: "The highest type of old maid has made no sacrifice, nor is she in any sense a victim, for marriage as a state is not necessary to her idea of happiness . . . She is the woman who has never met with her ideal, and who has never been cunningly persuaded to accept anything short of it."[36]

Even W. R. Greg's censorious "Why Are Women Redundant?" rests on this distinction between authentic spinsterhood and the "natural"woman who happens to be unmarried. Greg exempts single servant girls from the fearful new race of women he sees springing up in England, because servants retain a functional identity with wives: *"they are supported by, and they minister to, men."*[37] Though he will not see the authentic single woman as the exalted, elastic creature *Blackwood's* describes, he fears her as virtually a new species. In 1884 an article in the *Westminster Review* placed both the jeremiad of Greg and the discriminating appreciation of *Blackwood's* in their true context of evolutionary thought. Considering the old maid in the authoritative idiom of modern science, the *Westminster* finds in her "an important variation in the types of womanhood": "The unmarried woman of to-day is a new, sturdy and vigorous type. We find her neither the exalted ascetic nor the nerveless inactive creature of former days. She is intellectually trained and socially successful. Her physique is as sound and vigorous as her mind. The world is before her in a freer, truer, and better sense than it is before any individual male or female."[38]

As Florence Nightingale had done earlier, this important article borrows Milton's solemn initiation of humanity into the new world, removing it from the couple to consecrate with it the single woman alone. As a "type" of her age and of the coming race, she alone is associated with those mighty personifications, history and evolution. Frances Power Cobbe proudly quotes a similar benediction in her autobiography, when Sir Charles Lyell graced her at a dinner party with the most gallant compliment I have heard paid to a Victorian woman. The topic was evolution: "Suppose *you* had been living in Spain three hundred years ago, and had had a sister who was a perfectly commonplace person, and believed everything she was told. Well! your sister would have been happily married and had a numerous progeny, and that would have been the survival of the fittest; but *you* would have been burnt at an *auto-da-fè*, and there would have been an end of you. You would have been unsuited to your environment. There! That's Evolution! Goodbye!" (Cobbe, *Life*, p. 447). In his exemplum of the old maid as a higher type, evolving as society does, Lyell moves the iconography of the two sisters from popular fiction to evolution; the private heroic boasts of letters, memoirs, and journals, the intrepid single heroines of fiction and romance, become the scientist's hope of the coming race.

The sudden prevalence of old maids in the fiction of the 1890s grows from the heroic myth that had a subterranean life throughout the century; but in the bleak anatomies of transition of George Moore and George Gissing, the old maid is placed in an explicitly evolutionary context. Moore's Mildred Lawson, in *Celibates*, struggles toward a freer world and a higher state of consciousness. But because neither her environment nor her own talent permits her to become an independent artist, she bitterly succumbs to marriage: "I am not suited to marriage; but from marriage there does not seem to be any escape. All girls must marry, rich and poor alike; there seems no escape, though it is impossible to say why. I have tried all my life to find escape from marriage, and here I am back at the same point."[39] In Moore's *A Drama in Muslin* the rage and despair of the spinsters for whom there are no men left to marry, but no future without marriage, typify the paralysis of their Irish homeland. Both works thrust their heroines into an historical and evolutionary cul-de-sac: in both, marriage has become an obsolete destiny for women, but the age of heroism that can foster authentic old maids is powerless to be born.

George Gissing's "The Foolish Virgin" (*The Yellow Book* 8 [January 1896]) and *The Odd Women* are infused with a stronger, if bitter, faith in the new age. In the former, the desperation of vain, pretentious Rosamund Jewell to marry any man who will have her is forcibly transmuted into a bleak redemption by the "new gospel" of work. At the end she is nothing more rewarding than a servant; still, she has at least evolved, in the story's terms, from a "parasite" to a "rational combatant," and is thus closer to evolutionary triumph than she would be had she realized her dream of marrying Mr. Cheeseman. *The Odd Women* is a more heroic account of pioneering single women who are harbingers of the death of marriage, presiding over an ennobled future of work and solitary faith. The evolutionary visions of Moore and Gissing take definition from their emphasis on old maids. Moore's pray for a grand new world to live in; Gissing's body forth the new dispensation in their own severe mutations.[40]

The myth of the old maid culminates in the grim "scientific" realism of the nineties, while it flowers as well in its most florid romances. George MacDonald's Lilith and Rider Haggard's Ayesha may be the most authentic old maids we have met, in that they are unimaginably old (both have reigned over their magic worlds for over two thousand years) and yet they are literally "maids," not merely virgins but magically young. The impassioned and protracted virginity of both is the source of their power to rule; the celibacy they lament provides them with heroic immortality. In her more self-pitying moods, Ayesha might inhabit a realistic novel by Moore or Gissing: "Thus, even thus, have I lived for full two thousand years—for some six-and-sixty generations, as ye reckon time—in a Hell, as thou callest it—tormented by the memory of a crime, tortured day and night with an unfulfilled desire—without companionship, without comfort, without death, and led on only down my dreary road by the marsh-lights of Hope, which though they flickered here and there, and now glowed strong, and now were not, yet, as my skill foretold, would one day lead me to my deliverer."[41]

Two thousand years is longer than most novelists would make the old maid wait for her destiny, but as Haggard's readers saw the twentieth century coming into view, Ayesha must have seemed an apt harbinger of a new age in which the old maid was no longer to be "delivered," but emerged as deliverer herself. In *She* Ayesha tries to deliver the men who love her, but at the last moment they fear the fire-baptism through which she will lead them to transfiguration and immortality. In shrinking away from the flames they suffer Ayesha to fall from her supreme position on the evolutionary pinnacle, forcing her to wait for her next cycle of ascendancy.

Haggard's strong men could not measure up to the transfigured future Ayesha embodied; still the old maid's promise rang clearly at the end of two thousand years. In the myth Darwin sanctioned this "new type" became an evolutionary harbinger more powerful than Tennyson's mid-century vision of the redeemer Arthur Henry Hallam, whose passing and possible luminous return were cast in the regretful form of the elegy. Vividly present, the old maid announced her coming in the mixed and experimental form that belonged to her age—that of passionate, if stammering, prophecy.

V

The Rise
of the Fallen
Woman

THE HEROIC MYTHOLOGY of spinsterhood led what amounted to an underground life in the nineteenth century; we must search for it behind a mask of sad subservience. In contrast, the fallen woman, heartbreaking and glamorous, flourished in the popular iconography of America and the Continent as well as England. Her stance as galvanic outcast, her piquant blend of innocence and experience, came to embody everything in womanhood that was dangerously, tragically, and triumphantly beyond social boundaries. As Sally Mitchell puts it, she is a creature "ungoverned by law. She stands alone, pure woman."[1]

Yet in both art and life we find intense alliances between the old maid and the fallen woman, each in her own way an exile from woman's conventional family-bounded existence. We have seen in such literature as Christina Rossetti's "A Triad" and Annie E. Holdsworth's *Joanna Trail, Spinster* the strenuous journeys of soul-making on which fallen woman and spinster embark together, leaving wives to their materialistic incomprehension. In a better-known work, Ellen Wood's phenomenally popular *East Lynne,* this alliance is more covert, not less intense. Cornelia Carlyle, Lady Isabel's strong-minded spinster sister-in-law, assumes tyrannical control of her brother's household, forcing Lady Isabel into the transfiguring humiliation of the fallen woman; the novel absolves her paternalistic husband of any responsibility for his wife's flight. When Isabel returns as "Madame Vine," she has come eerily to resemble Miss Carlyle, both in her grotesque floppy hats and in her jealous exclusion from family bliss; it is no wonder that Miss Carlyle, who has remade her, is the first to pierce her disguise. The real domestic drama of *East Lynne* is the fierce interchange of identities between old maid and fallen woman, a marriage from which the husband in his noble befuddlement is thoroughly excluded.

The heart of a seemingly quite different work, Elizabeth Barrett Browning's feminist hymn *Aurora Leigh,* is the grand sisterhood the solitary literary woman Aurora discovers between herself and Marian Erle, a monumental Madonna whose "fall" through rape is celebrated as a grand purification. They sanctify their union by their common refusals to marry Romney Leigh, a hero as obtusely noble as Ellen Wood's Archibald Carlyle. In a dark ending, Aurora does return to Romney when he is broken and blinded, but Barrett Browning's true epithalamium is the mutual salvation of Marian and Aurora, a beatitude Romney is helpless to create or to partake of. Barrett Browning treats with feminist and religious ardor a subversive junction between old maid and fallen woman that is not hers alone; it is part of a complex cultural vision.

In Victorian painting as well, virgin and fallen woman unite iconographically, as Susan P. Casteras has shown.[2] The "courting wall," that pervasive and ambiguous motif of womanhood, secludes the nun as it ostracizes the fallen woman; purity and experience are iconographically associated, though Casteras finds little evidence that wives and mothers were painted against the wall. Dante Gabriel Rossetti brings this intensely exclusive union to life: *Ecce Ancilla Domini,* his early painting of the Annunciation for which his worshiped sister Christina posed, shows the newly empowered Virgin huddled against a wall (Figure 27); in *Found,* his later, unfinished study of a fallen woman, the lush Fanny Cornforth takes refuge in a similar way against a similar wall (Figure 35). The visions of poets and

27. *Dante Gabriel Rossetti, "Ecce Ancilla Domini."*

painters, stern cautionary tales and feminist paeans, seem to merge in this powerful association of two women beyond the pale of family.

This visionary alliance in art was the transfigured reflection of social experience. Reclamation of fallen women was one of the few respectable activities available to philanthropically minded Victorian spinsters. Artists perceived the subversive implications of this sisterhood, though complacent arbiters of mores did not. The Anglican sisterhoods struggling to be born in the 1850s dutifully justified their moral utility by the restoration of fallen women, which was considered "the particular work of the early nineteenth-century sisterhoods."[3] Such exemplary spinsters as Christina Rossetti (wearing a nunlike habit) and Dorothea Beale were transported to visions of religious exaltation by their private work in Magdalen homes. The inspiration of this new sort of community caused Dorothea Beale to write ecstatically in 1885 of "a Union of women which should embrace and work with the existing organisations, such as the Girls' Friendly, the Metropolitan Association, and the Christian Young Women,— . . .Women band themselves together to go out to nurse in the armies—once that was thought impossible . . . Perhaps I am talking of what is impracticable. It is hard to keep calm enough to see clearly, when such visions hover before one."[4]

This stunning apprehension of possible female community, transcending the unions Dorothea Beale had tirelessly administered in her girls' schools, is in part a mystical translation of the common, ambiguous social situation old maid and fallen woman shared. Not only did both exist amorphously beyond women's traditional identities as daughter, wife, and mother, but both were associated with exile in all its resonant confusion between criminal degradation and missionary heroism: as old maids were exhorted for conflicting reasons to emigrate to the colonies, so prostitutes were commonly transported there. Both were defined as essential strangers in England, and both were associated with the promise and the terror of a new world. Embracing this mission of heroic exile, epic apologias such as Florence Nightingale's defined the pioneering state of spinsterhood by appropriating Milton's myth of the fortunate fall. As the spinster in her despised respectability knows in private defiance that the

28. 29. 30. *Augustus Egg's popular parable of a quintessentially Victorian fall.* Above, *"Misfortune."* Opposite, *"Prayer."*

world is all before her, so the fallen woman flamboyantly acts out the spinster's seditious, if submerged, heroic myth.

In June 1858 Augustus Egg exhibited at the Royal Academy a trilogy that shocked its audience by animating their deepest fears of family blight: *Past and Present (Misfortune,* Figure 28; *Prayer,* Figure 29; and *Despair,* Figure 30), an allegory of the domestic havoc wreaked by the fallen wife. The narrative was accompanied by this solemn gloss: "August the 4th. Have just heard that B— has been dead more than a fortnight, so his poor children have now lost both parents. I hear *She* was seen on Friday last near the Strand, evidently without a place to lay her head. What a fall hers has been!"[5]

"What a fall hers has been!" This tenderly punitive note, in which admiration mingles with condemnation, recurs again and again in Victorian treatments of the fallen woman; her prone form becomes so pervasive an image that it crowns our mythic

pantheon. At first glance the Victorian myth of the fallen woman seems even more harshly degrading than its literary archetype in *Paradise Lost:* Milton's Eve gives powerful argumentative voice to her longing to reign rather than serve, while the Victorian fallen woman is usually depicted even in literature as a mute, enigmatic icon, such as Dante Gabriel Rossetti's Jenny, who sleeps through the poem that probes her nature. Milton's Eve will survive in the triumphant ascending woman whose heel will bruise the serpent's head, while Victorian conventions ordain that a woman's fall ends in death. It seems that an age of doubt has grafted the doom of Milton's Satan onto the aspirations of his Eve, generating a creature whose nature it is to fall—the sexual trespass that produced that fall is almost always elided in British treatments—and whose identity defines itself only in that fall.

This groveling figure lies at the heart of some of the most powerful literature and art the age produced. Not only does the titanic outcast Madonna Marian Erle dominate and determine the action of Elizabeth Barrett Browning's epic *Aurora Leigh,*

30. *"Despair."*

but the bardic prophecies of England's most influential poets, Browning's *The Ring and the Book* and Tennyson's *Idylls of the King,* depict a society brought down by the ambiguous, revolutionary power of a fallen woman. Like Egg's trilogy, *The Ring and the Book* (1868–69) is the saga of a fallen wife, though Browning's more subversive treatment is set in the hotter emotional climate of the Florentine Renaissance. The bartered child-bride Pompilia flees her respectable husband with a handsome young priest, only to be slaughtered with her newborn son by her husband's henchmen. This sensational material is refracted through a series of partisan narrators, tried in street and courtroom, until the verdict of the saintly old Pope stills the confusion by pronouncing Pompilia an angel of purity and her husband a Satanic monster. Guido, pillar of family, Church, and state, undergoes the poem's most radical and genuine fall; the touchstone of his wife's martyrdom exposes the demonic brutality of the society whose respectability he embodies and, by implication, of Browning's own society as well. Like Marian

Erle's, Pompilia's fall leaves her "whiter than white" and her society festering in its own lies. Pompilia's death is as excruciating as any Augustus Egg might have envisioned for her, but her fall is a vindication, for it brings down the institutions that oppressed her, justifying in the ensuing action her self-sanctifying dying words: "and I rise."

In Tennyson's *Idylls of the King* (1842–1885) Guinevere does not rise so easily from groveling at the feet of the "blameless king" whose authority her infidelity has emasculated. Tennyson's Guinevere is little more than a sinister, suffering shadow in the background of the action, apparently untouched by either Arthur's rectitude or Lancelot's doomed lust for honor; her consuming activity is her own, and Camelot's, fall. Her subversive avatars, of whom we see far more, are Elaine, the purity of whose passion for Lancelot exposes his essential dishonesty, making of her a death's-head portending the fall of the kingdom; and Vivien, the serpent woman who causes the fall of Merlin, Camelot's inspiration and soul. Guinevere's flamboyant alter egos initiate much of the action, generalizing upon both the degradation and the potency of the fallen Queen. The proliferation of fallen, seemingly fallen, or falling women in the *Idylls* transmutes a woman's fall from a personal to a national event, one that inspires and symbolizes Victorian England's epic portrait of its own doom. In both poems that counterpoint to the fallen woman—the semi-divine hero, or risen man, for whom Carlyle supplied the paradigms—is helpless to arrest the action's essential descent; he is forced into the role of choric ancillary to the woman's irresistible tragic activity.

For Browning and Tennyson the fallen woman becomes the abased figurehead of a fallen culture; her imaginative resonance justifies the punishment to which she is subjected. But Victorian social reformers found her as painful a presence as do contemporary feminist critics. Then and now she seems to enlightened minds a pitiable monster, created by the neurosis of a culture that because it feared female sexuality and aggression enshrined a respectably sadistic cautionary tale punishing them both. To redeem the fallen woman from degradation, sympathetic critics in her day and in our own have turned from the denunciations of epic and myth to the more flexible reality of history.

One group of nineteenth-century philanthropists wanted to

demythicize the fallen woman by making her victim rather than agent. Such documents of poverty as Thomas Hood's "The Bridge of Sighs" and Henry Mayhew's *London Labour and the London Poor* focus on the fallen woman as beaten-down prostitute, practicing one of the few trades available to Victorian females. She is defined economically rather than morally, emitting no special aura of destruction and doom but joining the poor seamstress and the shabby-genteel governess in the ranks of capitalist victims. William Acton goes further in his iconoclastic *Prostitution* ..., elevating many fallen women from practitioners of a dismal trade to apprentices at the nobler profession of marriage:

> I have every reason to believe, that by far the number of women who have resorted to prostitution for a livelihood, return sooner or later to a more or less regular course of life ... Incumbrances rarely attend the prostitute who flies from the horrors of her position. We must recollect that she has a healthy frame, an excellent constitution, and is in the vigour of life. During her career, she has obtained a knowledge of the world most probably above the station she was born in. Her return to the hearth of her infancy is for obvious reasons a very rare occurrence. Is it surprising, then, that she should look to the chance of amalgamating with society at large, and make a dash at respectability by a marriage? Thus, to a most surprising, and year by year increasing extent, the better inclined class of prostitutes become the wedded wives of men in every grade of society, from the peerage to the stable.[6]

In the light of Acton's sanguine common sense, the mobility of actual social life reverses the popular myth of a woman's implacable fall, introducing us to the bouncy heroine who is able to fall up. Later, controversial and "dangerous" authors adapted to their own uses Acton's new, worldly convention. Thomas Hardy's "Ruined Maid" (1866) returns home in triumph— " 'Some polish is gained with one's ruin,' said she"— while George Moore's Esther Waters also rises through her fall above the life of her martyred mother and can boast at the end of her stolid typicality: "She was only conscious that she had accomplished her woman's work."[7]

Feminist critics writing today about the fallen woman are as eager to demythicize her as forward-looking Victorians were, constructing the same morally purged models of victim and survivor. Françoise Basch and Frances Finnegan insist with

Mayhew on the prostitute's identity as exploited worker, limited to a wretched trade by the harsh realities of capitalist economics and sexual power. Judith Walkowitz sees the prostitute as Acton did, as a healthy adaptor, plagued by no special sense of sin but turning to prostitution as a part-time job among others on the path to eventual marriage and respectability. In the corrective vision of all these social historians the fallen woman is no longer an outcast from society; as martyr or social climber, she is at home in the world that bred her.[8]

Contemporary feminists share the discomfort of Victorian liberals at the irreversible sin and doom Egg's trilogy represents; in conjunction, though by different routes, they deny that the fallen woman existed at all. "What do I think will become of me?" retorts a "kept mistress" interviewed by Mayhew, "What an absurd question. I could marry tomorrow if I liked."[9] Nineteenth-century reformers were as drawn as we are to this vision of a flexible, open, nonretributive world, but in imaginative literature the myth persisted. No documentation could exorcise the titanic outcast, doomed and dooming, who seems to have been, like Marley's ghost, an undigested morsel of the Victorian bad conscience, familiar social reality cast into phantasmagoric and avenging shape, a woman readers could neither live with nor escape.

No doubt the Victorian imagination isolated the fallen woman pitilessly from a social context, preferring to imagine her as destitute and drowned prostitute or errant wife cast beyond the human community, because of her uneasy implications for wives who stayed home. Characteristically, Victorian literature plays with her professional alliance with virtuous wifehood only to snatch the two apart at the last minute. In painting, in what Linda Nochlin calls the "secular pictorial imagery of the fallen woman,"[10] she is associated with sweeping vistas of space and with impersonal urban masses, as in Egg's trilogy, never with snug domestic interiors. Thackeray and Dickens bring her to the fringes of the family, hinting at the interchangeability of the bought woman and the possessed wife, but at the last moment she is always ostracized from the sanctity of the hearth. In *Vanity Fair* Becky Sharp purchases respectability with shadiness, but her murder of Jos Sedley allows the pure, if equally heartless, domestic angel Amelia to shrink away from her at the end. In *Dombey and Son* Dickens' prostitute Alice

Marwood struts like a bird of ill omen after the future Edith Dombey as she is paraded on the marriage market. But Alice soon dies in a rage of penitence, and Edith, who has figuratively murdered the Dombey family and almost becomes the literal murderess of Carker, is ostracized to Dijon; neither shadows the pageant of blissful marriages with which the novel ends. Generally the fallen woman functions emblematically rather than economically in fiction; her appearance is the memento mori of a bad marriage, but her economic exploitation of and by a patriarchal society is not allowed to infect a good one.[11] Rather than associating the home and the marketplace, as the prostitute did in fact, she must destroy or be cast out of the home. The fallen woman in whom the Victorian imagination crystallizes transcends Mayhew's economic categories of pauper, working woman, and wife, wailing alone with Dickens' outcast Martha in *David Copperfield*, "Oh, the river!"

We are understandably embarrassed by the phantoms of our ancestors. In this case many of our ancestors were themselves embarrassed by the inherent cruelty of this image. Feminist criticism and broad cultural studies pride themselves on having shaken off the attitudes that created the fallen woman, without examining her myth itself very closely. Yet unconscious or half-formulated cultural myths are not always the enemy of enlightened historical understanding, nor can history and statistics always exorcise them. If we examine this figure as a haunting Victorian type in whom angel, demon, and old maid converge, she may remind us that the mind's changing transmutation of social fact is the only "true history" we know.

One constant element in the myth of the fallen woman, reaching back to the Old Testament and to Milton's epic recasting of it, is the absolute transforming power of the fall. At Eve's fall, Milton tells us, "Earth felt the wound, and Nature from her seat / Sighing through all her Works gave signs of woe, / That all was lost" (*Paradise Lost*, IX, 781–784). In Victorian revisions it is the woman alone who is wounded, sighs, laments, and is lost; indifferent Nature simply reclaims her. Once cast into solitude, the fallen woman, like Milton's Eden, is irretrievably metamorphosed, as even the enlightened modern Hardy insists in *Tess of the d'Urbervilles:* "Almost at a leap Tess thus changed from simple girl to complex woman."[12] In Ellen

Wood's *East Lynne* the fallen wife also changes her identity "almost at a leap," moving from glamorous and petted child-wife to unrecognizably haggard governess, her fall acting as a physical and social crucible. For Wilkie Collins the fallen woman is so entangled in visions of radical metamorphosis that his *No Name* (1862) and *The New Magdalen* (1873) anatomize her as an actress with an uncanny skill at disguise. In the former, Magdalen Vanstone is actually the daughter of a fallen woman, but her name and her ominous identity as "a born actress" associate her with her mother's hidden fall. When her illegitimacy is revealed and she and her sister are left nameless and disinherited, Magdalen assumes a dazzling series of names and disguises in order to marry the new heir and reclaim her fortune and her name. *The New Magdalen* reprises this motif: Mercy Merrick, a former prostitute who began life in her mother's profession of strolling actress, steals the identity of a respectable woman and performs her role with more feeling and skill than the true woman possessed. Magdalen and Mercy are implausibly reclaimed back to "truth" and marriage at the end; but the novels deal with their fallen lives, which are compounds of mobility and metamorphosis explicable only by the freedom of inspired acting.

Though in life the division between fallen and respectable woman might have been reasonably fluid, art allows no return to the old familial boundaries of identity. Generally the fallen woman must die at the end of her story, perhaps because death rather than marriage is the one implacable human change, the only honorable symbol of her fall's transforming power. Death does not simply punish or obliterate the fallen woman: its ritual appearance alone does her justice.

If we look again at the fallen wife in Augustus Egg's trilogy, in whom it seems ritual abasement could go no further, we become aware of her power as well as her humiliation. In *Misfortune* her offstage sexual sin aggrandizes as it shames her; not only does her sharp diagonal line slash insistently through the regularity of verticals and horizontals that constitutes her home, defining the painting's composition and knocking down her daughters' house of cards as it does so, but it aligns her with the painting's solidest, most substantial mass: the spreading floor. Her fall empowers her to break through the design of her world; in the two subsequent paintings, as in *Paradise Lost* and *Idylls of the King*, the fall seems to open out space, suggesting the pioneering desolation of new worlds. The mirror's flat and enclosed perspective gives way to the new depths of the window in *Prayer* and then to the sweep through the arch of the bridge in *Despair*. In both, the dead paterfamilias along with the walls of his house seems replaced by the waxing moon as the guiding symbol of the family.

As Raymond Lister suggests, the moon may hint at a reconciliation between mother and daughters, who appeal to it at the same moment.[13] Iconographically, it is more complex. Traditionally, it stands for changeableness, connoting not simply the wife's perfidy but the fallen woman's inherent power of metamorphosis which allows her to destroy and reconstruct her world. In such Victorian feminist writers as Charlotte Brontë the moon brings with it matriarchal potency, as in *Jane Eyre* when Jane's dead mother appears in the moon, commading Jane to flee Rochester, or in *Villette*'s final paean to the moon "all regnant" presiding over the city's triumphant female cabal. The moon is similarly regnant in the expanded world of women that the wife's fall generates in Egg's trilogy, as it will be in a later, and wittier, Victorian vision of a woman-ruled world: Aubrey Beardsley's wicked frontispiece to Oscar Wilde's *Salomé*, whose "Woman in the Moon" frightens those she shines on. Egg's cautionary genre piece carries intimations of ascendant female power along with its explicit images of abasement and despair and suggests a hidden potency in the fallen woman's fall made explicit in works that did not commit themselves to the Royal Academy's respectable walls.

It lacks a moon, but G. F. Watts's stark *Found Drowned* (Figure 31) seems a distillation of the dominant effects of Egg's trilogy. Reduced here to a corpse, the fallen woman again seems to epitomize helpless abasement, but in the diagonal line of her body and the Christlike stretch of her powerful arms she, too, brings a new, discordant, and enlarged sense of space to a composition otherwise restricted to stiff verticals and horizontals. Apart from the star with which she seems to exchange glances, her face is the painting's only source of light. This monumental corpse takes to herself the illuminating and shaping role of Egg's moon, exposing the painting's grim structural principle as she transcends it.

Perhaps because of its challenge to the sexual double standard, Ford Madox Brown's *Take Your Son, Sir!* (Figure 32),

31. George F. Watts, "Found Drowned."

whose majestic fallen woman "thrusts forward her naked child, demanding that responsibility for the conception of the child be shared," was never finished or exhibited.[14] Brown created this accusing image two years before Egg's moral fable was exhibited; yet one feels that here Egg's errant wife has freed herself utterly from the cumbersome design of her world and has appropriated its furniture, including its vacant mirror, to her own uses. She is here in full possession of all available space, swelling into enigmatic monumentality. Her white garment and the audacious folds through which she seems to pluck the child from her womb allow her to combine associations of animality, of maidenhood, and of wifely respectability. She, like all Victorian fallen women, is alone in her world; she seems to embody the defiant powers of all womanhood in the face of little men who would disown them.

Not only is she free from the conventional posture of abasement, but the viewer is abased before her. The source of the awe she generates is a daring combination of anatomy and religion: the large unfinished block of her drapery and the mirror haloing her head give her the air of a looming, outsize Madonna, asserting her powers to God, perhaps, as well as man. Like Watts's drowned corpse and more obviously than did Egg's fallen wife, she seems to have gained power over size and scale, reducing the cur who impregnated her along with the

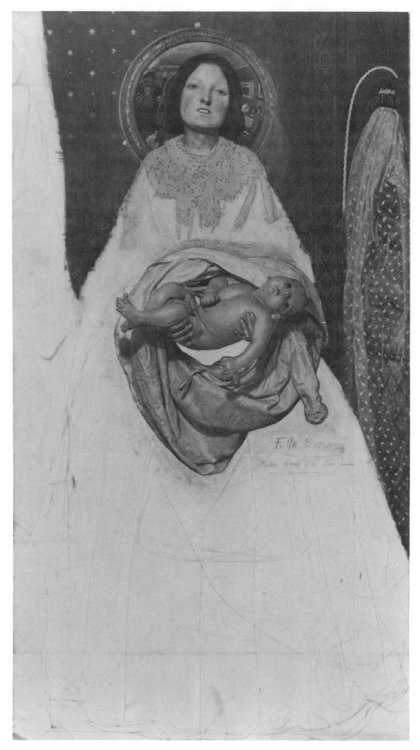

32. *Ford Madox Brown, "Take Your Son, Sir!"*

viewer to a diminutive figure in the mirror. Conventionally holy and defiant, her pose insists upon the simultaneity of her fall and apotheosis as she grows into the magus/God of her world, mocking by her size male claims of power over her.

British novels shun such challenging presentations of fallen women. To find an analog in nineteenth-century fiction for this defiant icon, unapologetic in its self-presentation, its purity and subversion, we must turn to an American heroine, Hester Prynne, whose majestic presence diminishes the gaping spectators that include the reader of her story:

> The young woman was tall, with a figure of perfect elegance, on a large scale. She had dark and abundant hair, so glossy that it threw off the sunshine with a gleam, and a face which, besides being beautiful from regularity of feature and richness of complexion, had the impressiveness belonging to a marked brow and deep black eyes. She was lady-like, too, after the manner of the feminine gentility of those days; characterized by a certain state and dignity, rather than by the delicate, evanescent, and indescribable grace, which is now recognized as its indication. And never had Hester Prynne appeared more lady-like, in the antique interpretation of the term, than as she issued from the prison. Those who had before known her, and had expected to behold her dimmed and obscured by a disastrous cloud, were astonished, and even startled, to perceive how her beauty shone out, and made a halo of the misfortune and ignominy in which she was enveloped.[15]

Hester's stature, her regality, to which her "halo of . . . misfortune and ignominy" adds an additional power, suggest the simultaneity of fall and apotheosis that are the verbal equivalents of Watts's and Brown's monumental paintings. From this opening tableau to the conclusion of Hester's "legend," where we stare at the cryptic symbolism of her tombstone, Hester presents herself pictorially, insisting on our scrutiny. Like her own elaborately wrought letter, she becomes an outsize and troublingly ambiguous work of art whose visual power outshines our ability to "read" her. Hester's self-created potency is made manifest when the narrator dubs the scaffold on which she is forced to stand "her pedestal" (p. 49), adding intimations of art's reigning power to Chillingworth's scathing description of her "standing up, a statue of ignominy, before the people" (p. 57). In Hawthorne's portraiture Hester's fall alone enables her to "stand up," imbuing her with the overweening power of creator and created object.

Insofar as Hester's career in *The Scarlet Letter* is a series of penitential renunciations, Hawthorne obeys the conventions we have seen in British literature which depict the fallen woman as prone and punished. Yet, more explicitly than in British fiction, the novel's visual symbolism forms a counterpoint to its moral structure; Hawthorne's deliberately difficult artistry suggests the possibility of hidden dimensions in England's more muted literary analogues. In this novel about a theocratic community, where sin is less a violation of social mores than of the might of souls, Hester's fall is the novel's one unequivocally religious activity. The adultery that precipitated it long before the beginning of the novel seems real only as a catalyst for Hester's ensuing spiritual power. As in Browning's *The Ring and the Book*, the unquestioned demonism of Hester's respectable husband, Roger Chillingworth, whose evil is, like Guido's, a reliable barometer for the ambiguity of the other characters, calls the status of her adultery into question. The novel makes Hester's sexual sin so abstract and problematic that her fall is made to seem the one available medium of spiritual life.

Unlike Gaskell's Ruth, whose infantine purity we shall examine, Hester's spiritual strength does not transcend her fall but arises from it. Her stigma, the letter itself, is transmuted into her own dazzling creation, then into her vocation—"The letter was the symbol of her calling . . . They said that it meant Able; so strong was Hester Prynne, with a woman's strength" (p. 117)—and finally, at her death, into her "engraved escutcheon," its passage from art to vocation to election reflecting her own rise. "Hand in hand with Ann Hutchinson," we learn, Hester "might have been a prophetess" (p. 119) had her unlawful child not prevented her; by the end she has become a feminist saint, the vehicle for "a new truth" of empowered and transfigured womanhood. Hawthorne's American parable explains one power of this myth over the nineteenth-century imagination, transcending its overtly sadistic cautionary message. Like Hester's "fantastical" needlework, which "then, as now, [was] almost the only [art] within a woman's grasp" (p. 61), a woman's fall is imagined as almost the only avenue through which she is allowed to grow.

Flaubert's fastidiously spiritual Emma Bovary, whose fall is inseparable from her exalted religious yearnings and craving to become "a Sister of Mercy," might almost be a parody of Hester Prynne, but in British fiction the fallen woman is forbidden the audacious self-presentation of these dark Madonnas. Yet their ambiguous spirituality, their artist's ability to make their worlds shrink by their statuesque presence, align them with a miniature object of impassioned and ambiguous worship: Lewis Carroll's Alice, a figure of simultaneous majesty and abasement in a world seemingly created by the catastrophe of her fall. "Down, down, down," Alice's story begins. "Would the fall *never* come to an end?" In the power of the fallen woman to infiltrate Victorian England's most beloved children's story, it may seem as if the fall never did, for Alice's fall seems almost a parody of our cultural myth, though nonsense, whimsy, and sentiment defuse it. Like those of Collins', Egg's, and Brown's women, Alice's fall ignites her capacity for metamorphosis; she mutates continually as she travels through Wonderland, growing when necessary into an object as intimidating as Hester Prynne presiding from her pedestal. Her fall transforms the reader's expectations of predictable reality, so that both Alice and our perspective are expanded by an act that seems to diminish them both.

Alice is both outcast in and creator of her newly expanded world, and, like that of some of the bloodstained fallen women we shall meet later, Wonderland is ruled by potentially murderous women. The Queen of Hearts, the Duchess, the Cook, and the Cheshire Cat insofar as it functions as a dream-version of Alice's female cat, Dinah, all suggest the varieties of female fury a pure girl's fall can energize.[16] Carroll's book may seem a surprising addition to our adult context, but in so potent a cultural myth, one containing so many intense and unexamined feelings about womanhood, it should not surprise us if extremes meet, and the demonic energy of the fallen woman share some of the preternatural purity Carroll located in little girls. Moreover, if we recall the inscrutable sensuality that suffuses Carroll's own illustrations to *Alice's Adventures Under Ground* and his photographs of little girls, we see that the fall brings out a certain perversity within Alice's apparent purity (see Figures 33, 34); as the fallen woman animates the mobile child, so juxtaposition with a little girl's apparent innocence should remind us of the spirituality with which the Victorian fallen woman is endowed. In the worlds of Egg, Brown, Watts, and Hawthorne, as well as

33. 34. *The unselfconscious sensuality of Lewis Carroll's nude photographs highlights the sexual power of the pure little girl he immortalized.*

Lewis Carroll, the woman's fall transfigures her, making her the God of her world, the vehicle of a potency which underlies her tribulations in Victorian fiction as well as art.

Bearing in mind the dual perspective of these works—an explicit narrative that abases the woman, an iconographic pattern that exalts her—I want to look again at three well-known fallen women in British fiction: Elizabeth Gaskell's Ruth, Thomas Hardy's Tess Durbeyfield, and George Eliot's Hetty Sorrel. I have chosen these novels because all were widely read and influential—though *Ruth* and *Tess of the d'Urbervilles* had an aura of controversy and scandal, while *Adam Bede* was wholesome and beloved—and because they seem to contain the spectrum of possible attitudes toward "fallen" heroines. Gaskell lovingly exonerates her pure heroine from the appearance of sin; the more aggressively iconoclastic Hardy flings his heroine's purity as a gauntlet at hypocritical social taboos; George Eliot seems to condemn Hetty Sorrel's ambitious sexuality with unyielding austerity, though Hetty is a more challengingly complex figure than the narrator wants her to be. For all their diversity, however, each novel is in its own way a variation on its culture's central myth.

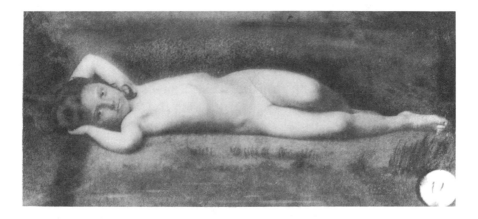

Hetty Sorrel is presented as fallen from her first lush and sensuous appearance in the novel, but Ruth and Tess seem initially under their authors' special protection. Gaskell's Ruth is too sublimely innocent to understand the fact of her own fall: through seduction and betrayal, unwed pregnancy and motherhood, she remains the victim of her destitution, her unprotected, orphan state, her sexual ignorance, and the Phariseeism of respectability that generates all three. Until the ending's abrupt reversal, Gaskell practices what liberal reformers preached: she defiantly reclaims this sweet soul for reintegration and respectability.

Dubbed by the subtitle "a pure woman," Hardy's Tess also seems vindicated by her narrator from having fallen at all. As was Ruth, she is allowed an implausible degree of innocence and passivity in her affair with Alec, suggesting that according to Victorian sexual ethics the true sin lies less in the act than in willing one's own fall. An absurd society condemns Tess, but natural growth is always her friend: her affinities with burgeoning nature, her incorrigible will to renewal and joy, seem to exempt her from the fallen woman's guilt and sorrow. Like Hetty and Ruth, Tess is given a certain psychic integrity, a fidelity to her own nature, that raises all three above the moral flaccidity of their seducers. The singleness of being of these three heroines seems to resist the myth that would transform them from characters into types of sin.

Yet each novel conforms to its strictures in the end. As Ruth is on the brink of respectability, her history is revealed, she and her son are ostracized, and she dies a penitential death nursing her cowardly seducer through typhus fever—a sacrificial ending that infuriated such feminist readers as Charlotte Brontë.[17] In *Adam Bede* Hetty's sexual fall is compounded by infanticide: she murders her illegitimate baby, confesses her guilt under Dinah Morris' noble influence, and is dramatically rescued from the gallows only to die anticlimactically after empty years of transportation. Tess, too, compounds sexual experience with murder, and there is nobody to rescue her from the ceremonial butchery of death by hanging. No doubt this addition of murder to sexuality eased Eliot and Hardy's final conformity to Victorian conventions: the execution of a killer was not yet revolting to society's liberal guilts and fears.

It is easy to denounce the punitive endings of these novels, as Charlotte Brontë did, to condemn the moral timidity of their authors in the face of publishers' and readers' pressures. Still, one component of their fascination comes from the tension between social possibility, in which the community, more elastic than it seems, absorbs the fallen woman comfortably, and a social myth that aggrandizes the outcast. The gestures and confessions of guilt, the ritual slaughters with which all three novels end, are less betrayals of the social realism of Victorian fiction than expressions of its powers to clarify and create the myths of its culture.

Gaskell's Ruth vehemently rejects marriage to her seducer, conventional salvation through respectability, in favor of a saint's life and a martyr's death. On our first view she is marked off from her environment by moonlight: she passes wearily through "a commonplace-looking shop" past "a window (through which the moonlight fell on her with a glory of many colours)."[18] Despite her pregnancy, her fall seems devoid of sexuality and will, consecrating her as the moon through the window does; as with the wife in Egg's *Despair*, that which isolates her from society assures her kinship with the moon. As Ruth moves through the novel toward exposure and death, she seems refined beyond anger, conflict, and physicality. "She was bodily wearied with her spiritual buffeting" (p. 288), suggesting that her essence is distilling itself into immateriality alone. With the further dilution of her sexuality, her sole remaining kinship with animalism is the instinct of fear: "Ruth lifted up her eyes for the first time since the conversation began, the pupils dilating, as if she were just becoming aware of some new agony in store for her. I have seen such a look of terror on a poor dumb animal's countenance, and once or twice on human faces. I pray I may never see it again on either!" (p. 336).

Ruth's "fall," like that of Brown's accusatory Madonna in *Take Your Son, Sir!*, touches her only as a benediction, allowing her to transcend the animal, and thus the human, condition; her martyr's death is the fullest expression of her rarefied life rather than a denial of it. Her fall is so spiritualizing that she dies long before the end of the novel, having refined herself, like Dickens' fallen Nancy in *Oliver Twist*, to a pair of eyes that avenge and compel simultaneously. Like the phantom of Nancy, she has left the body to become not a part of the community but its overseer and its scourge. Once again the transforming power of the fall lends spiritual potency to the woman it destroys.

Ruth's fall becomes an allegory of the triumph of spirit over life; that of Tess Durbeyfield suggests initially the triumph of life over spirit. Abetted by the knightly cadence of her name in the title and the vivid insistence on her sheer physical presence in virtually every episode, Tess seems to tower over the arbitrary conventions that label her a sinner, especially as they are embodied in the callow and vacillating Angel Clare. Yet despite Hardy's radical air and idiom, his Tess seems from another perspective the most pitiably abased of all our fallen women. With all her supposed purity, perspective and language insinuate images of a somewhat unsavory and guilty thing. Not only does a famous passage present her as "a fly on a billiard-table of indefinite length, and of no more consequence to the surroundings than that fly" (p. 89), but, like Kafka's Joseph K., Tess seems a consciousness born to guilt: " 'Now, punish me!' she said, turning up her eyes to [Alec] with the hopeless defiance of the sparrow's gaze before the captor twists its neck. 'Whip me, crush me; you need not mind those people under the rick! I shall not cry out. Once victim, always victim—that's the law!' " (p. 275). Despite Hardy's ambivalently protective commentary, the reader is infected by Tess's own unremitting sense of sin.

Tess of the d'Urbervilles seems to fling a gauntlet at the myth of the fallen woman's ever-accelerating guilt and sorrow; but the structure of its narrative is as subservient to the myth as Tess is to Alec. Following the orthodox pattern, Tess begins in hopeful innocence, but goes from bad to worse after her fall divorces her from her girlhood self, her increasingly estranged condition aligning her with bare and open landscapes until her murder of Alec consummates her identity as outcast. From first to last, more than any of our heroines, Tess is marked off from the human community. Gaskell's Ruth was engulfed by the sympathetic faith of the Bensons, as George Eliot's Hetty was by Dinah Morris'; but for the most part, Tess attracts sympathetic understanding only from objects: "The wall felt warm to her back and shoulders, and she found that immediately within the gable was the cottage fireplace, the heat of which came through the bricks. She warmed her hands upon them, and also put out her cheek—red and moist with the drizzle—against their comforting surface. The wall seemed to be the only friend she had. She had so little wish to leave it that she could have stayed there all night" (p. 235).

From one point of view the friendship Tess draws from the wall is the ultimate gesture of Victorian pathos: tenderness lies only in the senseless exterior of the family that casts her out. But through the friendship of the wall she imbibes life and grandeur from her surroundings, taking her stature from objects as human beings conspire to reduce her. Similarly, when we first meet Tess a hedge frames her solitude in opposition to the uniformity of the country dance. In the florid Eden of Talbothays a cow's flank sets off her profile so vividly that Angel is driven to declare his passion. At the wasteland of Flintcomb-Ash the featureless faces to which Hardy likens the staring emptiness of earth and sky set off Tess's own mangled face after she cuts her eyebrows off to avoid molestation. She finds her ultimate "home" not in her posthumous reconciliation with Angel, but at the empty altar of Stonehenge where she waits to be arrested, receiving through this final setting architectural, historical, and divine recognition. Things give Tess an epic life, belying her recurrent humiliations. Ruth's triumph was spiritual, Hetty's, as we shall see, natural and cosmic, but Tess's is in large part compositional. By stationing her against large and grand objects Hardy gives her a borrowed magnitude which defies human measurements of her fall.

In his placement of Tess against his own ironic version of a courting wall, Hardy provides a telling gloss on the fallen woman in Dante Gabriel Rossetti's *Found* (Figure 35), who

35. *Dante Gabriel Rossetti, "Found."*

crouches against a wall despite the urging of her former suitor. The wall in *Found* has the same double nature as the wall in *Tess.* In the explicit narrative it bears the pathos of a last retreat to unfeelingness, overshadowing the woman as the net imprisons the lover's calf. But simultaneously, the wall is an escape from that very net, represented by the lover's clutch. Retreating from compassion, Rossetti's fallen woman is aligned through the strength of the wall with the most substantial masses in the painting: the sweep of the bridge, the touched-in wall at the right, the wheelbarrow, the solid cannon beneath it whose firmness contrasts with the wrinkles on the lover's boots, the ripples in his tunic. The lover is the dominant human figure in the triangle, yet his wrinkles and ripples give him a suggestion of instability, while the woman's cloak drops solidly to the ground, as if it were sculpted rather than painted. Linda Nochlin reminds us that the first sketches for *Found* used a wispy, starved-looking model; the woman became increasingly substantial and strong once Rossetti brought in as his model the florid Fanny Cornforth.[19] In counterpoint to the pathos of his explicit narrative, Rossetti, like Hardy, endows his fallen woman with the strength of the forms that surround her. As with Tess, we are only subliminally aware of her power in the painting's composition, but it is in large part the power of each woman, endowed and oblique though it is, that has kept both works alive for so long.

Hetty Sorrel's power in *Adam Bede* is even more oblique than that of Ruth and Tess, in part no doubt because George Eliot endows her with no spiritual or physical gifts that will draw the reader's sympathy. Unlike the others, Hetty is emotionally insentient and intensely aggressive, falling not because she is lulled passively into a sexuality associated with sleep, but because she wills to possess the social glamour and power Arthur embodies. The way in which the novel's rhetoric forbids the reader to like Hetty must have something to do with the novelist's own fierce suppression of the impulse to self-pity and apologia, for unlike the eminently respectable minister's wife or the polemical defender of luscious womanhood, George Eliot was herself born into artistry by "falling." Forbidding, perhaps, her own sympathy with Hetty as well as ours, Eliot enmeshes her with similes linking her with lower forms of life; at various times Hetty is associated with a pound of butter, kittens, small downy ducks, babies, rose-petals, a young calf, a butterfly, a blossom, a bud, a peach, a brooklet, a spaniel, a bird, a pet, a "thing," a canary, a water-nixie, "a pictur in a shop-winder," a "round, soft-coated pet animal," a brute, a "Medusa-face," a stone, and death. Her association with small, spiritually depleted forms of life seems to deprive her fall of a corresponding ascent we can admire.

But other, more implicit links are forged around Hetty's selfish and solitary little figure. Her nature and destiny align her strangely with her cousin, the spiritual paragon Dinah Morris, to whom she seems initially no more than a sensuous foil: "What a strange contrast the two figures made! Visible enough in that mingled twilight and moonlight. Hetty, her cheeks flushed and her eyes glistening from her imaginary drama, her beautiful neck and arms bare, her hair hanging in a curly tangle down her back, and the baubles in her ears. Dinah, covered with her long white dress, her pale face full of subdued emotion, almost like a lovely corpse into which the soul has returned charged with sublimer secrets and a sublimer love. They were nearly of the same height; Dinah evidently a little the taller as she put her arm round Hetty's waist, and kissed her forehead."[20]

That kiss by moonlight seals an association more radical than the obvious pictorial contrast. In the course of the novel Hetty will don Dinah's Methodist garb as a joke, but as an abandoned wanderer her flush will disappear, replaced by an intensifying pallor until she becomes the corpse Dinah resembles here. Correspondingly, Dinah will get rounder and ruddier, finally to marry Hetty's fiancé Adam and discard her Methodist garb. In the plot the strapping figure of Adam brings the two women together, but the kiss here hints at a more fundamental complicity between purity and fallenness than he can understand, as in a subtle sense they drain each others' identities and exchange natures.

At the beginning Hetty and Dinah meet in the context of the Hall Farm, that fecund emblem of domestic rootedness, where both are disapproved of because they are unsettled wanderers by nature and vocation. The narrator instructs us to disapprove of Hetty by botanical analogy: "There are some plants that have hardly any roots: you may tear them from their native nook of rock or wall, and just lay them over your ornamental flower-pot, and they blossom none the worse. Hetty could have cast all her past life behind her, and never cared to be reminded of it again" (p. 132). Mrs. Poyser laments Dinah's similar, though more high-minded, indifference to settled family virtues: "if everybody was to do like you, the world must come to a standstill; for if everybody tried to do without house and home, and with poor eating and drinking, and was allays talking as we must despise the things o' the world, as you say, I should like to know where the pick o' the stock, and the corn, and the best new-milk cheese 'ud have to go. Everybody 'ud be wanting bread made o' tail ends, and everybody 'ud be running after everybody else to preach to 'em, istead o' bringing up their families, and laying by against a bad harvest. It stands to sense as that can't be the right religion" (p. 68). Later on, Mr. Poyser gives us a pithy echo of his wife in this dark picture of leaving home: "We should leave our roots behind us, I doubt, and niver thrive again" (p. 294). But initially, Dinah as well as Hetty denies this inexorable fate by the fervent determination to be rootless and to thrive.

In this Wordsworthian novel, built on the primacy of interrelation, Hetty is subtly attached both to the "higher" nature of Dinah and, in her equation with a plenitude of insentient things, to the web of life that is the novel's more equivocal, personified Nature. Two key chapters in *Adam Bede* are entitled "Links" and "More Links," and ironically, despite her rejection of community, Hetty is the novel's primary linking principle. The definition of a character through her "links" or lack of them is a device Hawthorne used dramatically in *The Scarlet Letter*, a book that influenced *Adam Bede*, but Hester's one remaining "iron link of mutual crime" emphasizes by contrast Hetty's boundless connectedness: "The links that united [Hester] to the rest of human kind—links of flowers, or silk, or gold, or whatever the material—had all been broken. Here was the iron link of mutual crime, which neither he nor she could break. Like all other ties, it brought along with it its obligations" (p. 116).

Hetty craves the solitude of the social climber, but the novel never allows her links to her world to break. Hester appeared first as a solitary icon, stared at by crowds, but when we first see Hetty in the dairy, her dimpled fleshliness makes her the equivalent of her environment of butter and cream; she embodies her world rather than transcending it. Once she has fallen into the role of outcast and solitary, her very alienation makes her the equivalent of a larger environment defined by "the agony of the Cross" in a pastoral landscape:

> and surely, if there came a traveller to this world who knew nothing of the story of man's life upon it, this image of agony would seem to him strangely out of place in the midst of this joyous nature. He would not know that hidden behind the apple-blossoms, or among the golden corn, or under the shrouding boughs of the wood, there might be a human heart beating heavily with anguish;

perhaps a young blooming girl, not knowing where to turn for refuge from swift-advancing shame; understanding no more of this life of ours than a foolish lost lamb wandering farther and farther in the nightfall on the lonely heath; yet tasting the bitterest of life's bitterness.

Such things are sometimes hidden among the sunny fields and behind the blossoming orchards; and the sound of the gurgling brook, if you came close to one spot behind a small bush, would be mingled for your ear with a despairing human sob. No wonder man's religion has such sorrow in it: no wonder he needs a Suffering God.   (pp. 305–306)

More successfully than the spiritually aspiring Dinah, Hetty is linked to the novel's single divine principle, that of a god become tragically human, suffering alone in nature's ironic blossoming. Her very isolation, which the narrator initially uses against her, becomes her strongest link to the novel's somber vision of divine humanity.

In her solitary suffering Hetty achieves a connection to divine humanity that the nobler characters fail to reach. Nevertheless, she is equated as well with the ironic fertility of George Eliot's personified Nature, most importantly by a trait often used to dismiss her from our moral consideration: her revulsion against children, motherhood, and nurturing, culminating in her abandonment of her own child. A facile reading might lead us to think that Mrs. Poyser, who fusses incessantly over her own swarm of children, is the novel's "natural" woman, but in fact Nature is, like Hetty, an indifferent mother: "There are so many of us, and our lots are so different: what wonder that Nature's mood is often in harsh contrast with the great crisis of our lives? We are children of a large family, and must learn, as such children do, not to expect that our hurts will be made much of—to be content with little nurture and caressing, and help each other the more" (p. 247).

Like her own mother, Nature, Hetty nurtures only herself, proving truer to the design of her world than the novel's solicitous believers in the absolute virtue of family and farm. No doubt it is Hetty's fidelity to the cosmic design of the novel's world that gives her fall the power to diminish the family at Hall Farm and the larger familial community of Hayslope; like the wife in Egg's *Past and Present*, she opens the composition from enclosure to vastness, "away from the familiar to the strange" (p. 309). She is all the more structurally potent in that her links with larger cosmic and natural forces are unconscious; her one article of faith is the mirror before which she postures. But this mirror is linked to the magic well of the novel's central shaping principle, the instrument of the sibylline artist herself: "With a single drop of ink for a mirror, the Egyptian sorcerer undertakes to reveal to any chance comer far-reaching visions of the past. That is what I undertake to do for you, reader" (p. 5). Typically, Hetty's mirror is explicitly condemned as vanity but implicitly aligned with the oracular instrument of narrative art: "my strongest effort is to avoid any such arbitrary picture, and to give a faithful account of men and things as they have mirrored themselves in my mind. The mirror is doubtless defective . . . but I feel as much bound to tell you as precisely as I can what that reflection is, as if I were in the witness-box narrating my experience on oath" (p. 150). It is fitting that Hetty become the artist's chief ally, so intricately woven is she into the design of the novel's world. As with the other fallen women we have examined, the materials of her abasement define her magnitude. Her junction with the cohesive power of *Adam Bede*'s universe and its vision is subtler and more insidious than in our other novels because, creating to such a large extent from within the myth rather than making a case from without, George Eliot is under no liberal compulsion to make her outcast character attractive.

Demeaned and exalted, Hetty is the most dramatic manifestation of this peculiarly Victorian vision of the fortunate fall, and characteristically, for all her sexual promise, her abundant interactions with the natural world, Hetty is oddly devoid of erotic life. George Eliot reminds us constantly that she is ambitious, not passionate, and is thus all the more subversive of her hierarchical community. This radical sexlessness distinguishes British representations of fallen women, and it may seem at first to diminish them further. If we recall the symbolic use of horses in novels about fallen women from three different countries, we may be depressed by the dearth of glamour, of ecstatic animal intensity, in our British example.[21]

In a charged episode of Leo Tolstoy's *Anna Karenina* (1878), Count Vronsky rides his horse Frou-Frou in the officers' steeplechase. We experience with Vronsky the aristocratic magnificence of the horse, her consummate sensitivity to the nuances of the race, foreshadowing his finely bred dream-mistress Anna. Through clumsy riding Vronsky betrays his eloquent horse: she breaks her back and is shot. The episode is essentially a foreboding morality play, yet its glamour and intensity are stressed above all. The intoxication of public triumph as it passes imperceptibly into defeat, of ardor as it modulates into cruelty and disease, are epitomized in the fall of the glorious Frou-Frou, who embodies, with Anna, Tolstoy's essence of grace betrayed. Similarly, Émile Zola's *Nana* (1880) places the climax of the courtesan's career at the Grand Prix de Paris, won in an upset by a golden filly named after Nana. The pervasive glamour of the sunshine, the triumph of a perfect animal accompanied by Nana's "swaying . . . thighs and hips," obscure in their vitality the underlying corruption of the race. The glorious horse does full justice to her namesake, the "Golden Beast" who is the true ruler of a decaying Paris.

In their sensuous celebrations of triumphant horses both Tolstoy and Zola commemorate their heroines' animality and the poignant glamour of its fall. George Moore's *Esther Waters* is dominated by racehorses, but they are meager beasts with none of the luster of their foreign counterparts. Esther's first impression of a racehorse is characteristically laconic: "He rode a beautiful chestnut horse, a little too thin, Esther thought, and the ugly little boys were mounted on horses equally thin" (p. 14). As the novel becomes progressively somber, so the horses become pathetic: "Esther, her print dress trailing, watched a poor horse striving to pull a four-wheeler through the loose heavy gravel that had just been laid down" (p. 255). Not only are the animals shorn of glory, but the novel's racing scenes emphasize the financial desperation of betting, never the physical intoxication of victory. Esther resembles an animal only in her stolidity, her dumb instinctive tenacity, never in aristocratic pride of the flesh. She is allowed no celebration of her sexual power through horses, but only broken reminders of her own doggedness.

In all our British works the love stories seem similarly remote if not inconceivable. Gaskell's Ruth seems oblivious of any sexuality beyond her indefatigable nursing of her lover; her pregnancy seems a miracle of spontaneous generation, so unaware is she (and we) of what led up to it. Tess has only contempt for Alec, the agent of her fall, reserving her hope of passion for disembodied, ultimately unattainable Angel, though, as we saw, her deepest sympathies spring from the inhuman potency of objects in the landscape. Moreover, the lovers fade out of the action at crucial moments in the heroines' histories, returning only when it is too late: destiny has been determined without them. Neither Egg, Brown, Watts, nor Rossetti bothers to include in his paintings the love affairs that generated the falls, only their fruits in the women's tortured postures. No doubt this omission was imposed by Victorian propriety, but it has the interesting result of making each fallen woman essentially autonomous and her own agent. Their sexlessness, expressed in the iconographic kinship between the fallen woman and the pure little girl, becomes another avenue whereby these women grow as they fall and take possession of their worlds.

On the one hand, as all these works remind us immediately, the fallen woman is captured in various stages of abasement, proneness, and self-laceration. No doubt like some of the more sadistic boarding-school literature, these scenes fed their audiences' well-known relish for flogging and tales of flogging. These works of art could punish women more effectively for an offstage and unnamed trespass than civilized society was permitted to do. Yet what they lose in sensuality and human interest, they gain in ambiguous suggestiveness. By excising love and passion from the fall, and by subtle modulations of power in the fallen woman, they encompass both the pity of the woman's fall and the transforming power, not of her redemption but of her will to rise. They mediate between abasement and exaltation, hiding images of woman's triumph in representations of her punishment.

The shaping power of this myth intensifies when we examine its impact, not just on art, but on the lives of two writers we know well: Charles Dickens and George Eliot. In the novels of both, the equivocal figure of the fallen woman is a recurrent, troubling presence, while in their lives, she grows into a symbol of wished-for, almost magical transformations.

Dickens' was a life that defined itself through its obsessions. Beyond his enchanter's magic as novelist he was possessed in turn by four forces that seemed to him replete with transforming power: philanthropy, the magical science of mesmerism, the theater, and love. Each of these is galvanized by its association with the metamorphic promise of fallen women.

Dickens' plots in the 1840s generally center on the purification of a tainted protagonist. In the same spirit, in 1847 Dickens and the wealthy philanthropist Angela Coutts opened a Magdalen Home, Urania Cottage, which was to bring about the redemption of its charges through their eventual marriages in the colonies.[22] The reclamation of fallen women was a popular philanthropy, but Dickens' grandiose vision of colonial emigration distinguishes Urania Cottage from such relatively modest missions as William Gladstone's furtive attempts to effect private and particular conversions through fireside nourishment and good words. Dickens was less interested in domesticating his women than in transfiguring them. Urania Cottage was less a haven than a crucible, affecting transformations as magical as any that conclude his books. Under its aegis the young women would undergo the dual metamorphosis of transportation and marriage.

Dickens' dream of the potential alchemy of emigration associates his magdalens with a host of pioneering spinsters as criminals, heroes, and harbingers of a stronger, saving race. Later in his life Dickens' Prospero-like vision of emigration as transfiguration was applied to his own fallen household: an embittered paterfamilias, he sent two of his disappointing sons to Australia and two others to New Zealand, hoping vainly that exile would change them as wonderfully as it did his dearer creatures Wilkins Micawber and Abel Magwitch. The magic potential of his fictions and the domestic salvation he dreamed for his sons rely upon the blueprint for fallen women that Dickens had tried to institutionalize in the 1840s.

Two years before the founding of Urania Cottage, Dickens had been possessed by another Prospero-like role. This one involved incessant experiments with mesmerism, in which his attempts to "heal" a Madame de la Rue became so frenzied that his wife jealously ended the sessions. Here, too, Dickens' ascension as healer and savior became entangled in the need, not merely to possess a woman, but, like the Victorian artist Freud later in the century, to engage her very soul in magic self-transformations. As doctor, Dickens drew on the same well of personal and cultural mythmaking that underlay his philanthropy:

both the mesmeric subject and the fallen woman promise a new and newly empowered selfhood.[23] Each is equipped to transcend galling and degrading human changelessness, the daily stolidity that had already begun to afflict Dickens in his marriage.

This core of mythic faith blazed out once more in Dickens' final lunge at metamorphosis: his affair with the actress Ellen Ternan, a more agonized and disruptive recapitulation of the mesmeric sessions with Madame de la Rue. The latter assumed the role of fallen woman only in the wounded imagination of Mrs. Dickens; Ellen Ternan played it in fact. Moreover, since the phrase "public woman" was still used interchangeably for performer and prostitute, Ellen's suggestive profession as actress and member of a theatrical family suffused her with the glamour of fallenness before the affair began.

Here, too, Ellen must have seemed the achieved reincarnation of Madame de la Rue, for, as Fred Kaplan reminds us, mesmeric subjects became stars in their own right: "Like great actresses, these 'prima donna'(s) of the magnetic stage played many moods and roles" (p. 118). Like Madame de la Rue, Ellen Ternan manifests herself as a vehicle of charismatic transformations, thus explaining Dickens' association of the two in the pet or code name whereby he designated Ellen as "the Patient."[24]

This love affair ignited when Dickens and Ellen Ternan appeared together in *The Frozen Deep*. Throughout its furtive course it was submerged in the stage, creating a background of masquerade, codes, and intrigues to Dickens' final, self-consuming theatrical triumphs; his compulsive onstage murders of the fallen woman Nancy were shadowed by his equally compulsive and theatrical offstage love of the fallen actress Nelly. As actress and "Patient" as well as mistress, Ellen Ternan aroused in the aging Dickens a last promise of the fallen woman's gift of destruction and restoration. This final obsession may have been fed by Wilkie Collins' dazzling associations of the magdalen with the actress, but its explosive confusions of passion and performance epitomized Dickens' own past as well. As philanthropist, mesmeric "healer," actor, and lover, as well as author, he seems to have been possessed by a belief in woman's metamorphic power that haunted his life even more than it did his books, crystallizing in the hidden and many-faceted promise of the fallen woman.

Dickens tried to institutionalize the myth of the fallen woman, to stage-manage it in the lives of others, and finally, it seems, in a hopeless exertion of his magnetizing will, to appropriate its powers to himself by possessing its agents. For George Eliot the myth brought a new, almost miraculous self-possession. In her second novel, *The Mill on the Floss*, she pours out on Maggie Tulliver all the sympathetic identification that was forbidden to *Adam Bede*'s Hetty Sorrel. In this explicitly autobiographical fiction the episode of an actual sexual fall becomes vestigial—Maggie's trespass is an illusion, existing only in its effect on the community and on other lives—for in her mélange of demonic and transforming power, Maggie seems a fallen woman by nature, in whom any activity is secondary to the intense ambiguous impact of what she *is*. Manifesting an eerie kinship to Ford Madox Brown's fallen Madonna, George Eliot's monumental autobiographical projection is both the witch Defoe imagines in his *History of the Devil*, spreading desolation and punished for it, and her community's legendary protector, the Virgin of the Flood, who sanctifies the spots she visits. The shifting mythic identities that George Eliot sheds upon her heroine suggest the almost magic metamorphosis the role of fallen woman brought to her own life.

In one of the few expressions of glee she allowed herself George Eliot wrote to Barbara Bodichon in the year of *Adam Bede*'s great success: "I am a very blessed woman, am I not? to have all this reason for being glad that I have lived, in spite of my sins and sorrows—or rather, by reason of my sins and sorrows."[25] Hetty and Maggie had to be destroyed for the transformations their sins and sorrows caused, but the transforming power of the myth brought gladness and grace to George Eliot. Whether deliberately, unconsciously, or accidentally, she seems to have composed her own life so that its fitful, rudderless, and self-doubting first half was alchemized into gold when the austere bluestocking became the fallen woman. In the period of relative ostracism after her elopement with George Henry Lewes the ugly duckling became a swan, the critic became an artist, and the awkward victim became the sibylline Madonna of the Priory and of England itself, as George Eliot was formed out of the mistakes of Mary Ann Evans.[26]

The role of fallen woman was so pivotal in Eliot's life, functioned so powerfully as the crucible in which unpromising beginnings were forged into unprecedented triumphs, that it is tempting to read her life as a mythic work of Victorian fiction. The apparent abasement and the hidden power of the fall crystallize here as they rarely do in her novels, suggesting that despite the role Lewes assumed as George Eliot's benign Pygmalion, her birth as an artist may have resulted from the power of her faith in the unstated implications of her own fall and its potential, not for redemption, but for renewal. When we look at her biography in this broader context, George Eliot's salvation as an artist seems to spring from her own awesomely intelligent appreciation of the conventional role she assumed.

We can never know a life as we think we know a work of art, but it is possible to find intimations of cultural mythology in the patterns such brilliantly receptive and self-dramatizing Victorians as Charles Dickens and George Eliot shaped in their lives. Just as actual spinsters extracted an awareness of destiny from their culture's heroic mythology, so the century's greatest novelists lived a myth that gives shaping energy to their fiction. For both novelists, assuming the role of fallen woman transfigured creator as well as character with the alchemical possibilities of the outcast. The self-transforming majesty of this character type borrowed some of its intensity from a larger belief underlying an age that feared belief was lost: the majesty of character itself and the ensuing immortality shed on those who played a character.

VI

Victorian Womanhood and Literary Character

T<small>HE PRETERNATURALLY</small> endowed creature who taunts conventional morality as angel and demon, old maid and fallen woman, seems alien to the approved model of womanhood Victorians were bred to revere. Officially, the only woman worthy of worship was a monument of selflessness, with no existence beyond the loving influence she exuded as daughter, wife, and mother. By contrast, the woman I claim is at the center of Victorian woman worship seems a monster of ego. As angel, she is militant rather than nurturing, displacing the God she pretends to serve. As angelic demon, she becomes the source of all shaping and creative power, dropping the mask of humility as she forecasts apocalyptic new orders. As old maid, she simulates meekness while proclaiming that the world is all before her new dispensation. As fallen woman, she spurns meekness for the glory of her own apotheosis. Oddly, these subversive paradigms are only incidentally feminist. They infuse the writings of women and men alike, dominating works famous and obscure, radical and conventional, experimental and popular. They are not limited to the underground code of an oppressed female tradition; they pervade the Victorian imagination. How can we explain their divergence from official self-sacrificial womanhood? What does the imaginative dominance of these ego-driven isolates tell us about the canonical worshiped woman with no life beyond family?

Properly seen, these are the many faces of a single image. The mobile and militant woman is the source of the placid self-renouncing paragon of official veneration; the demonic angel rises from within the angel in the house. The motto of this book is Maxine Hong Kingston's speculation: "Perhaps women were once so dangerous that they had to have their feet bound." In the Victorian imagination the danger of woman's special powers produced the foot-binding of her officially approved image. Feminist and nonfeminist writers about Victorian England have seen the foot-binding but not the perceived danger at its source. In their examination of familiar figures in the context of a new mythology, the preceding chapters remind us that the diluted woman of acceptable convention was one peculiar outgrowth of a broad mythography in which woman, potent, primary, and alone, appropriates all the magic left in her world.

Because danger and repression are interdependent participants in a continuous process, it is virtually impossible to distinguish "official" from "subversive" visions of Victorian womanhood: perceptions of power cannot be untangled from the impulse to suppress it. If, for example, we examine an apparently repressive definition of womanhood, we see that the myths anatomized above animate it in covert form. For the anti-feminist Eliza Lynn Linton "womanliness" is meant to be a bulwark against the New Woman's push beyond her proper domestic sphere:

> We call it womanliness when a lady of refinement and culture overcomes the natural shrinking of sense, and voluntarily enters into the circumstances of sickness and poverty, that she may help the suffering in their hour of need; when she can bravely go through some of the most shocking experiences of humanity for the sake of the higher law of charity; and we call it womanliness when she removes from herself every suspicion of grossness, coarseness, or ugliness, and makes her life as dainty as a picture, as lovely as a poem. She is womanly when she asserts her own dig-

nity; womanly when her highest pride is the sweetest humility, the tenderest self-suppression; womanly when she protects the weaker; womanly when she submits to the stronger.[1]

Linton's selfless minister seems nobly remote from the ego-fueled solitaries with which my book is concerned. When considered closely, however, they tend to merge; all that distinguishes them is the high-mindedness of Linton's lady, who translates her own impulses into the needs of others. Nonetheless, she, too, is a mobile creature who defines herself in verbs. The Victorian essay reaches for active verbs when it tries to define womanhood; even Linton's retrograde and restrictive definition does the same. Her womanly woman overcomes, enters, helps, goes, removes, makes, asserts, protects, then submits. Like her verbs, she is not only active but the sole instigator of action. As her world's sole motive principle, even when choosing to submit at last, she leads rather than obeys.

In accordance with the language, the first half of Linton's paragraph is appropriately odyssean. Womanliness is not an emotional state, but a series of difficult journeys and passages. As with the myth of the old maid as heroic exile, the life of Linton's good woman finds expression in odyssey. As with the old maid, her journeys are not a mere motion from place to place, but a remaking of herself. Like the grand Pre-Raphaelite angel-demons, though more fastidiously than they, she can aggrandize her life into a work of art. Her essential powers are those of Rossetti's Beata Beatrix, who in translating her womanhood to beatitude with no need of a divine male intercessor metamorphoses into a self-created icon.

Linton's womanly woman can make not only herself but space as well: the available space in this passage expands or contracts according to what she does with it, widening to accommodate her motions in the first half and fitting itself to her dimensions in the second. Her capacity to open out space or to mold it to her own figure aligns Linton's pure woman with our fallen woman. As she wills, the world opens out or becomes her dominant form. She is the source of her own and her world's change. Intended as an emblem of immutable femininity, like our more seditious paradigms, she asserts herself in metamorphoses. Thus, even so fiercely reactionary a theorist of womanhood as Eliza Lynn Linton imagines a mobile and dominant woman with peculiar powers over herself and her world. An image from the main culture becomes one with that which subverts it, for only Linton's saccharine vocabulary and her creature's determinedly unselfish motives distinguish upright womanhood from her more radical fallen counterparts. In the same way, our mythography of womanhood is less a challenge to the main currents of Victorian culture than it is an expression of its shaping vision.

The repressiveness of Victorian culture is a measure of its faith in the special powers of woman, in her association with mobility and unprecedented change, with a new and strange dispensation, with an unofficial but widely promulgated and frightening mythology. This mythology was inextricable from visions of power in actual life. As Adrienne Rich reminds us, a credible myth is shaped by our apprehension of the known: "As the classical anthropologist Jane Harrison once expressed it, a myth is not something that springs 'clean and clear' out of the imagination (if anything can be said to do that) but is rather a response to the environment, an interaction between the mind and its external world."[2] The myths that crystallize in the literary imagination are the buried lives of women whose lives are themselves further emboldened by these same myths.

Embodying both danger and dilution in her own little person was the intractable and seemingly immortal figure of the Queen. Victoria's official statements about womanhood may have been wails of needy femininity, but her transfigured, mythic presence set the pattern of her time despite herself. A statement about the Elizabethan age is more dramatically applicable to the age of Victoria: "The woman ruler is a spur to feminism because her position forces men to ask questions about the relation between femininity and power."[3] In the nineteenth century the dialectic between womanhood and power was so central and general a concern, one so fundamental to the literature, art, and social thought of the period, that it is misleading to pigeonhole it as "feminist" as though it were the concern of one interest group alone. Legally and socially women composed an oppressed class, but whether she was locked in the home, exiled to the colonies, or haunting the banks of the Thames, woman's very aura of exclusion gave her imaginative centrality in a culture increasingly alienated from itself.[4] Powerful images of oppression became images of barely suppressed power, all the more grandly haunting because, unlike the hungry workers, woman ruled both the Palace and the home while hovering simultaneously in the darkness without. Assuming the power of the ruler as well as the menace of the oppressed, woman was at the center of her age's myth at the same time as she was excluded from its institutions.

The mythic power of womanhood fueled the lives of the outstanding women which retain exemplary power today. It is an oversimplification to call Florence Nightingale, Charlotte Brontë, or George Eliot rebels against a restrictive culture, for as they assimilated to their own lives a social mythology that endowed the female outcast with virtually magical powers, they transformed themselves into the vivid personae who still haunt our imaginations. Their lives remain at least as compelling as their works, not merely in their solitary battles against their age but in their exploitation of the mythic properties of womanhood which was so tenacious a belief in that age. Just as great lives were sufficiently sensitive to their time to form themselves from the faith that was at hand, so more obscure women seem to have felt a similar sense of undefined power. In their memoirs and autobiographical fiction little-known spinsters paid lip service to humility, while quietly celebrating their power to rule and shape. As we become more sensitive to the lives of women who never became famous, we may perceive a similar awareness of a triumph that was tabooed but undeniable.[5] We are so accustomed to facile generalizations about the squeezed, crushed, and egoless Victorian woman, to whom the age's geniuses present an absolute and inexplicable contrast, that we have barely begun to consider the ways in which an essentially literary mythology might have animated her consciousness, if not her official behavior.

Victorian Characters

Like all living myths, ours is inseparable from history, from culture, and from lives. We have seen the sudden convergences between mythology and lived reality, though the relationship between belief, consciousness, and history can never be fully charted in its subtlety and depth. Just as belief cannot survive without roots in history, so our elaborate mythography of womanhood cannot be detached from the larger phenomenon of Victorian religious humanism.[6] Womanhood has never been placed in the context of this eminently Victorian spiritual effort. We learn only that the most advanced thinkers abandoned, and felt abandoned by, official revealed religion; that to lose one's faith was the equivalent of our identity crisis as the obligatory rite of passage toward harmonious adulthood.[7] We know, too, that nineteenth-century sages invested compensatory faith in the godlike possibilities of man, only to be as disillusioned as they deserved to be. We have seen the exhaustion of a religious ideal without granting its peculiar kinds of triumph.

The authentic awe divine-demonic womanhood aroused was not the only counterpoint to Victorian failures of faith. A popular variant of Victorian humanism flourished spontaneously, if almost unconsciously, at least until 1910: a belief in the immortal life, not of tarnished daily humanity, but of its transfiguration into fictional character. If mankind, that grand abstraction and disheartening reality, failed as an object of worship, its essence distilled into fiction triumphed. Mr. Pickwick retained his magic long after his creator was exposed as a corrupted idol. I associate literary character with Victorian womanhood because in a spiritual landscape of fallen gods, both came to symbolize a genuine, if instinctive and virtually unformulated, faith in the metamorphic potential of transfigured humanity. In our easy dismissals of the fatal compromises of Victorian religion, we neglect the potent, spontaneous life of these unofficial beliefs.

The self-consecration of literary character declares itself most forcefully through commentary that does not present itself as religious. Thus, a periodical essay that ostensibly analyzes Sir Walter Scott's novel *Rob Roy* is a covert hymn to the twinned powers of womanhood and character. In T. E. Kebbel's invocation of Scott's Diana Vernon, awe at grand, self-sustaining womanhood swells into a celebration of fictional character whose vivid humanity is in a perpetual process of self-translation into magic. Kebbel's vision of the mutually consecrating alliance between the power of womanhood and the majesty of character is a more immediate expression of religious humanism than were the official creeds of Anglicanism or agnosticism.

"Diana Vernon" does not call itself religious.[8] Like most Victorian literary criticism, it is a reverent scrutiny of a grand freestanding character extracted from its surrounding textual medium. This intense concentration on a figure who was never quite alive has come to seem naive or eccentric, but these acts of aesthetic idolatry produced intense and diverse varieties of worship, culminating perhaps in the passage of Freud's case histories from that of his own loved and hated, half-invented Dora to that of Ibsen's tortured heroine Rebecca West, which beneath its scientific vocabulary brings the same awed tribute to the infinite variety of character. "Diana Vernon" is representative of a major movement of mind, in the force with which it celebrates a character transcending text and context and in its instinctive association of that character with the solitary grandeur of womanhood.

The essay recasts Diana Vernon as a multidimensional figure with a range of choices and identities beyond her role in Scott's novel. Her life is so large, so rich, that the essay never mentions *Rob Roy* itself; its elaborate intrigues appear only insofar as they impinge upon Diana's larger life. She alone has a spacious past and future manifest in the intricate series of tenses she is allotted: "Would she have so spoken after she had known that she was in love with him?" (p. 286). To accommodate these multiple possibilities, the essay believes in a "true" Diana with an identity beyond the circumstances Scott contrives for her: "Now, Diana Vernon was essentially a *genuine* girl. Fast or slow, original or conventional, virtuous or vicious, she would always have been her own self, and would never have jeopardized her self-respect for the sake of being called 'jolly.' This was her true nature. But even this might have suffered from the life she was obliged to lead and the company she was obliged to keep, but for the very circumstances which made her situation so painful" (p. 286).

Kebbel's faith in Diana's essential reality has been bred out of readers of our own century, but her multiple and flexible existence in complex planes of time her novel cannot share, her ability to step out of Scott's frame to possess her own destiny, make her a vivid epitome of Victorian transcendence. Like the monumental women conceived by Ford Madox Brown, Dante Gabriel Rossetti, and George Frederic Watts, Diana Vernon alone determines the scale of her world. Her reality defines its fictionality; only she has access to a higher, freer plane where woman and character meet.

Transcending the text of her novel, she transcends her author as well, possessing an autonomous life independent of Scott's conception: "And here we have arrived at what we conceive to be the real merit of this character, although perhaps even Sir Walter Scott himself was unconscious of it. We are constantly told in novels of the present day that love and marriage are the be-all and end-all of a woman's existence. The history of Diana Vernon is a flat contradiction of this theory" (p. 288). In literature at least, the immortal creature can surpass her perishable creator. Scott may be bound by his age's pieties about women, but his character is free of them. As woman and character, Diana Vernon is realer than her fiction, wiser, stronger, and freer than the historical man who imagined her; her independence of love and marriage leads her to transcendence of all that does not enhance her own enlarged existence. She alone possesses an infinitely expanding life, animating by the richness of her presence those limited beings, her novel, her author, and her reader. The freedom she promises is both aesthetic and cosmic, a grand and tantalizing hint of possible human divinity.

Such criticism imagines character as art's sole link with eternity. Character here is not frozen and exemplary, but perpetually vital, capable of infinite dimension and change. Like Diana Vernon, it takes possession of a heightened and perennial time, inhabiting a medium that bridges permanence and transience, more durable than duration, but humanly richer than eternity. In *The Sense of an Ending* Frank Kermode meditates upon such an aesthetic and spiritual medium, *aevum:* "It contains beings (angels) with freedom of choice and immutable substance, in a creation which is in other respects determined. Although these beings are out of time, their acts have a before and an after. *Aevum,* you might say, is the time-order of novels. Characters in novels are independent of time and succession, but may and usually do seem to operate in time and succession; the *aevum* coexists with temporal events at the moment of occurrence, being, it was said, like a stick in a river."[9]

For Kermode *aevum* is where religion and fiction, angels and characters, meet. This transcendent but never static medium thus becomes the home of two creatures who haunted the Victorian imagination, seeming to promise an immortality that did not involve extinction of the known. In the iconographic revolution of the nineteenth century, visions of angels and of women became inseparable. Similarly, literary characters of both sexes provided the same image as women did of a magic life within yet beyond the human. The religious and the literary imaginations converge in woman to envision a transcendence that does not involve the death of time. In such evocations as that of the mighty Diana Vernon stepping out of her frame, the power of womanhood feeds and is fed by the transcendent attributes of character.

Even in its nonliterary sense the word "character" is endowed with striking incantatory resonance when used by such a popular sage as Samuel Smiles. For Smiles the word resides somewhere between the moral and the numinous, bearing no relation to the "identity" or "selfhood" we thirst after today. Rather than invoking a dark and involuntary inward voyage, it exhorts a strenuous climb to that summit Matthew Arnold called "the best self." Smiles begins his *Character* with an exhortation from the Book of Daniel:

> Unless above himself he can
> Erect himself, how poor a thing is man!

As the age understood it, character is not the given self but the self as it makes itself. For Smiles it is not nature but grandeur: "In its noblest embodiments, [character] exemplifies human nature in its highest forms, for it exhibits man at his best."[10] Though Smiles has little apparent interest in literature, his idea of character is essentially literary in that character, like fiction, is created, formulated, constructed. A person of character is not endowed by birth or circumstances; he is an artist over his own human nature. Once character erects itself, its possessor is transfigured, like Kebbel's Diana Vernon, into an empowered and transcendent being: "The crown and glory of life is Character. It is the noblest possession of a man, constituting a rank in itself, and an estate in the general good-will; dignifying every station, and exalting every position in society. It exercises a greater power than wealth, and secures all the honor without the jealousies of fame."[11]

In life as well as literature character is transfiguration, the transcendence of temporal conditions. To have it is earthly grace; to lose it is to be denied salvation. It is suggestive that in Samuel Smiles's *Character*, quasi-religious hymns to this attribute consistently give way to apparently digressive exaltations of noble womanhood. Though he never links womanhood and character explicitly—he seems squeamishly to feel that the two are incompatible—they are associated in the dual focus of his book. Smiles's florid tributes to womanhood may simply be defensive responses to contemporary feminist agitation about woman's right to a life outside the home, yet it may be as well that in his veering between character and womanhood, those two poles of transcendence, he is responding in a profound if unconscious association to his culture's central myths.

The magic power of character, together with its tenuous relation to one's given selfhood, reach an extreme point in the Victorian vernacular whereby "character" comes to mean both "reputation" and "professional reference." Here economic reality aligns itself with myth, for "a character" is the primary requisite for survival in the marketplace. Some scattered phrases from Wilkie Collins' *The New Magdalen* bring home this tougher and more concrete meaning: "And *he* would be the sufferer, for *he* had a character.—a clergyman's character—to lose." "Who would trust their children to a woman without a character?" "It was useless, in the face of the facts, to declare my innocence. I had no character to appeal to."[12]

In its literary, its moral, and its socioeconomic connotations, this rich word conveys redemption. As Collins' speakers bitterly know, it is attached only incidentally to our everyday lives and actual identities, yet it is the source of their survival. Even in its least literary context, it is so fundamentally an art of selfhood that the ideal seems to reach one grotesque culmination in such a late work as Oscar Wilde's *The Picture of Dorian Gray.* Here the achieved perfection of character becomes utterly detached from its human source, shaping itself into a self-sustaining work of art. Dorian Gray's character assumes autonomous life in his magnificent portrait, while Sibyl Vane's creates itself in her Shakespearean performances, which are sublime as long as she herself remains emotionally hollow but insufferable once the woman's natural passion confuses itself with the characters she creates. The characters of both Dorian and Sibyl are such inspired creations that they become doppelgängers, so transcendent of given humanity that they live mockingly free of it. Samuel Smiles's ideal of character as self-transcendence finds its logical, if perverse, consummation in Lord Henry Wotton's chilling epitaph for the human race: "Art [has] a soul but . . . man [has] not."[13] In *The Picture of Dorian Gray* character, the foundation of art and the last home of the soul, has detached itself utterly from the humanity it promised to transfigure. For Wilde the quintessence of character is the triumph of art over recognizable life, a triumph so complete that in a novel dancing with linguistic play, even the word "character" has become extinct.

Before Wilde took this buoyant Victorian myth to its mordant conclusion, whereby character becomes such a consummate creation that his people lose their own souls pursuing the art of self-perfection, this new image of temporal immortality shaped not only the imagination but even the relaxation of Victorian England. For writers like Smiles character is the art of secular beatitude, hallowing the self in its ordinary life. Madame Tussaud's extraordinarily popular waxworks exhibition displayed similarly hallowed characters, transfigured as they lived. Her advertisements emphasize the imperceptible boundary between humanity as it lives and dies in history and the transcendence she bestows in wax: "the original figures of BURKE and HARE (taken from their faces, to obtain which the Proprietors went expressly to Scotland); which have excited intense interest from the peculiar nature of their crimes, and their approach to life, which renders it difficult to recognize them from living persons."[14] The eerie vividness of death masks, which hover between the living and the eternal, became family edification under the art of this drab, mysterious Frenchwoman. Like the fictional characters who became centers of popular cults, Madame Tussaud's kings and criminals were grotesquely compelling manifestations of religious humanism, immortalizing divine-demonic humanity without extracting it from our concrete, breathing world.

Madame Tussaud moved her waxwork exhibition to London in 1834, the year Dickens was serializing *Sketches by Boz* preparatory to releasing his own mythic gallery of characters upon the Victorian imagination. Understandably, Dickens was both fascinated and repelled by her necromantic "history in wax": "I had passed this building a thousand times, without once being struck by the fact, that the greatness of which I had all my life been dreaming, was there in visible presence: not merely sculpted in marble, or pourtrayed on canvas, but actually wearing the habit in which it lived; a thing to be walked close up to and examined; to be looked at behind and before; to be handled—no, that was a mistake of mine, as I afterwards discovered; to be face to face with, and yet, not altogether to be borne down."[15] It is the simultaneous intimacy and distance that captivate Dickens: like his own characters, Madame Tussaud's figures are at once accessible to life and untouchable by it. Appropriately, in *The Old Curiosity Shop* Dickens had already given his angel Nell a temporary haven in Mrs. Jarley's Waxworks. This earlier, equally ambivalent tribute to Madame Tussaud aligned his angel-child with this powerful, if ineffably ridiculous, female creator. For all the feebleness of the one and the extravagance of the other, both are empowered to possess history, humanize, and transfigure it.

Dickens' "History in Wax" taunts Madame Tussaud for her obsequious Royalism, but as a quiet chronicler of the French Revolution, she was in fact a diligent turncoat, making death masks of Royalists and Revolutionaries alike.[16] Demurely resurrecting the greatest upheaval of her age as a pageant of faces and characters, animating it with a human intensity beyond bland and transient daily existence, Madame Tussaud is a further manifestation of her century's mythology. Translating history into character, she is the magic vehicle of immortality, transcending the slaughters and the factions of the times she alone can immortalize in the last immortality those times accept.

The National Portrait Gallery, which opened in 1856, is another quintessentially Victorian tribute to the myth immortalizing history as character. Like Madame Tussaud's, the National Portrait Gallery makes icons of its great men and women by highlighting their preternaturally vivid faces. Just as Madame Tussaud founded an institution on the popular nineteenth-century art of the death mask, the National Portrait Gallery took its idiom from the caricature, that easily reproduced heightening of the most individual features in famous faces. The death mask and the caricature both locate their subjects somewhere between immortality and particularity, the heroic and the comic. Like Dickens' characters, each is an apotheosis of individuality, within which the immortal type resides.

The National Portrait Gallery's celebration of greatness, not as an abstraction but as a pageant of human diversity, is one more Victorian exaltation of character as the bridge between the human and the divine. Wilde was not the only Victorian for whom portraiture was so powerful a distillation of character that it possessed its own soul. On May 1, 1848, John Ruskin wrote of a portrait of his generally severe father: "the portrait is becoming more and more alive every day, and it gladdens me to see my father smiling on me." Perhaps it was particularly in portraits of women that the line between the daily mask and the immortal soul wore thin. In 1894 the feminist Josephine Butler sat to George F. Watts for his Hall of Fame and wrote of the process to her son: "He said he wanted to make me looking into Eternity, looking at something no one else sees, because—he says—I look like that; and he has certainly given that idea. It is not at all pretty, and the jaw and head are strong and gaunt. I don't think my friends will like it. But then he is not doing it for us, but for posterity; and no doubt it will convey an idea of my hard life work."[17] We have seen that the source of the spiritual mobility of the angel/demon lies in her face as portraiture apotheosizes it. Here an actual sitting is invested with such spiritual power that it takes on some attributes of the Gothic magic portrait. Painter and sitter share the faith that the soul—embodied for the devoted Josephine Butler in her "hard life work"—will emerge through the mystic transcription of living character, for, as both know, the magic of portraiture springs less from the painter's genius than from the potential human magic of the sitter.

The same faith inspired Julia Margaret Cameron's innovational portrait photographs in the 1860s and 1870s. Paying homage to genius as it declared itself in outsize faces made magical, Julia Cameron translated the new science of photography into an act of human worship. Like Madame Tussaud, the eerie and indefatigable maker of effigies, the imperious photographer tyrannized over her sitters to immortalize them, finding in the intractable material of technology new forms for the creation of character which constituted modern worship.

Until it was challenged by James Whistler's shockingly iconoclastic transformation of portraiture to a triumph of paint over person, the potent element of portraiture was found in the sitter's soul rather than in the portraitist's skill: the great painter or photographer is a mere medium through whom the divine art of character comes into its immortal life. The National Portrait Gallery is a shrine to this reverent aesthetic. The religious exaltation of portraiture becomes explicit when literary characters rather than actual persons are represented, as we see in the rapture with which a contemporary art critic praises John Everett Millais' painting of Scott's heroine Effie Deans: "A glance of a moment satisfies us that we are in the presence of a supreme achievement. We are hushed and awed, even before we are delighted, by a sense of the glamour of genius. Here, realized for us for ever by deeply imaginative art, and by the very mastery of art power, are the dear creatures whom we have known so long and loved so well in Scott's peerless tale; and the magic of the painter is felt to be equal to the magic of the poet novelist. We stand before one of the highest, purest, noblest productions of modern art ... Has not Millais seized the 'indescribable expression?'—indescribable in words, but capable of depicture in painting—has he not realised the essence of Scott's character?"[18]

In this critic's awe before a story painting dismissed by art historians in our own century, the sister arts of poetry and painting grapple, not for aesthetic perfection, but for the most perfect expression of an essentially religious vision whose object is the independently existing literary character. The transfigured Effie Deans, and not a living man or woman, is the ultimate subject of portraiture, because Effie Deans never lived and is always alive. Her transcendent presence in and beyond Scott's novel challenges the religious humanism of Victorian art to capture the soul while remaining true to the mobile, indescribable particularity of face.

Thomas Carlyle is one stern father of these new Victorian icons; his precepts underlie the vision institutionalized at Madame Tussaud's and the National Portrait Gallery of history as a pageant of transfigured characters. His lectures *On Heroes and Hero Worship* bear the tablets of his age's new myth whereby history becomes biography: "For, as I take it, Universal History, the history of what man has accomplished in this world, is at bottom the History of the Great Men who have worked here."[19] In his deification of the great man, it is not surprising that Carlyle was one of the early trustees of the National Portrait Gallery, claiming in support of the new enterprise that a portrait was worth a dozen biographies.[20]

Carlyle was among the first and loudest prophets of a myth of history mighty because it is human, but his myth of the hero diverges in important ways from the myth of character that so illuminated the Victorian imagination. For one thing, Carlyle has little concern with our myth of womanhood; his history is grandly empty of women. Womanhood came to stand for humanity heightened into supreme mobility, capable of transforming itself and its world into radical new shapes, but the Carlylean hero is a monolithic creature with no trace of this mobile individuality. He is bare of all distinguishing contour: "This Universe, ah me—what could the wild man know of it; what can we yet know? That it is a Force, and thousandfold Complexity of Forces; a Force which is *not we*. That is all; it is not we, it is altogether different from *us*. Force, Force, everywhere Force; we ourselves a mysterious Force in the centre of that" (p. 246).

The hero is most receptive to this nonhuman Force. His essence is found not in his flexible and self-sustaining individuality but in his kinship to abstractions and to things: "The Hero is he who lives in the inward sphere of things, in the True, Divine, and Eternal, which exists always, unseen to most, under the Temporary, Trivial: his being is in that; he declares that abroad, by act or speech as it may be, in declaring himself abroad. His life, as we said before, is a piece of the everlasting heart of Nature herself: all men's life is,—but the weak many know not the fact, and are untrue to it, in most times; the strong few are strong, heroic, perennial, because it cannot be hidden from them" (p. 384). Carlyle's hero is so attuned to mighty abstractions that, like the comic-book protagonists of our Star Wars series, he has virtually ceased to be a man at all: his character, his humanity, dissolve in the Force which is the nonhuman essence of things. His humanity is not glorified, but forfeited, together with that individuality which for most Victorians made character immortal. In Carlyle's apocalypse, distinguishing individuality would not preside, but would vanish utterly in a world of heroes: "In all this wild revolutionary work, from Protestantism downwards, I see the blessedest result prepearing itself; not abolition of Hero-worship, but rather what I would call a whole World of Heroes. If Hero means *sincere man*, why may not every one of us be a Hero?" (p. 358).

In his conquest Carlyle's hero, like Matthew Arnold's later, equally abstract and hypothetical critic, will reign because he is indistinguishable from all men and from the Force that is grander and less human than we. England remained untransformed, and at bottom unbelieving, in part because no women preside over Carlyle's faceless and transfigured world, and in Victorian mythography woman in her revolutionary potential as well as in her power to make new orders is the source of sincere and authentic belief. Even for Carlyle himself parades of heroes were insufficient to prevent the howls of despair that constitute his later work. His *Reminiscences* are in large part an act of contrition to the grand, transfigured presence of a woman he had banished: his suppressed and suffering wife, who in death dislodged his hero as the mystic maker of his imagined world. Carlyle's hero-worship provided the blueprint of his age's new myth, but the vehicle of the hero proved empty and untenable even to its creator. His recantation in favor of the female, the particular, and the vivid, brings this thwarted prophet into the community of Victorian faith.

Shakespearean Characters and Victorian Visions

The boast of Carlyle's hero is the submergence of his humanity in the Force to which the privileged have access. The triumph of the literary character is his achievement of perpetual humanity, together with an eternal vitality denied to the merely living. John Blackwood's urbane editorial encouragement to the unknown author of *Adam Bede* is suffused by this faith in the vital and particular: "The story is altogether very novel and I cannot recollect anything at all like it. I find myself constantly thinking of the characters as real personages, which is a capital sign. It will be very different from anything that has ever appeared in the Magazine."[21] Blackwood's belief in the reality of burgeoning character is a more intimate and instinctive expression of his age's faith than is the collective will to believe in the sublime abstractness of the Carlylean hero.

As his culture's best-loved magus, Dickens, the creator of men and women, assumed a semi-divine stature inaccessible to Carlyle, dyspeptic imaginer of heroes. The blended literary and religious wizardry of character creation is central to the iconography Dickens generated during his life: his chief emblem is a host of tiny characters springing from the brain of a large central figure. Sometimes, as in Hablot K. Browne's frontispiece to *Martin Chuzzlewit* (Figure 36), the creator is himself a character in the novel, further purging character of its taint of mortality. Here saintly Tom Pinch dreams the novel's characters

36. *Tom Pinch dreaming his creator's world.*

in his organ music, along with such extraneous exuberances
as a birdcage with dancing legs. These whimsical hybrids point
up the hybrid nature of literary character itself, as it grafts the
divine to the human, the timeless to the changing. In other

37. *Dickens dreaming the characters who give him life.*

variations, such as Robert W. Buss's "Dickens's Dream" (Figure 37), Dickens himself becomes the central dreaming creator: the magic of portraiture raises him above the flesh to partake of the eternal interactions of his own creations. When Dickens enters the frame in his own person he simultaneously controls his little people and becomes transfigured to their state: as author, the man will perish, but as dreamer, his humanity transcends itself to become one with character.[22] The double deification of this iconography, whereby Dickens is supernaturally endowed in his godlike role as creator of characters as well as in his implied beatification by these characters, dramatizes as vividly as Wilson's paean to Millais' portrait of Effie Deans the quickening of the religious imagination artistic images of literary character excited. But Dickens' fragility as creating God, his fear of possession by his own independently existing creations, find despairing expression in a letter of 1857, written shortly after his meeting with Ellen Ternan, who seemed to have lept whole out of his fictional imagination: "I am the modern embodiment of the old Enchanters, whose Familiars tore them to pieces."[23]

When he is deified or damned, then, Dickens' creations become the agency of his spiritual life. Thus, inevitably, his characters outlive him. In Luke Fildes's obituary portrait, "The Empty Chair" (Figure 38), they swarm bewilderedly about his now-deserted workroom, defining the favorite motif in his obituaries, that of a host of orphan characters searching for their father.[24] The literary character possesses immortality, but is not sufficiently godlike to bestow it. His gift is to exude pure being in eternal temporality, abandoning to time his creator and reader. G. K. Chesterton offers a moving account of the eternity hidden in Dickens' characters: "As it happens, the book ends after Mr. Pickwick has taken a house in the neighborhood of Dulwich. But we know he did not stop there. We know he broke out, that he took again the road of the high adventures; we know that if we take it ourselves in any acre of England, we may come suddenly upon him in a lane."[25]

It is part of the myth of literary character that the creation cannot return eternal life to his creator. It may have been this doom that drove the rapidly aging Dickens to the stage, where he thrust himself into each of his creations in turn. If these compulsive metamorphoses into his own characters did not prove to be a talisman against death, they may have provided a final transfiguration, for the assumption of a character upon the stage was as close to the mystery of incarnation as most unbelieving Victorians would penetrate.

If literary character is magical in its blend of human with supernatural vitality, there is a necromantic intensity in the representation of character. The proximity of actors to this cultural mythology explains the particular urgency of the feelings they aroused: "acting as an art and actors as people were charged with an extraordinary symbolic increment which in our own time (except as regards the actor's personal life) has evaporated."[26] The magic of character made of the actor an awesome figure, the vagaries of whose private life were irrelevant. In a censorious age Ellen Terry attracted a general reverence that ignored her liaison with Edward Godwin and their two illegitimate children. Having become Shakespeare's heroines, she was by definition an untouchable amalgam of the demonic and divine.

38. *Luke Fildes, "The Empty Chair."*

George Eliot never ascended a stage, but she, too, was increasingly drawn to the theater and theatricality. She flourished when in life she played the literary role of the fallen woman; toward the end of her career, as the sibylline Madonna of the Priory, she acted her own magnificence, expunging her "fall" in her new, grand priestliness. Matilda Betham-Edwards wrote of a visit to the Priory: "There in the centre of the room, as if enthroned, sat the Diva; at her feet in a semicircle gathered philosophers, scientists, men of letters, poets, artists—in fine, the leading spirits of the great Victorian age."[27] Assuming the magic prerogatives of her sex, this ungainly woman, unlike Dickens, did not snatch at transcendence under the mantle of characters; like her diva, Alcharisi, in *Daniel Deronda*, "she acted her own emotions" until, like many Victorian women, she assumed the magnitude of a literary character in life. George Eliot's hidden proclivity for acting and role-playing, her evolution from a censorious Evangelical girl who shunned the theater into a sanctified diva, dramatize a theatricality at the essence of her religious humanism. For her as for Dickens, the art of translating oneself into a character was an act of devotion to the self's latent, and awesome, powers. Self-aggrandizement becomes a last prayer for immortality.[28]

It is in the Victorian theater, dominated by the overpowering individuality of the actor, and in the sorts of writing the theater inspired, that our myths of womanhood and of literary character converge most visibly. Acting was one of the few professions whereby a woman could transcend her prescribed social function of self-negating service to live out her own myth: to an intelligent, passionate woman the stage offered authority and fame, wealth, glamour, emotional and sexual freedom, and even, in the "Ibsenized" theater of the 1880s and 1890s, a network of feminist thought and activity.[29] The questionable social position of the early Victorian actress enhanced her mythic freedom. While the use of the phrase "public woman" for performer and prostitute alike was a social liability, it endowed the actress with the fallen woman's incendiary glory without dooming her to ostracism and death.

Wilkie Collins celebrated the public woman with ambivalent intensity in the 1860s in *No Name* and *The New Magdalen*, two melodramas featuring performing, and thus, perhaps, by definition, fallen, heroines. In each novel the logic of the plot condemns as sinful the uncontrolled role-playing of the gifted magdalen; yet each heroine is the dazzling center of her novel, transcending the mechanics of morality which make of the other characters lifeless shadows. In each novel the actress-magdalen alone steps outside the moral frame in her fidelity to the rich fluidity of self which precepts of honesty falsify and constrain. When they renounce acting for the repentance of a worthy marriage, they collapse into suicidal self-effacement. Predicated on a belief in the transcendent truth of the public, performing woman, the novels can only fade away into unease once they reduce her to sincerity.

By virtue of her public identity, her self-transforming power, and her association with myths of fallen women and with literary character, the actress unleashes divine-demonic womanhood. George Bernard Shaw's worship of actresses was more unwavering, if no less impassioned, than Wilkie Collins'. Shaw's intimately reverential correspondence with Ellen Terry, whom he fled from meeting offstage, are the outpourings of a Victorian acolyte, though this fiercely modern iconoclast would no doubt have bristled at the suggestion. Like Oscar Wilde's Sibyl Vane, or Collins' repentent magdalens, the real and perishable Ellen can only deny her multiple, transfigured performing self. Fussing about her rouge, Ellen fusses at the division between her mortal and her immortal identities: "Darling, I've not read your letter, but I must tell you I dislike folk who are not reserved, and will tell me of your *Janets* and things and make me mad, when I *only* want to know whether they think you would, if we met, have a horrible dislike of me when you found me such an old thing, and so different to the Ellen you've seen on the stage. I'm so pale when I'm off the stage, and rouge becomes me, and I know I shall have to take to it if I consent to let you see me. And it would be so pathetic, for not even the rouge would make you admire me away from the stage. Oh what a curse to be an actress!"[30] Like Dickens', Ellen Terry's only immortality is a fleeting gift from the characters she creates, for no rouge can bridge the gap between a real woman living in time and her own infinite potential as acting a character epitomizes it. The "curse" of acting is the double face of a Faustian pact: the actress' transcendence of time and circumstance is manifest in the brilliant worship of Shaw's prose, while the off-stage woman is stripped of her characters' magic immunity.

Ellen Terry remains our most vivid exemplar of the mythic luminosity of the Victorian stage, in part because she made her reputation performing Shakespeare's heroines. For Victorian audiences Shakespearean characters represented the apotheosis of selfhood and a glorification of womanhood in particular. Striving to win respectability in a manner Ellen Terry never bothered about, the actress Helen Faucit saw it as her duty "to put in living form before her audience the types of noble womanly nature as they have been revealed by our best dramatic poets, and especially by Shakespeare."[31] Despite this right-thinking effort to make of Shakespeare an exemplary moral influence, the quintessential Victorian image was closer to myth than to homily: Shakespeare was the supreme instance of the artist as magus, revered as his own Prospero creating flights of imperishable characters. While the artist faded into time, Shakespearean characters moved beyond the boundaries of his life, and even of the plays which enclosed them, to become Victorian national divinities, believed in more tenderly than were living men and women who would die. The afterlife promised by official religion may have become impalpable, but the eternal life of Shakespearean characters was a vivid fact.

John Singer Sargent's life-size portrait "Ellen Terry as Lady MacBeth," which still occupies a wall of honor in the National Portrait Gallery, pulls together our myths of portraiture, of the actress, of womanhood, and of Shakespearean character (see Figure 39). The portrait represents, not Shakespeare's Lady Macbeth, but the apotheosis of Ellen Terry as she crowns herself with Shakespeare's character. Sargent ignores Shakespeare's life-denying "fiendish queen" and her subordination to her warrior husband; while the play's Lady Macbeth craves the crown only for Macbeth, exhibiting no touch of personal ambition even in soliloquy, Sargent's creation overwhelms all thought of a mate as she crowns herself in grand solitude. The moral ambiguity of this consecration of the divine Ellen Terry into the diabolical Lady Macbeth, a composite creature who seems about to step out of her frame and force the viewer to kneel before her, crowns our icon of divine-demonic woman. Shakespeare is the catalyst for Sargent's vision of a monumental Ellen Terry at her moment of self-transfiguration, but his play is left far behind in this exaltation of the awesome powers of self-creating womanhood. Oscar Wilde brought this regal vision to a consumma-

39. *John Singer Sargent, "Ellen Terry as Lady MacBeth."*

tion beyond either Shakespeare or Sargent when he apotheosized Ellen Terry in costume driving past his house to Sargent's
nearby studio for sittings: "The street that on a wet and dreary
morning has vouchsafed the vision of Lady Macbeth, in full re-
galia magnificently seated in a four-wheeler, can never again be
as other streets; it must always be full of wonderful possibilities."[32] Transforming magic issues from the queenly union of
woman and character stepping out of her frame to make a myth
of the street.

Sargent's portrait is one variant of religious humanism. In it
a literary character embraces and fuels the self-glorification of
the woman who portrays her. In popular criticism as well
Shakespeare is generally approached through the transfigured
medium of womanhood. Deified as England's Prospero-like
creator of immortal characters, Shakespeare was most re-
verently appreciated in Victorian England when the magic life
of his characters converged with the magic of womanhood.
Though most twentieth-century critics would deny that the
Victorian Shakespeare was appreciated as a conscious artist, his
female portraits rather than his verbal ingenuity earned him the
dearer title of National Bard.

Victorian criticism of Shakespeare adopts the viewpoint of
Sargent's Ellen Terry, who invokes, not Shakespeare's spirits of
evil and ambition, but the divine-demonic presence of Lady
Macbeth herself. The best-known works of Victorian Shake-
speare criticism share this incantatory quality. Such beloved
and popular books as Mary Cowden Clarke's *The Girlhood of
Shakespeare's Heroines* and Andrew C. Bradley's *Shakespearean
Tragedy* are steeped in necromantic suggestion as they attempt
to resurrect Shakespeare's people as the animating spirits of
their own works. The critic's business is at one with the actor's.
A contemporary review of *Othello,* comparing Booth and
Irving, reminds us that the actor is a less real presence than
Shakespeare's character is: "Iago is no unnatural monster, no
chaos of irreconcilable opposites; he is a man, and a natural
man enough, if one looks carefully at his character, not as this
actor or that may have conceived it, but as Shakespeare has
drawn it." The actor's job is mediumistic. He is not to act or in-
terpret, but to possess himself of the character's spirit. Thus,
Irving's Othello is praised because "Mr. Irving gets nearer, we
think, to the true man."[33]

"The true man" is not the living actor but the deathless character who immortalizes him. A modern survey of Shakespearean criticism makes explicit this association between the reality of character and the mediumistic actor's perspective: "If Stoll [who debunked Victorian faith in the reality of character] knew the theater better, if he perhaps tried to recreate in stage actions the characters he criticized, he might have learned to yield to their humanity."[34] The humanity of the play is inseparable from its stage life, which was in turn inseparable from a peculiarly intense form of faith that sprang from the needs of an age. Eminently Victorian forms of holy demonism animate the bardolatry that seems so strange a phenomenon to later, nonbelieving critics.

Nowhere is this faith more intense than in the proliferating celebrations of Shakespeare's heroines. In Victorian tributes to Shakespeare we see the twin theologies of character and womanhood converge. The heroes were also centers of worshipful cults, but womanhood is the inspiriting force behind most Victorian exaltations of Shakespeare. When, in "Of Queens' Gardens," Ruskin invokes Shakespeare's mighty women as authority for his own exaltation of female powers, he is being neither eccentric nor escapist. His paean joins a well-known tradition of literary worship: "Such, in broad light, is Shakespeare's testimony to the position and character of women in human life. He represents them as infallibly faithful and wise counsellors,—incorruptibly just and pure examples,—strong always to sanctify, even when they cannot save."[35]

In using Shakespearean characters as his text for the worship of peculiarly female powers, Ruskin pays homage to a popular female tradition of his age, in which women extract Shakespeare's heroines from the texts of their plays and exalt them as womanhood's inspiration. Anna Jameson's *Shakespeare's Heroines: Characteristics of Women, Moral, Poetical, and Historical* is suggestively titled, for it assumes equivalence between Shakespearean character and living womanhood: "O Nature! O Shakespeare! which of ye drew from the other?"[36] For Jameson as for Ruskin, the transfigured nature from which character springs is interfused by art. She moves easily from comparing Portia and Isabella to different sorts of trees to hymning the Countess of Rousillon as a Titian, Cordelia as an Italian Madonna, Cleopatra as a graceful and fantastic piece of antique

Arabesque, or painting "the gothic grandeur, the rich chiar-oscuro, and deep-toned colours of Lady Macbeth" (p. 378). Character and womanhood, art and nature, blend into a crucible which produces a new dimension incorporating all these but larger than they: the permanent vitality of myth.

Jameson's colony of mythic women frees its heroines from the plays in which they are generally subordinate to the heroes and to the demands of the plot. No Shakespearean play takes its title from its heroine alone, but Jameson's mythmaking releases the heroines from their contexts of love and intrigue, marriage and death, allowing them to exist perennially in the conditional tense. "In the convent . . . Isabella would not have been un-happy, but happiness would have been the result of an effort" (p. 39); Desdemona and Ophelia would have reacted differently had they inhabited each others' plays; Shakespeare's other hero-ines would also have loved Hamlet; and so on. Living a larger life than their plays allow, these heroines and the womanhood they exemplify are granted by this freedom of the conditional tense a mobility and spaciousness that exist only in the domain of myth.

Freed from their texts, these heroines never submit their in-dividuality to the conventions of types. Like all Victorian cele-brants of Shakespearean character, Anna Jameson minutely dis-tinguishes her heroines from each other: "Viola is, perhaps, in a degree less elevated and ideal than Perdita, but with a touch of sentiment more profound and heart-stirring" (p. 121). The deli-cate distinctions upon which these commentaries insist free the characters from reliance upon a larger creator. The emphasis on their individuality, their uniqueness, even their idiosyncracies, suggests that their transcendence is self-generated: they are the sole agents of their own survival. Like the faces in the National Portrait Gallery, no one of which could become anyone else, Shakespearean heroines achieve immortality not as their artist's gift but as the insatiable force of their own individuality.

For Jameson the "truth and nature" of her portraits take precedence over any "moral lesson" (p. 124), as she once again releases her heroines from any merely typical or exemplary function. The subjects of Mary Cowden Clarke's *The Girlhood of Shakespeare's Heroines* may be paragons of womanhood even more exalted than Anna Jameson's—their histories are repeated demonstrations of their moral purity in the face of male assaults

—but Clarke's format emphasizes still more insistently the immortal vitality of the heroines that overwhelms their role as moral vehicles. Clarke's lively best-seller is a series of ingenious novellas tracing the lives of the heroines from childhood to their first entrance in Shakespeare's play. Through these imagined biographies, which fall somewhere between the spiritual history of the bildungsroman and pre-Freudian case history, we learn the origins of their character, the why of their heroism. Such a character as Desdemona has little scope to reveal herself in Shakespeare's play, existing almost entirely to be falsely murdered, but Clarke depicts her early history with such density that we swim in her consciousness, her experiences, granting her a structural and psychic primacy that obliterates the noble fool of a hero who will marry, murder, mourn, and upstage her. More completely even than Jameson, Clarke frees the heroines from the boundaries of their plays, endowing them with rich lives of their own whose autonomy is impinged on by neither Shakespeare nor the man his play will make them love.

Clarke's emphasis on richly perceived origins endows her characters even more than Jameson's with two key attributes of transcendence: contingency and individuality. These heroines are rescued from the predetermined sequence of Shakespeare's borrowed stories; like Jameson's, they move freely in the conditional tense. Desdemona might have altered her fate had she been raised differently: "Could the Lady Enminia have taught [Desdemona] the honesty as well as modesty of innocence,—the unflinching candour with ought to belong to goodness and greatness,—have inspired the courage of transparent truth, she would have invested her daughter with a panoply that would have proved her best protection against the diabolical malignity by which she was one day to be assailed, and borne her scathless through the treachery which wrought her fate."[37] The possibility of other lives for Desdemona elevates her above the single set of circumstances in which author and audience imagine her. The endowment of girlhoods frees Shakespeare's heroines from being puppets of heroes or of fate, enriching their lives with the accidents, the surprises, the dense possibility of choices, for which poetic drama has no room.

These girlhoods distinguish the heroines from each other far more than Shakespeare does, for in their own idioms all Shakespeare's nubile heroines are set to unravel the problems surrounding love and marriage. By stretching their lives back to widely divergent girlhoods, emphasizing their independent destinies at an age which ignores the finalities of marriage, Clarke highlights the vivid individualities of the heroines, allowing us to forget their common fate. Until her history is ended and begun by Shakespeare's words, each heroine lives as herself alone, appropriating fleeting suggestions in Shakespeare's text to her own richly unfurling life.

The overwhelming popularity of Mary Cowden Clarke's long emendations reminds us of the widespread intensity with which the autonomous literary character was believed in, winning deference even from the time-honored language and actions of Shakespeare's plays and from the worshiped figure of the bard himself. Character and womanhood break free of bardolatry to inaugurate their own faith, sanctified by the religious language of Ellen Terry's lectures on Shakespeare's "triumphant" and "pathetic" heroines: "An actress must be in a state of grace to make [Juliet's potion] speech hers! She must be on the summit of her art where alone complete abandonment to passion is possible!" Ellen Terry lends authority to her own apotheosis through Shakespeare's heroines by quoting Coleridge, though her age endowed his tribute with an iconoclasm he may not have foreseen: "In Shakespeare all the elements of womanhood are holy."[38]

Anna Jameson, Mary Cowden Clarke, and Ellen Terry all assimilate Shakespeare to their age's religion of womanhood. In their accounts womanhood and Shakespearean character sanctify each other, mingling nature and art to create a holy medium of perennial vitality beyond the play. Both Jameson and Clarke employ the format of Carlyle's *On Heroes and Hero Worship*, structuring each chapter upon a biographical exaltation of character, but their different assumptions crystallize the distinctions between the "new mythos" of Carlylean hero-worship and the true mythos of Victorian womanhood. The divergent sorts of worship Carlyle's heroes and Shakespeare's heroines inspire define the different sorts of powers men and women were imagined to possess.

Carlyle's heroes lack the contingent dimension that allows Shakespearean heroines to transcend their texts. They plod on in obedience to a higher reality, barred from the conditional tense. Carlyle's tribute to Mahomet applies to them all: "Direct from the Inner Fact of things;—he lives, and has to live, in daily communion with that" (p. 281). Carlyle's Mahomet lives at the command of his author, while Desdemona takes life from her own holy essence, freed from her author's single-minded cause.

Forced into "daily communion" with ultimate reality, denied contingency and autonomy, the Carlylean hero is allowed no space for distinguishing individuality. Emanating from the great Force or Inner Fact, he disappears into his own archetypal nimbus, indistinguishable from his kindred heroes and from the potential heroism in all men. While the Shakespearean heroine takes her life from her distinctiveness, the hero finds his in this larger unity of Force. He takes identity from his historical and spiritual antecedents; she exists on her own account.

Finally of course the Carlylean hero is a creature of history made mythic, the Shakespearean heroine of a powerful and national literary myth whose impact becomes historical. He depends upon our memory of his actual life in time, however aggrandized by the oracular voice of Carlyle; her vividness springs from her transcendence of time. The Carlylean hero is resurrected from the past to trumpet a Utopian future, but in the present he is merely a reproachful ghost of what was and a cloudy promise of what might be. Dwarfed by no historical past and no apocalyptic future, the Shakespearean heroine lives alone in a perpetual Now, glorified by her rich uniqueness and her capacity for many lives. If, unlike her male counterpart, she has no identity in history, she is a more powerful object of belief than he. He is a changeless puppet of eternity thrust periodically into time; she inhabits an eternity made to her own dimensions, taking from time only what will feed her boundlessly changing nature.

The Victorian myth of womanhood, which so powerfully shaped its age's imagination and activities, takes on clearest definition as part of the contemporary theology of literary character, particularly Shakespearean character. Man, in the person of his most imposing representative, the Carlylean hero, acts stalwartly in history and time, but he lacks woman's power to create and restore herself, instigating a personal transcendence that immortalizes her ever-changing nature, inhabiting an intermediate eternity of literature-in-life. Like the literary character as its age imagined it, womanhood transcends time while retaining her powers of mutability, remaining always vital, always alive, immune from the decline that marks what is human. She is less than human in her immunity from history, more than human in her transcendence of and potential control over it. From her own magic sphere she takes life from and shapes a world she cannot quite join.

These differences emerge poignantly in Andrew C. Bradley's classic *Shakespearean Tragedy*, where the critical methods used earlier to delineate Shakespearean heroines are sharply modified in their application to heroes. *Shakespearean Tragedy* is so eloquent and complete an expression of the Victorian myth of character that future commentators have had no alternative but to react against it, marking it as the end of an episode of faith as well as of a literary tradition. In our study of Victorian mythic thinking, there is a vital link between Jameson's *Shakespeare's Heroines*, Clarke's *Girlhood of Shakespeare's Heroines*, and Bradley's *Shakespearean Tragedy*. This tradition may not truly end until 1954, with the publication of Ernest Jones's psychoanalytic *Hamlet and Oedipus*. But though each analysis extracts the central character from the plays, endowing him or her with a history beyond Shakespeare's language, the vision of character alters significantly when it moves from women to men. Jameson and Clarke celebrate their heroines' capacious lives, but Bradley's heroes fall wretchedly below their extratextual nobility, while Jones's Hamlet is crippled utterly by his life beyond the play.

Bradley's is the definitive formulation of Victorian assumptions about reading, and revering, Shakespeare. For one thing, though actual performances often fall short of the great imagined reality, his ideal unscholarly reader brings to the plays an actor's incantatory zeal, resuscitating the characters within himself: "Such lovers read a play more or less as if they were actors who had to study all the parts."[39] Obeying his own precept, Bradley, who performed his book initially in the classroom, resurrects the spacious presences of Hamlet, Othello, and the rest. Like his female predecessors, he finds their living essences in their distinguishing individuality, not in their common type: long, bravura discussions distinguish Hamlet from Iago, Macbeth from Lady Macbeth, Desdemona from Cordelia. Bradley pays homage to Mary Cowden Clarke in his assumption of Ophelia's bemused point of view regarding Hamlet's mad activities and in his sketch of Cordelia's desolate girlhood. His most passionate tributes to character are not the moral paeans to nobility found in Carlyle, but benedictions to indissoluble uniqueness: "Were we intended to remember, as we hear this last 'falsehood,' that other falsehood, 'It is not lost,' and to feel that, alike in the momentary child's fear and the deathless woman's love, Desdemona is herself and herself alone?" (p. 168).

As Bradley's title suggests, he departs from his female predecessors in that his book does not celebrate the individuality of heroines so much as it mourns the lost power of heroes. As befits the last and greatest disciple of a literary tradition that is also a creed, Bradley's book is essentially elegiac, a lament for the greatness of his heroes before the play descended to paralyze them: "For Hamlet, according to all the indications in the text, was not naturally or normally such a man, but rather, I venture to affirm, a man who at any *other* time and in any *other* circumstances than those presented would have been perfectly equal to his task; and it is, in fact, the very cruelty of his fate that the crisis of his life comes on him at the one moment when he cannot meet it, and when his highest gifts, instead of helping him, conspire to paralyse him" (pp. 92–93). Shakespeare's desiccated hero, so far from being the potent prince whose ghost Bradley evokes, is himself the spirit of tragedy, with its "sense of the soul's infinity, and the sense of the doom which not only circumscribes that infinity but appears to be its offspring" (p. 108).

For Bradley, with his emphasis on the decline and diminution of heroes, Shakespearean tragedy is no longer the gateway to an infinity of human plenitude. Its essence is rather a last and bitter glimpse of that infinity which the play inevitably retracts. Shifting his examination from the heroines, the abundance of whose vitality makes them comic even when they appear in tragedies, to the tragic heroes, Bradley finds the essence of Shakespearean character in a vision of waste: "Everywhere, from the crushed rocks beneath our feet to the soul of man, we see power, intelligence, life and glory, which astound us and seem to call for our worship. And everywhere we see them perishing, devouring one another and destroying themselves, often with dreadful pain, as though they came into being for no other end. Tragedy is the typical form of this mystery, because that greatness of soul which it exhibits oppressed, conflicting and destroyed, is the highest existence in our view. It forces the mystery upon us, and it makes us realise so vividly the worth of that which is wasted that we cannot possibly seek comfort in the reflection that all is vanity" (p. 29).

Using the methodology of female writers on Shakespeare's heroines, Bradley applies it to heroes and inverts it into a vision of irony and inescapable vulnerability. Popularly thought of as the epitome of Shakespeare "character criticism," his book tells over and over of the death of character. Rather than using character to celebrate whatever in the human soul is permanent and mysteriously potent, he laments the essence of human infinity in human dissipation. The soul's eternity of art and nature becomes the soul's waste. Shakespearean heroines were the vehicles of immortal freedom from their texts, but for heroes there is no such consummation in a human eternity. For Bradley the essence of a hero is the death of his soul, a death realized in our own century and one not limited to the man at the end of the play: it is the death of literary character itself.

Epilogue:
The Death of Character
and the Fight
for Womanhood

THE TRADITION of which Mary Cowden Clarke was the celebrant and A. C. Bradley the elegist gave more to its age, and took more from it, than our present critical enlightenment acknowledges. It is a quintessential Victorian, and quite moving, statement of faith. Clarke and Bradley's insistence on the reality of a character's life before the play began is a testimony to its continued existence after their play, and our own plays, must end. A conventional heaven is a discarded dream; yet literary character preserves the eternal dimension of humanity by moving beyond the boundaries of art and life. In this use of character as a final vessel of the soul, Victorian England evolved its own living, if cerebral and oblique, religion, counterbalancing the maddening hammers of the geologists and the nonhuman origin of the species.

The association of womanhood—that characteristically Victorian word, idea, and article of faith—with the divinity of character added more vitality and complexity to her existence than it removed. Today the unchallenged authority of the social sciences has withered the religious and literary imagination, making its exaltation of woman's special powers seem a mere insulting obfuscation. But in an age when religion and literature were primary and interdependent vehicles of apprehension, the illumination of womanhood and literary character produced a special endowment our own century has forgotten. The Victorian woman's power within a community of popular faith reveals her as central, not marginal, in the human inheritance. Uneasy Victorians often rationalized this felt power by diluting womanhood into the more self-sacrificial and digestible holiness of motherhood, but in her essence it is the woman alone who enlarges herself into demonic divinity: the angel/demon, the old maid, and the fallen woman, the paradigms in which she takes on her most vivid life, barely acknowledge conventional maternal properties. Today we are dispossessed of the centrality religion and fiction once possessed, and so we can barely empathize with the urgency and magic they bestowed on Victorian womanhood, stripped of her reassuring domestic confinements.

The spontaneous intensity with which this multifaceted religious humanism was believed in died with the Victorian age: in our own century the charged images of character and womanhood became, for the most part, icons to destroy. The loss of character was the loss of an intricate web of belief. As early as 1886, using *Crime and Punishment* as his text, Robert Louis Stevenson sensed that Modernism in the person of Henry James dictated a withdrawal from character as a source of endlessly renewing life: "Henry James could not finish [*Crime and Punishment*]: all I can say is, it nearly finished me. It was like having an illness. James did not care for it because the character of Raskolnikoff was not objective; and at that I divined a great gulf between us, and, on further reflection, the existence of a certain impotence in many minds to-day, which prevents them from living *in* a book or a character, and keeps them standing afar off, spectators of a puppet show. To such I suppose the book may seem empty in the centre; to the others it is a room, a house of life, into which they themselves enter, and are tortured and purified."[1]

For the Victorian Stevenson the refusal of faith in the human fullness of a book was a symptom of impotence. This refusal became austere dogma to a new generation of critics. Responding to the feel of an age which the Great War had cleansed of excess humanity, Shakespearean critics purged the plays. For L. C. Knights, attacking Bradley, Macbeth's despairing soliloquy gains authority only because it is "impersonal. It is the keystone of the system which gives emotional coherence to the play. Certainly the system will remain obscured if we concentrate our attention upon 'the two great terrible figures, who dwarf all the remaining characters of the drama,' if we ignore the 'unexciting' or 'undramatic scenes,' or if conventional 'sympathy for the hero' is allowed to distort the pattern of the whole." Literature has mutated into "system" and "pattern," not the boundless life-renewal of character, who becomes "merely an abstraction . . . brought into being by written or spoken words."[2] Streamlining literature of Victorian mythologies, modernist criticism of the 1930s is as virulent in disemboweling character as were Victorian intellectuals when they relentlessly humanized canonical divinity. For C. H. Rickword "character" is "merely the term by which the reader alludes to the pseudo-objective image he composes of his responses to an author's verbal arrangements."[3] As character decomposes into patterns of language, so does a last avenue to a human eternity.

The critical demolition of character in favor of a new myth of pattern and system is manned with an intensity reserved for destroyers whose target is religious as well as literary. Had he been alive, Matthew Arnold might well have derogated its tone as "acrid," a word with which he denounced all single-minded assaults upon once-living beliefs. Max Beerbohm's brilliantly funny story " 'Savonarola' Brown" could never be charged with acridity, but its exuberance and delight provide a more devastating finale to our Victorian myths than critical rage and righteousness could do.

" 'Savonarola' Brown" reduces to a perfection of absurdity Victorian idolatry of the theater, of Shakespeare, and of literary character, overwhelming the reverent reader with embarrassment at his dearest icons. Beerbohm's Brown, "a confirmed second-nighter," is writing a high-minded poetic drama about Savonarola. So exalted is he by his central character that his own name falls away (which is fortunate, for he was named after the suburb in which he was born) to be replaced by his hero's; like the Dickens of Buss's portrait, Brown is transfigured by his own creation. Willingly and gratefully he submerges himself within his creatures: " 'All sorts of people appear,' he would say rather helplessly. 'They insist. I can't prevent them.' I used to say it must be great fun to be a creative artist; but at this he always shook his head: 'I don't create. *They* do. Savonarola especially, of course. I just look on and record. I never know what's going to happen next.' "[4] Brown's earnest faith is a pale memory of Dickens writing in fierce possession by his characters, terrifying his eavesdropping daughter by making hideous faces at himself in the mirror, studying himself, and writing on. Beerbohm's Brown is not an isolated poseur, but an earnest disciple of the Victorian mediumistic artist whose mortality is transfigured when his characters possess him.

But it is 1917, and when Brown dies a ridiculous death, so does Savonarola. The ingenuous narrator is appointed literary executor of the unfinished play, but with the best will in the world he can find no life in this garble of Shakespeare by way of Browning and Edward Lear: "Lo! my soul's chin recedes, soft to the touch / As half-churn'd butter. Seeming hawk is dove, / And dove's a gaol-bird now. Fie, out upon 't!" (p. 132). Like the "impotent" Henry James as Robert Louis Stevenson indicts him, the modernist narrator withdraws his belief from the fullness of character, thus making a puppet show of this product of faith.

Brown's characters have no power to justify their creator's obsessed life. The relentlessly clear-eyed Max is his only heir. We last see him waiting for the characters to reappear with a child's skeptical patience: "They did absolutely nothing. I sat watching them, pen in hand, ready to record their slightest movement. Not a little finger did they raise. Yet I knew they must be alive. Brown had always told me they were quite independent of him. Absurd to suppose that by the accident of his own death they had ceased to breathe" (p. 140). As Hardy's *Jude the Obscure* puts it more somberly, "Nobody did come, because nobody does."[5]

Luke Fildes's obituary drawing for Dickens, "The Empty Chair" (Figure 38), was a Victorian resurrection hymn in that Dickens' characters continued to swarm around that chair though their creator was gone. Here the death of the author is also the death of his personified belief, whose life cannot outlast his own: Savonarola is only Brown after all. Published in the middle of the First World War, which boasted of the myths it had killed, Beerbohm's apparently unobtrusive story is a more uncompromising obituary than Fildes's, for it is the final expression of a national belief that arose in an age of doubt, only to decline into the tragicomedy of a confirmed second-nighter's personal obsession.

Savonarola's devolution into the quixotic brain of Brown marks the end of a faith. As character lost its self-generated life, so did its concomitant icon of divine-demonic womanhood, harbinger of a transfigured humanity. A new generation of women expected joyful liberation from Victorian expectations and taboos, but succumbed instead to psychic and political depression. According to Elaine Showalter, the novelists of the 1880s and 1890s who first tried to free themselves from their culture's myths of womanhood became the first generation of suicides, while the female aesthetic of the post-World-War-I novelists is notable for its renunciatory, self-annihilating drift.[6] For actual women, freedom from Victorian mythic constructs seems to have produced more loss than gain.

Vera Brittain's autobiography *Testament of Youth,* exemplifies this loss of spirit in women that accompanied the loss of Victorianism. Portraying herself as a representative of the generation born in the 1890s and blasted by the First World War, Brittain begins the book as a scrappy young feminist at odds with her provincial surroundings, determined to make a glamorous and triumphant career at Oxford. The War, which takes up most of her memoir, brings her new freedom and loss of selfhood. She leaves Oxford to volunteer as a nurse, coming to live solely through the men she loves, all of whom are killed. For the matured and scaled-down Vera, her own life and achievements lose consequence before the giant reality of the idealized male dead: "I couldn't see that it mattered to myself or anyone else if I caught and even died from one of my patient's dire diseases, when so many beautiful bodies of young men were rotting in the mud of France and the pine forests of Italy."[7] She lives on to become a writer and marry another man, but this guilt-ridden self-mortification dominates the second half of the book. A legacy of Victorian confidence is replaced by pervasive self-hate: in her postwar breakdown she imagines with the utmost horror that she is growing a beard and turning into a man. Vera Brittain's memoir seems a testament to horrors other than war's.

Her comparative egolessness and self-doubt once she has been freed from Victorianism hint at the secret strength our mutable myth of womanhood brought to its subjects. Though the lives of such postwar women seem free and enlightened—they could vote, work, organize, associate easily with men without elaborate chaperonage, experiment sexually, and, a more radical change, talk about sex—these lives seem depleted as well. The lost Victorian taboos had furtively empowered women by endowing them with a sense of their dangerous potential. As women shore up the fragments of their history today, it may be wise to include the myth that inspired as well as retarded it.

This self-defeating exhaustion that drains women's lives as the complicated beliefs of the Victorians die reminds us how rich in vigor and conviction that age was even for those who seem its victims. The imaginative appeal of its mythologies pervades the literary criticism of Virginia Woolf, who was on the surface the most anti-Victorian of emancipated modernists. In fact Woolf rather than Max Beerbohm is generally thought to have killed the idea of character as the Victorians understood it by her pert, proudly modern dictum: "on or about December 1910 human character changed."[8]

Woolf's "Mr. Bennett and Mrs. Brown" seems a blow at the heart of the Victorian myth of character; but in fact she deftly redeems the myth, without emphasizing its essential Victorianism, from the elephantine externality of her Edwardian predecessor Arnold Bennett. Beerbohm's gloating obituary for "Savonarola" Brown celebrates an authentic death, but Woolf's celebration of the eternal life of Mrs. Brown insists upon a stubborn resurrection. With feminist as well as artistic wisdom, Woolf's essay preserves the Victorian myth she seems at first to be killing.

For one thing, the iconoclastic challenge of Woolf's assertion that human character changed "on or about December 1910" is in essence a tribute to the past. No Victorian sensitive to the implications of his own obsessions would have been shocked by a radical change in character, for the essence of character is its capacity for incessant change within timelessness. Like womanhood, character reflects the perpetual metamorphoses of history without history's attendant deaths and oblivion. The change in character is not character's death, but its startling and recurrent self-assertion.

In equating the magic of character with a personification of womanhood, Mrs. Brown, Woolf perpetuates the Victorian vision of Anna Jameson and Mary Cowden Clarke. In deference to modern idioms she replaces their Shakespearean frame with a railway carriage—an eminently Victorian as well as a modern setting—and Shakespearean self-assertion with a "threadbare" little lady bearing an anonymous name. Yet Mrs. Brown as much as Rosalind is the triumphant essence of character, ignored by the self-absorbed Edwardian predelection for opulent settings and abstract Utopias. The Edwardian Bennett is a spurious modern, for Mrs. Brown is the past in conjunction with the future: "With all his powers of observation, which are marvellous, with all his sympathy and humanity, which are great, Mr. Bennett has never once looked at Mrs. Brown in her corner. There she sits in the corner of the carriage—that carriage which is travelling, not from Richmond to Waterloo, but from one age of English literature to the next, for Mrs. Brown is eternal, Mrs. Brown is human nature, Mrs. Brown changes only on the surface, it is the novelists who get in and out—there she sits and not one of the Edwardian writers have looked at her" (p. 16).

Like Victorian critics, Virginia Woolf imagines an alliance between character and womanhood that unifies time into a perpetually mobile eternity. As an image of constancy that moves through time and space, changing incessantly but "only on the surface," the train is a perfect analog for the Shakespearean play, keeping its essence of character intact as it mutates through centuries of performance. Like Shakespeare, the train is the heir of the ages when it carries Mrs. Brown. Woolf's final oracular warning to novelists perpetuates the mobility of the past against a false modernity: "You should insist that she is an old lady of unlimited capacity and infinite variety; capable of appearing in any place; wearing any dress; saying anything and doing heaven knows what. But the things she says and the things she does and her eyes and her nose and her speech and her silence have an overwhelming fascination, for she is, of course, the spirit we live by, life itself" (p. 24).

Woolf's seemingly iconoclastic essay is our most eloquent and comprehensive assertion of the Victorian association between mythic character and womanhood. The first, most self-aware literary feminist of the modern generation writes a pioneering essay in preservation of the essence of Victorian belief.

The apparent traditionalism of Beerbohm's " 'Savonarola' Brown" masks a real relish to destroy the past; the surface irreverence of Woolf's "Mr. Bennett and Mrs. Brown" cherishes the heart of a queer-looking old myth. The instinctive conservationism of Woolf's feminism sets out to expose fictions of womanhood, but it never betrays the central myth of its inheritance, the profound alliance between womanhood and fiction, which properly conjoined are infinite and infinitely resilient: " 'The proper stuff of fiction' does not exist; everything is the proper stuff of fiction, every feeling, every thought; every quality of brain and spirit is drawn upon; no perception comes amiss. And if we can imagine the art of fiction come alive and standing in our midst, she would undoubtedly bid us break her and bully her, as well as honour and love her, for so her youth is renewed and her sovereignty assured."[9] The personified "she" tells us as much about women as it does about Woolf's imagination of fiction, for while men like Bennett create fictions about women that ignore their living essence, so do women feed on apparent fictions about themselves that provide the resilience to nourish life and art. The perpetual regenerative capacity of Woolf's female personifications is her tribute to a myth that enlivens the past and animates the future by aligning the powers of womanhood with the living transcendence of fiction.

In defiance of the facile anti-Victorianism that characterized the early decades of the new century, and in partial defiance of her own modernist manifesto, Virginia Woolf transmutes for her own generation the most powerful Victorian distillation of womanhood. Her impulse to preserve the heart of a literary idea against the degradations of contemporaneity was the beginning of a corporate feminist attempt, still with us, to secrete through the generations the valuable essence of woman's usable past as a talisman against a sleekly complacent modernity that continually threatens new disenfranchisements. In her personification of literary character as an indomitable woman, Woolf steals for the besieged and rarefied community of modern feminists an image that had once been animated by a widespread Victorian need to believe.

Today, if this image is not dead for most of us, it seems to be undergoing a wearyingly long dying. The novel and the theater have lost their mass fascination; a general boredom with language has replaced the icon of fictional character with that of the star. Ellen Terry obsessed Victorian audiences with her power to transfigure herself into a Shakespearean character; Marilyn Monroe obsesses us in herself alone, as we read countless awed biographies (including those by our most Dickensian novelist, Norman Mailer) invoking the luminous "real" woman whose essence was violated by the characters she was made to play. Judy Garland still haunts us not because she was sufficiently magic to possess little Dorothy's innocent power to dream Oz, but because lurking somewhere within Dorothy we find the ravaged "real" and spoiled Judy of the later years. In our new mythology character is a virtually transparent screen between the awed viewer and the authentic holy presence of the star.

As the actress in her own person is transfigured into a star, no longer needing the magic of character to consecrate her, so, too, is the writer. Television talk shows have encouraged authors to upstage their own characters. Norman Mailer and Erica Jong are stared at on the street by rapt fans who cannot identify a single character in their novels. No mythic Savonarola dignifies Brown. The creator emerges in his own person, free of his intercessory demi-divinity, but shorn of the immortality that intercessor radiated.

The transfer of power from character to creator/star strips our myth in its present incarnation of religious promise. In the United States at least, with immortality stricken from stardom, twentieth-century actors and authors tend to achieve mythic fulfillment through their deaths rather than their surviving creations: Marilyn Monroe, Judy Garland, Janis Joplin, Lenny Bruce, James Dean, John Lennon, Ernest Hemingway, Sylvia Plath, John Berryman, even, for some devotees, Virginia Woolf, all are granted ultimate transfiguration by their deaths, acts of self-sanctification to which their living works are secondary. Death, and not the perpetual resurrection of character, is the central fact in our contemporary myth of stardom, as if the loss of character can find its essential meaning only in its own mortality.

The magic of character lay in its self-creation; endowing selfhood with magic leads only to glorifications of the death of self. Our century of wars may now be feeling that it has killed too much: even our most resolute deconstructionists cling to the essence of the transfiguring myth they want to think they have slain. The anti-character theorists Alain Robbe-Grillet, Leo Bersani, and Hélène Cixous recall the deconstructing magus Freud with whom we began. Freud seemed to have decomposed Dora into the labyrinth of her own dreams, but she sprang to life with defiantly renewed energy. Similarly, in the twentieth century, the myth of character renews itself through critical attempts to destroy it, for, to transpose Virginia Woolf's celebration of the giant female form of fiction, character's self-renewing resilience "[bids] us break her and bully her, as well as honour and love her, for so her youth is renewed and her sovereignty assured."

Thus, almost twenty years ago Robbe-Grillet's *For a New Novel* set out to kill an obsolete divinity who refuses to die: "How much we've heard about the 'character'! Moreover, I swear we haven't heard the last. Fifty years of disease, the death notice signed many times over by the most serious essayists, yet nothing has yet managed to knock it off the pedestal on which the nineteenth century had placed it. It is a mummy now, but one still enthroned with the same—phony—majesty, among the values revered by traditional criticism." The language of Robbe-Grillet's diatribe itself commemorates the irrational indestructibility of this icon: its mixed tone brings deconstructor and celebrant together beneath the pedestal.

While mocking the supposed respectability of the nineteenth-century character, Robbe-Grillet taps energies he can explain only by calling them modern: "One may, for variety's sake, to give oneself some impression of freedom, choose a hero who seems to transgress one of these rules: a foundling, a vagrant, a madman, a man whose uncertain character harbors here and there some small surprise . . . One must not exaggerate, however, in this direction: that is the road to perdition, which leads straight to the modern novel."[10]

Perhaps, but it also leads straight to Victorian celebrations of character as the embodiment of freedom and surprising change. In attacking the fossilized remains of our myth, Robbe-Grillet formulates the energizing source of this worship of an outcast from time. In the same way, Bersani's brilliant deconstructionist polemic *A Future for Astyanax* attacks fossilizations of character to recover the energy at the source of Victorian worship of character. For him, character is one with the explosive mobility of unsublimated desire. He may want to equate with pre-modern notions of character the "structured, socially viable and verbally analyzable self" to whom he opposes his image of the authentic, deconstructed, and metamorphosing Astyanax; yet his Astyanax, like Woolf's Mrs. Brown, is a contemporary recasting of Victorian mythology. "The self as a potentiality for metamorphoses"[11] is the fundamental vision of Victorian transfiguration, casting its magic on women and fictional characters alike. As with Robbe-Grillet, the futurity Bersani posits for his myth leads us secretly back to our Victorian past.

An unconscious ancestral association may have led writers of the 1970s to rediscover womanhood at the same time as critics reinvestigated the idea of character with a strange ambivalent wistfulness.[12] These twin myths of the past took on a new, complex, and simultaneous life in the last decade just as they had done in the last century. These gestures toward reconstruction in contemporary literary studies may reflect a saturation in our culture as a whole with icons of death and the changelessness of death, a longing for a time when the objects of our worship were not human enough to die, but whispered of perpetual metamorphoses. The mortality that comprises our present divinities may inspire Cixous' apparent defiance of character, which she associates with the bounded past: " 'I' must become a 'fabulous opera,' and not the arena of the known."[13]

Cixous claims to be stepping boldly into a mythless future, yet her self-apotheosis as a "fabulous opera" reminds one above all of the Ellen Terry Sargent painted, crowning herself into the boundlessness of Lady Macbeth. For it was the nineteenth century that revealed character to be ecstatic and defiant self-transfiguration in the absence of a transfiguring creator. Like Virginia Woolf, Alain Robbe-Grillet, and Leo Bersani in their manifestos to the future, Hélène Cixous celebrates the demonic energy of literary character by destroying the boundaries that constrict its mythic pride.

Feminists like Woolf and Cixous celebrate the eternal energy of character as perpetual metamorphosis, though the wisdom of their age insists that character in the old, grand sense is lost. For women, whose own myth was so entwined in that other, larger myth, character remains the promise of a "fabulous opera," holding the inspiration of becoming the creature of one's own creation, of stepping out of an imposed frame. We can never again worship literary character with Victorian intensity, for fiction can never regain its nineteenth-century primacy; yet the idea of character has been part of woman's legacy as well as literature's, its very fictionality hinting of an unbounded future that includes the powers of our unregarded past.

Notes

I. The Myth of Womanhood: Victims

1. See Theo Aronson, *Victoria and Disraeli: The Making of a Romantic Partnership* (New York: Macmillan, 1977); Robert Blake, *Disraeli* (New York: St. Martin's, 1967), p. 587, for an account of Disraeli's influential myth of the Suez Canal crisis, which for over a century attracted more credibility than did diplomatic reality; and D. A. Hamer, "Gladstone: The Making of a Political Myth," *Victorian Studies* 22 (Autumn 1978), 29–50.

2. Kate Millett's *Sexual Politics* (New York: Doubleday, 1970) sees myth exclusively as a male assault upon women. Elizabeth Janeway offers more subtle and sophisticated denunciations in *Man's World, Woman's Place: A Study in Social Mythology* (New York: Morrow, 1971), and *Between Myth and Morning: Women Awakening* (New York: Morrow, 1975). Recently, however, even Janeway has called cautiously for a new mythos; see her "Who is Sylvia? On the Loss of Sexual Paradigms," *Signs: Journal of Women in Culture and Society* 5 (Summer 1980), 573–589.

3. Sandra M. Gilbert and Susan Gubar, *The Madwoman in the Attic: The Woman Writer and the Nineteenth-Century Literary Imagination* (New Haven and London: Yale University Press, 1979). Following this new impulse, two recent feminist critics appropriate to their own uses Neumann's celebration of the mythic Psyche, on whom they project their own revi-

sionist images of heroic womanhood; see Rachel Blau duPlessis, "Psyche, or Wholeness," *The Massachusetts Review* 20 (Spring 1979), 77–96, and Lee R. Edwards, "The Labours of Psyche: Toward a Theory of Female Heroism," *Critical Inquiry* 6 (Autumn 1979), 33–49. Carolyn Heilbrun's *Reinventing Womanhood* (New York: Norton, 1979) calls for an expanded female mythos incorporating characteristics that had been reserved for male heroes alone.

4. Generally writers accept a mythic dimension in American literature and culture that they have denied to the English. For analyses of the interfusion between popular myth and subversive reality as they converged in the creation of American womanhood, see especially Barbara Welter, "The Cult of True Womanhood: 1820–1860," *American Quarterly* 18 (Summer 1966), 151–174; Nancy F. Cott, *The Bonds of Womanhood: "Woman's Sphere" in New England, 1780–1835* (New Haven: Yale University Press, 1977); and Ann Douglas, *The Feminization of American Culture* (New York: Knopf, 1977). Until recently students of British culture have ignored the prevalence of mythic constructs in this seemingly solid world. For some innovative exceptions, see Alexander Welsh, "The Allegory of Truth in English Fiction," *Victorian Studies* 9 (September 1965), 7–28, anatomizing one myth of womanhood in British fiction; George Levine, "Realism, or in Praise of Lying: Some Nineteenth-Century Novels," *College English* 31 (January 1970), 355–365; U. C. Knoepflmacher, *George Eliot's Early Novels: The Limits of Realism* (Berkeley and Los Angeles: University of California Press, 1968); John R. Reed, *Victorian Conventions* (Athens: Ohio University Press, 1975); and George P. Landow, *William Holman Hunt and Typological Symbolism* (New Haven and London: Yale University Press, 1979).

5. Frances Power Cobbe, "Dreams as Illustrations of Involuntary Cerebration," in *Darwinism in Morals, and Other Essays* (London: Williams & Norgate, 1872), pp. 337–338.

6. Andrew C. Bradley, "Old Mythology in Modern Poetry," *Macmillan's Magazine* 44 (May 1881), 28–47.

7. For a wonderful reanimation of the complex ethos of the 1890s, see Linda Dowling, "The Decadent and the New Woman in the 1890s," *Nineteenth-Century Fiction* 33 (March 1979), 434–453.

8. Mario Praz, *The Romantic Agony* (Oxford: Oxford University Press, 1933); Frank Kermode, *Romantic Image* (New York: Vintage, 1957), pp. 49–91. Jerome J. McGann, "The Beauty of the Medusa: A Study in Romantic Literary Iconology," *Studies in Romanticism* 11 (1972), 3–25, is a closer, more suggestive and sophisticated examination of the deathly femme fatale in nineteenth-century poetry, but he fails to note her vital significance in Victorian culture as a whole, perhaps because he allegorizes the femaleness of this magical figure out of existence. Hélène Cixous' vision of feminist apocalypse, "The Laugh of the Medusa" (trans. Keith and Paula Cohen, *Signs: Journal of Women in Culture and Society* 1 [Summer 1976], 875–893), laughs at all writers and heroes who forget the triumphant femaleness of this seeming monster.

9. George du Maurier, *Trilby* (1894; rpt. London and New York: Everyman's Library, Dutton, 1977), p. 337. Future references to this edition will appear in the text.

10. Josef Breuer and Sigmund Freud, *Studies on Hysteria*, trans. and ed.

James Strachey (1895; rpt. New York: Basic Books, 1957), p. 61. Future references to this edition will appear in the text.

11. Recent vampire films are beginning to incorporate this underlying dynamic in Stoker's novel. In the most recent Hollywood *Dracula* (1979), directed by John Bodham, Frank Langella's Count quite pales before the aggressive ardor of Kate Nelligan's Lucy. In Werner Herzog's *Nosferatu, the Vampyre* (1979) Isabelle Adjani's Lucy takes the entire story into her hands, overriding the inscrutable passivity of hero and villain alike.

12. Bram Stoker, *Dracula*, ed. Leonard Wolf (1897; rpt. New York: Ballantine, 1975), p. 38. Future references to this edition will appear in the text.

13. Welsh, "The Allegory of Truth," discusses at length the hallowed iconographical tradition wherein Truth is represented as a woman. My own interest lies in the subversive implications within this traditional emblem.

14. Quoted in Philip Rieff, *Freud: The Mind of the Moralist* (New York: Viking, 1967), pp. 181, 138. For a provocative analysis of the congruence between Haggard and Freud, see Norman A. Etherington, "Rider Haggard, Imperialism, and the Layered Personality," *Victorian Studies* 22 (Autumn 1978), 71–87.

15. Quoted in Ernest Jones, *The Life and Work of Sigmund Freud: The Formative Years and the Great Discoveries, 1856–1900*, 3 vols. (New York: Basic Books, 1953), I, 177–178.

16. Sigmund Freud, *Dora: An Analysis of a Case of Hysteria*, trans. James Strachey (1905; rpt. New York: Collier, 1963), p. 75. Future references to this edition will appear in the text.

17. See Philip Rieff's introduction to the Collier edition of *Dora*, pp. 15–18, as well as his more general remarks on Freud's ideas of womanhood in *The Mind of the Moralist*, pp. 178–181; and Steven Marcus, "Freud and Dora: Story, History, Case History," in *Representations: Essays on Literature and Society* (New York: Random House, 1975), pp. 247–310.

18. See Elaine Showalter, "Guilt, Authority, and the Shadows of *Little Dorrit*," *Nineteenth-Century Fiction* 34 (June 1979), 38–39.

19. On the face of it, Freud's actual achievements in these years are our clearest reminder that the myth is not true: his eleven-week analysis of Dora took place in 1900, by which time he had completed his laborious self-analysis and his seminal *Interpretation of Dreams*, using his own dreams as the primary source of both. But if we consider his ensuing drained depression of which he writes to Fliess, not to mention (dare one say it?) his essentially masturbatory role as both dreamer and interpreter, the anguished undercurrent of his failure with Dora, as well as his gleeful harping on her childhood masturbation, gain emotional if not objective coherence.

20. See, for instance, Marcus, "Freud and Dora," p. 306, and Felix Deutsch, "A Footnote to Freud's Fragment of an Analysis of a Case of Hysteria," *Psychoanalytic Quarterly* 26 (1957), 159–167.

21. H. D., *Tribute to Freud; Writing on the Wall; Advent* (1956; rpt. Boston: David R. Godine, 1974), p. 100. Future references to this edition will appear in the text.

22. Letter dated 5-11-97. *Sigmund Freud: The Origins of Psychoanaly-*

sis: Letters to Wilhelm Fliess, trans. Eric Mosbacher and James Strachey (New York: Basic Books, 1954), p. 228.

23. Freud's psychic recasting of ancient mythology lies at the heart of his "new science," but we are just gaining perspective on his responsiveness to the mythologies latent in his own culture. Lee Sterrenburg's "Psychoanalysis and the Iconography of Revolution," *Victorian Studies* 19 (December 1975), 241–264, traces Freud's appropriation of "a nineteenth-century myth of our cannibalistic and revolutionary origins" that now "lives on in the guise of psychoanalytic discourse" (p. 264). More recently, Frank Sulloway's *Freud: Biologist of the Mind* (New York: Basic Books, 1979) analyzes the degree to which Freud's interest in magic and mythmaking has affected our understanding of his role in the history of science. Like Sterrenburg's intellectual tapestry of science, myth, and magic, Sulloway's conclusion that "myth rules history with an iron grip" (p. 503) recovers A. C. Bradley's apprehension in 1881 that mythmaking lies at the heart of scientific modernism.

24. H. D., *Helen in Egypt* (New York: Grove, 1961), pp. 113, 161, 260.

II. The Myth of Womanhood: Queens

1. H. Rider Haggard, *She* (1887; rpt. New York: Hart Publishing Co., 1976), p. 156. Future references to this edition will appear in the text.

2. George MacDonald, *Lilith* (1895; rpt. New York: Ballantine, 1969), p. 31.

3. The crucial interrelation between these paradigms of victim and queen, and among the paradigms I shall anatomize later on, suggests that the social prejudices of our own day have oversimplified our awareness of our past, placing misleading emphasis on woman's unalloyed isolation. Elizabeth Janeway, for example, insists that Western society has traditionally offered only two paradigms of womanhood which "have existed in a balanced polarity of good and bad, sacred and profane," lust and chastity. See Elizabeth Janeway, "Who is Sylvia? On the Loss of Sexual Paradigms," *Signs: Journal of Women in Culture and Society* 5 (Summer 1980), 574. But women have a richer inheritance than such polar oppositions suggest. A fuller acceptance of female power in the present may free our responsiveness to the paradigms of past cultures.

4. Quoted in Richard D. Altick, *The Shows of London* (Cambridge, Mass.: Harvard University Press, 1978), p. 335.

5. Bruno Bettelheim, *The Uses of Enchantment: The Meaning and Importance of Fairy Tales* (1975; rpt. New York: Vintage, 1977), p. 236.

6. Quoted in Adeline R. Tintner, "The Sleeping Woman: A Victorian Fantasy," *The Pre-Raphaelite Review* 2 (November 1978), 18. Tintner examines the sleeping woman motif in Victorian painting with a censorious eye, criticizing the "condition of thinghood" sleep brings about in women and the motif's general aroma of escapism.

7. See Helen O. Borowitz, " 'King Lear' in the Art of Ford Madox Brown," *Victorian Studies* 21 (Spring 1978), 333.

8. George MacDonald, *At the Back of the North Wind* (1871; rpt. New York: Schocken, 1963), p. 46.

9. Loren Eiseley, *Darwin's Century: Evolution and the Men Who Discovered It* (1958; rpt. New York: Anchor, 1961), p. 6.

10. For Stanley Edgar Hyman, Darwin's female Nature is central to his creation myth; see *The Tangled Bank: Darwin, Marx, Frazer and Freud as Imaginative Writers* (New York: Atheneum, 1962), pp. 37–38; but see also Walter F. Cannon's contentious refutation of Hyman in "Darwin's Vision in *On the Origin of the Species,*" in George Levine and William Madden, eds., *The Art of Victorian Prose* (New York: Oxford University Press, 1968), p. 158.

11. *Westminster Review* 66 (October 1856), 442–461, and 67 (January 1857), 1–42. Both essays are reprinted in *Essays of George Eliot*, ed. Thomas Pinney (New York: Columbia University Press, 1963), pp. 317, 371. Future references to Pinney's edition will appear in the text.

12. John Stuart Mill, *The Subjection of Women* (1869; rpt. Cambridge, Mass.: MIT Press, 1970), p. 57. Future references to this edition will appear in the text.

13. John Stuart Mill, *On Liberty* (1859; rpt. New York: Norton, 1975), p. 56.

14. Kate Millett, *Sexual Politics* (New York: Doubleday, 1970), pp. 89–108. But see David Sonstroem's astute and sympathetic "Millett Versus Ruskin: 'Of Queens' Gardens,'" *Victorian Studies* 20 (Spring 1977), 283–297, which aligns Ruskin with such twentieth-century feminist heroines as Adrienne Rich in his elevation of woman's special powers.

15. This and the quotation preceding it are from John Ruskin, *Sesame and Lilies* (1865; rpt. Philadelphia: Henry Altemus, 1894), pp. 84, 137. Future references to this edition will appear in the text.

III. Angels and Demons: Woman's Marriage of Heaven and Hell

1. Roland Mushat Frye, *Milton's Imagery and the Visual Arts: Iconographic Tradition in the Epic Poem* (Princeton: Princeton University Press, 1978), p. 182, and "The Vision of Angels," pp. 169–188.

2. Walter E. Houghton, *The Victorian Frame of Mind, 1830–1870* (New Haven and London: Yale University Press, 1957), p. 393.

3. Sandra M. Gilbert and Susan Gubar, in *The Madwoman in the Attic* (New Haven: Yale University Press, 1979), p. 17, quote Virginia Woolf's murderous aesthetic in *Professions for Women*: "Before we women can write, declared Virginia Woolf, we must 'kill' the 'angel in the house.'" Carol Christ, "Victorian Masculinity and the Angel in the House," in Martha Vicinus, ed., *A Widening Sphere: Changing Roles of Victorian Women* (Bloomington and London: Indiana University Press, 1977), pp. 146–162, sees the angel as herself a murderous counterpoint to the strenuous work ethic of Victorian culture. Alexander Welsh's brilliant anatomy of "The Bride from Heaven" in *The City of Dickens* (Oxford: Clarendon, 1971), pp. 141–228, manages simultaneously to kill the angel and to apotheosize her homicidal role as angel of death.

4. Sir Leslie Stephen's *Mausoleum Book*, ed. Alan Bell (Oxford: Clarendon, 1977), p. 53. Houghton, *Victorian Frame of Mind*, pp. 389–390,

also quotes part of this letter, but he makes of it an essentially negative response to doubt while I see it as an active declaration of iconoclastic faith.

5. Frye, *Milton's Imagery*, p. 70. See also, for example, R. E. L. Masters, *Eros and Evil: The Sexual Psychopathology of Witchcraft* (1962; rpt. Baltimore: Penguin, 1974), which defines traditional demonism as a hugely phallic male devil luring a helpless human female into witchcraft.

6. Sir Walter Scott, *Letters on Demonology and Witchcraft*, 2nd ed. (London: John Murray, 1831), pp. 76–77.

7. "Maturin's Fatal Revenge," *Quarterly Review* 3 (May 1810), 339–347; and *Blackwood's Edinburgh Magazine* 2 (March 1818), 613–620. Both essays are reprinted in *Critical and Miscellaneous Essays of Sir Walter Scott, Bart.*, vol. I (Philadelphia: Carey and Hart, 1841).

8. Peter Brooks, "Virtue and Terror: *The Monk*," *ELH* 40 (Summer 1973), 249; René Girard, *Violence and the Sacred*, trans. Patrick Gregory (Paris, 1972; rpt. and trans. Baltimore and London: The Johns Hopkins University Press, 1977), p. 111.

9. Edward George Bulwer-Lytton, *The Last Days of Pompeii* (1834; rpt. New York: Van Nostrand Reinhold, 1979), p. 158.

10. David Sonstroem, *Rossetti and the Fair Lady* (Middletown, Conn.: Wesleyan University Press, 1970), pp. 28, 197. Helene E. Roberts, "The Dream World of Dante Gabriel Rossetti," *Victorian Studies* 17 (June 1974), 371–393, is a vivid survey of the woman-worship motivating Rossetti's paintings, though Roberts' insistence that Rossetti's paradigmatic goddess can be reduced to his imagined mother seems to me to diminish the spiritual integrity of this worship.

11. Henry Esmond's worship of Rachel as a heavenly Madonna is explicitly linked to Father Holt's early and intense Jesuitical influence. John Henry Newman's *Apologia Pro Vita Sua* admits that Roman Catholic Mariolatry was his chief motive for hesitation in abandoning the stern patriarchal embrace of Anglicanism. In Charlotte Brontë's *Villette* Lucy Snowe associates the distasteful influence of the Catholic Church with the inflated icons of women that dominate school and city, as well as with M. Paul's ultimately fatal reverence of women. Charles Dickens was haunted by the spirit of his dead sister-in-law, Mary Hogarth, one inspiration for Little Nell, as excruciatingly as Dante Gabriel Rossetti was to be by the dead Elizabeth Siddal Rossetti or, in fiction, Heathcliff by the dead Catherine. In 1844 Dickens dreamed of Mary Hogarth "draped in blue like one of Raphael's Madonnas" and recommending his conversion to the Roman Catholic Church (Edgar Johnson, *Charles Dickens: His Tragedy and Triumph*, 2 vols. [Boston: Little, Brown, 1952], I, 518). Dickens' particular Blessed Damozel, who like Rossetti's manifests herself in the forms of Catholicism, is an uncharacteristic intrusion on an imagination singularly indifferent to the forms of religion.

12. See Mark Roskill, "Holman Hunt's Differing Versions of 'The Light of the World,' " *Victorian Studies* 6 (March 1963), 229–244.

13. See ibid., p. 229; and George Landow, *William Holman Hunt and Typological Symbolism* (New Haven and London: Yale University Press, 1979), pp. 45–46.

14. Mary Elizabeth Braddon, *Lady Audley's Secret* (1862; rpt. New

York: Dover, 1974), p. 194. Future references to this edition will appear in the text.

15. See Helene E. Roberts, "Marriage, Redundancy, or Sin: The Painter's View of Women in the First Twenty-Five Years of Victoria's Reign" in Martha Vicinus, ed., *Suffer and Be Still: Women in the Victorian Age* (Bloomington and London: Indiana University Press, 1972), pp. 48–51.

16. Welsh, in *The City of Dickens'*, provides a stimulating reconsideration of these two maligned heroines in the light of a peculiarly Victorian angelology, though his insistence that they are above all angels of Death overemphasizes, in my opinion, their association with passivity and obliteration of will.

17. For Welsh, ibid., p. 195, Dickens' implicit beliefs are closer to "primitive superstition" than to classical or Christian religion. Harry Stone, *Dickens and the Invisible World: Fairy Tales, Fantasy, and Novel-Making* (Bloomington and London: Indiana University Press, 1979), p. 275, uncovers a universe in *David Copperfield* that "is not religious but magical. Dickens is depicting a fairy-tale or anagogic universe, not a theocentric one." Stone's distinction seems true to the essential structure of Dickens' entire canon.

18. Charles Dickens, *The Old Curiosity Shop* (1841; rpt. Middlesex: Penguin, 1972), p. 405. Future references to this edition will appear in the text.

19. Frye, *Milton's Imagery*, p. 178.

20. George Eliot, *Silas Marner* (1861; rpt. New York: Harcourt, Brace and World, 1962), p. 160.

21. Charles Dickens, *David Copperfield* (1850; rpt. Middlesex: Penguin, 1966), pp. 288–289. Future references to this edition will appear in the text.

22. Donald D. Stone, *The Romantic Impulse in Victorian Fiction* (Cambridge, Mass.: Harvard University Press, 1980), p. 265.

23. Garrett Stewart makes this point in *Dickens and the Trials of Imagination* (Cambridge, Mass.: Harvard University Press, 1974), p. 98.

24. Welsh, *The City of Dickens*, p. 172, discusses the magical power of the angel's face.

25. Quoted in Gordon N. Ray, *Thackeray: The Uses of Adversity: 1811–1846* (New York and London: McGraw-Hill, 1955), p. 110.

26. William Makepeace Thackeray, *The History of Henry Esmond* (1852; rpt. Middlesex: Penguin, 1970), pp. 250–251. Future references to this edition will appear in the text.

27. Joan Garrett-Goodyear, "Stylized Emotions, Unrealized Selves: Expressive Characterization in Thackeray," *Victorian Studies* 22 (Winter 1979), 174.

28. William Makepeace Thackeray, *Vanity Fair* (1848; rpt. Boston: Houghton Mifflin, 1963), p. 617.

29. Merlin Stone, *When God Was a Woman* (New York and London: Harcourt Brace Jovanovich, 1976), p. 199.

30. Among other critics, Sylvia Manning, "Incest and the Structure of *Henry Esmond*," *Nineteenth-Century Fiction* 34 (September 1979), 207–209, discusses the essential kinship of Rachel and Beatrix.

31. See Elaine Scarry, "The Rookery at Castlewood," in Eric Rothstein and Joseph Anthony Wittreich, Jr., eds., *Literary Monographs 7: Thackeray, Hawthorne and Melville* (Madison and London: University of Wisconsin Press, 1975), for a brilliant analysis of Esmond's ontological instability.

32. George Lukács, *The Historical Novel,* trans. Hannah and Stanley Mitchell (1937; rpt. Boston: Beacon, 1963), pp. 201–206, contains a well-known indictment of Thackeray's reduction of history to privacy, though Lukács does not analyze the compensatory grandeur of the myth of womanhood in whose service Esmond writes.

33. Charles Dickens, *Hard Times* (1854; rpt. New York: Norton, 1966), p. 154.

34. See Gilbert and Gubar, *Madwoman in the Attic,* p. 293. But Leo Bersani, *A Future for Astyanax: Character and Desire in Literature* (Boston and Toronto: Little, Brown, 1976), offers a more radical description of Heathcliff's fundamental "slipperiness" of being, confounding the boundaries of family, gender, generation, and class.

35. Emily Brontë, *Wuthering Heights* (1847; rpt. New York: Norton, 1963), p. 115. Future references to this edition will appear in the text.

36. Robert Louis Stevenson, *Dr. Jekyll and Mr. Hyde* (1886; rpt. New York: Bantam, 1967), p. 85. Future references to this edition will appear in the text.

37. See John D. Rosenberg's introduction to *Swinburne: Selected Poetry and Prose* (New York: Modern Library, 1968), pp. xxiv–xxv.

38. Sheridan LeFanu, "Carmilla" (1872) in *Best Ghost Stories of J. S. LeFanu,* ed. E. F. Bleiler (New York: Dover, 1964), p. 277. Future references to this edition will appear in the text.

39. Elaine Showalter, *A Literature of Their Own: British Woman Writers from Brontë to Lessing* (Princeton: Princeton University Press, 1977), p. 163, accepts Margaret Oliphant's claim for Braddon's innovational use of angel characteristics for her demon heroine. Braddon is certainly a conscious and sophisticated parodist of male writers and artists—she often modulates into brilliant mimicry of writers like Dickens cooing over angelic womanhood—but I hope I have shown that hers was not an isolated feminist taunt but part of a peculiarly Victorian iconography employed by Thackeray, LeFanu, and Swinburne, as well as Tennyson and Browning, George Eliot, and Charlotte Brontë, along with numerous other writers and artists not mentioned here.

40. William Harrison Ainsworth, *The Lancashire Witches* (1848; rpt. Manchester: E. J. Morton, 1976), pp. 110–111.

IV. Old Maids and the Wish for Wings

1. Mary Daly anatomizes the mentality that instigated the burning of single women as witches; see her *Gyn/Ecology: The Metaethics of Radical Feminism* (Boston: Beacon, 1978), p. 184. For figures on the rising proportion of unmarried women in the Victorian age, see J. A. and Olive Banks, *Feminism and Family Planning in Victorian England* (Liverpool: Liverpool University Press, 1964), p. 27.

2. Quoted in Shirlene Mason, *Daniel Defoe and the Status of Women* (St. Alban's, Vt.: Eden Press, 1978), p. 82.

3. *Autobiography and Letters of Mrs. Margaret Oliphant*, ed. Mrs. Harry Coghill (1889; rpt. Leicester: Leicester University Press, 1974), pp. 16–17.

4. Charlotte Brontë's three letters are quoted in *Mary Taylor, Friend of Charlotte Brontë: Letters from New Zealand and Elsewhere*, ed. Joan Stevens (Auckland, New Zealand: Auckland University Press, 1972), pp. 17, 18, 23.

5. Catherine Sinclair, *Jane Bouverie; or Prosperity and Adversity* (Philadelphia: H. Hooker, 1851), p. iii. Future references to this edition will appear in the text.

6. See A. M. Allchin, *The Silent Rebellion: Anglican Religious Communities, 1845–1900* (London: SCM Press, 1958), p. 78; and Nina Auerbach, *Communities of Women: An Idea in Fiction* (Cambridge, Mass.: Harvard University Press, 1978), p. 195, n. 21.

7. 1861, reprinted in *The Writings of Anne Isabella Thackeray Ritchie* (New York: Harper & Brothers, 1870), p. 303.

8. Sally Mitchell, *The Fallen Angel: Chastity, Class, and Women's Reading, 1835–1880* (Bowling Green, Ohio: Bowling Green University Popular Press, 1981), conclusion.

9. See Auerbach, *Communities of Women*, pp. 77–97.

10. Quoted in Stanley Weintraub, *Four Rossettis: A Victorian Biography* (New York: Weybright and Talley, 1977), p. 101.

11. See Jerome J. McGann, "Christina Rossetti's Poems: A New Edition and a Revaluation," *Victorian Studies* 23 (Winter 1980), 237–254.

12. Lines 108–120 in *The Complete Poems of Christina Rossetti*, ed. R. W. Crump (Baton Rouge and London: Louisiana State University Press, 1979), I, 203.

13. See Ruby V. Redinger, *George Eliot: The Emergent Self* (New York: Knopf, 1975), pp. 105–159.

14. *The George Eliot Letters*, ed. Gordon S. Haight, 9 vols. (New Haven and London: Yale University Press, 1954–1978), I, 284.

15. Quoted in Josephine Kamm, *How Different From Us: A Biography of Miss Buss and Miss Beale* (London: The Bodley Head, 1958), pp. 34, 204, 237.

16. Ibid., p. 204.

17. Adrienne Munich, "Katisha's Elbow: The Domestication of Conquest in Gilbert and Sullivan," presented at the Northeast Victorian Studies Association, 1980, provides a pungent and witty analysis of the covert inspiration Queen Victoria provided for the large, commanding spinster who is a perennial type in Gilbert and Sullivan's operettas.

18. Cecil Woodham-Smith, *Florence Nightingale: 1820–1910* (New York and London: McGraw Hill, 1951), pp. 253, 348.

19. Quoted in ibid., pp. 53, 67.

20. Sarah C. Frerichs, "Elizabeth Missing Sewell: Concealment and Revelation in a Victorian Everywoman," in George Landow, ed., *Approaches to Victorian Autobiography* (Athens: Ohio University Press, 1979), p. 176.

21. Elizabeth Missing Sewell, *The Experience of Life* (1852; rpt. New York: Appleton, 1853), p. 14. Future references to this edition will appear in the text.

22. Elizabeth S. Haldane, *George Eliot and Her Times: A Victorian Study* (London: Hodder & Stoughton, 1927), p. 274.

23. Elizabeth S. Haldane, *From One Century to Another* (London: Alexander Maclehouse, 1937), p. vi. Future references to this edition will appear in the text.

24. *Life of Frances Power Cobbe* (London: Swan Sonnenschein, 1904), p. xxiv. Future references to this edition will appear in the text.

25. Frances Power Cobbe, "Celibacy V. Marriage," *Fraser's Magazine* 65 (February 1862), 233.

26. *A Record of Ellen Watson*, ed. Anna Jane Buckland (London: Macmillan, 1884), p. 89.

27. In "Why are Women Redundant?," 1862; reprinted in *Literary and Social Judgments* (Boston: James R. Osgood, 1873), pp. 274–308.

28. February 9, 1849. Quoted in Stevens, ed., *Mary Taylor*, pp. 80–81.

29. A. James Hammerton, *Emigrant Gentlewomen: Genteel Poverty and Female Emigration, 1830–1914* (Totowa, N.J.: Rowman and Littlefield, 1979), gives a rich picture of the contradictions out of which the institution of emigration arose.

30. As I do in *Communities of Women*, pp. 97–113.

31. Christina Rossetti, *Commonplaces and Other Short Stories* (London: F. S. Ellis, 1870), p. 6. Future references to this edition will appear in the text.

32. Annie E. Holdsworth, *Joanna Trail, Spinster* (New York: Charles L. Webster, 1894), p. 5.

33. Ellen Price Wood, *Mildred Arkell*, 2 vols. (Leipzig: Bernard Tauchnitz, 1865), II, 327. Future references to this edition will appear in the text.

34. Wilkie Collins, *The Woman in White* (1859–60; rpt. Middlesex: Penguin, 1974), p. 33. Future references to this edition will appear in the text.

35. See Elaine Showalter, *A Literature of Their Own: British Women Novelists from Brontë to Lessing* (Princeton: Princeton University Press, 1977), p. 162. But see, too, U. C. Knoepflmacher, "The Counterworld of Victorian Fiction and *The Woman in White*," in Jerome H. Buckley, ed., *The Worlds of Victorian Fiction* (Cambridge, Mass.: Harvard University Press, 1975), pp. 351–369, for a suggestive appraisal of Collins in a context of anti-cultural protest fiction.

36. Old Maids," *Blackwood's Edinburgh Magazine* 112 (July 1872), 97.

37. *Literary and Social Judgments*, p. 296; Greg's italics.

38. "The Future of Single Women," *Westminster Review* 121 (1884), 154, 158.

39. George Moore, *Celibates* (London: Walter Scott, 1895), p. 309.

40. For a fuller discussion of Moore and Gissing, see Auerbach, *Communities of Women*, pp. 141–157.

41. H. Rider Haggard, *She* (1887; rpt. New York: Hart, 1976), p. 207.

V. The Rise of the Fallen Woman

1. Sally Mitchell, *The Fallen Angel: Chastity, Class, and Women's Reading, 1835–1880* (Bowling Green, Ohio: Bowling Green University Popular Press, 1981), introduction.

2. Susan P. Casteras, "Down the Garden Path: Courtship Culture and Its Imagery in Victorian Painting," unpub. dis., Yale, 1977.

3. A. M. Allchin, *The Silent Rebellion: Anglican Religious Communities, 1845–1900* (London: SCM Press, 1958), p. 69.

4. Stanley Weintraub, *Four Rossettis: A Victorian Biography* (New York: Weybright and Talley, 1977), p. 112; Dorothea Beale, quoted in Josephine Kamm, *How Different From Us: A Biography of Miss Buss and Miss Beale* (London: The Bodley Head, 1958), p. 190.

5. Quoted in Raymond Lister, *Victorian Narrative Paintings* (London: Museum Press 1966), p. 54.

6. *Prostitution*, ed. Peter Fryer (New York: Praeger, 1968), pp. 72–73. This is an abridgment of the second edition (1870), whose full title reads *Prostitution, Considered in its Moral, Social, and Sanitary Aspects, in London and Other Large Cities and Garrison Towns. With Proposals for the Control and Prevention of its Attendant Evils*. The first edition appeared in 1857.

7. George Moore, *Esther Waters* (1899; rpt. New York: Duffield, 1953), p. 508. Future references to this edition will appear in the text.

8. Françoise Basch, *Relative Creatures: Victorian Women in Society and the Novel*, trans. Anthony Rudolf (New York: Schocken, 1974), pp. 195–268; Frances Finnegan, *Poverty and Prostitution: A Study of Victorian Prostitutes in York* (Cambridge: Cambridge University Press, 1979); Judith Walkowitz, "The Making of an Outcast Group: Prostitutes and Working Women in Nineteenth-Century Plymouth and Southampton," in Martha Vicinus, ed., *A Widening Sphere: Changing Roles of Victorian Women* (Bloomington: Indiana University Press, 1977), pp. 72–93.

9. Quoted in Basch, *Relative Creatures*, p. 204.

10. Linda Nochlin, "Lost and *Found*: Once More the Fallen Woman," *Art Bulletin* 60 (1978), 139.

11. The same pattern applies to Eliza Lynn Linton's stentorian attack on the brazen "girl of the period." Linton writes in horror that young women were neither shunning nor saving their fallen sisters but emulating their style in order to catch men. Yet this incorporation of the tactics of the street into the competition of the marriage market is withdrawn from her idealized good wives, whose sphere is a walled garden, not a marketplace. See "The Girl of the Period," *Saturday Review*, 14 March 1868, pp. 339–340.

12. Thomas Hardy, *Tess of the d'Urbervilles* (1891; rpt. New York: Norton, 1965), p. 84. Future references to this edition will appear in the text.

13. Lister, *Victorian Narrative Paintings*, p. 58.

14. Helene E. Roberts, "Marriage, Redundancy or Sin: The Painter's View of Women in the First Twenty-Five Years of Victoria's Reign," in Martha Vicinus, ed., *Suffer and Be Still: Women in the Victorian Age* (Bloomington: Indiana University Press, 1972), pp. 73–75. Arthur S. Marks offers

a more literal biographical iconography than Roberts': for Marks, the figures are Brown's common-law wife and their illegitimate child, a reinterpretation which emphasizes the richness in Brown's blend of sexual transgression with religious exaltation. See Arthur S. Marks, "Ford Madox Brown's 'Take Your Son, Sir!,' " *Arts Magazine* 54 (January 1980), 135–140.

15. Nathaniel Hawthorne, *The Scarlet Letter* (1850; rpt. New York: Norton, 1961), pp. 42–43. Future references to this edition will appear in the text.

16. Critics who discuss Alice as the ambiguous creator of Wonderland include Edmund Wilson, "C. L. Dodgson: The Poet-Logician," in *The Shores of Light*, 2nd ed. (1952; rpt. New York: Noonday Press, 1967), pp. 543–544; Nina Auerbach, "Alice and Wonderland: A Curious Child," *Victorian Studies* 17 (September 1973), 31–42; and James R. Kincaid, "Alice's Invasion of Wonderland," *PMLA* 88 (1973), 92–99.

17. Elizabeth Barrett Browning, who, like Brontë, was experimenting with feminist literary forms, echoed Brontë's protest at Gaskell's concession to punitive morality. See Aina Rubenius, *The Woman Question in Mrs. Gaskell's Life and Works* (Cambridge, Mass.: Harvard University Press, 1950), p. 211.

18. Elizabeth Gaskell, *Ruth* (1853; rpt. London: Everyman's Library, Dent, 1967), p. 3. Future references to this edition will appear in the text.

19. Nochlin, "Lost and *Found*," pp. 143, 147–148.

20. George Eliot, *Adam Bede* (1859; rpt. Boston: Houghton Mifflin, 1968), p. 136. Future references to this edition will appear in the text.

21. Basch, *Relative Creatures*, p. 268, condemns the infantilism of British Victorian fiction compared to the lavish sensuality with which Russian and Continental heroines fall out of the family and out of life.

22. Edgar Johnson, *Charles Dickens: His Tragedy and Triumph*, 2 vols. (Boston: Little, Brown, 1952), II, 594.

23. Fred Kaplan associates Madame de la Rue with the many other "little" women in fiction and life whose destinies Dickens wanted to mold. See *Dickens and Mesmerism* (Princeton: Princeton University Press, 1975), p. 82.

24. See Ada Nisbet, *Dickens and Ellen Ternan* (Berkeley and Los Angeles: University of California Press, 1952), pp. 56–57.

25. George Eliot to Madame Eugène Bodichon, May 5, 1859, in *The George Eliot Letters*, ed. Gordon S. Haight, 9 vols. (New Haven: Yale University Press, 1954–1978), III, 64.

26. In his review article "The Secrets of George Eliot," Alexander Welsh equates the secret of Lewes's household with the secret identity of George Eliot, novelist. This hidden and potent entanglement suggests that Mary Ann Evans' simultaneous metamorphoses into "Mrs. Lewes" and "George Eliot" could not have happened without each other. See *Yale Review* 68 (Summer 1979), 589–597.

VI. Victorian Womanhood and Literary Character

1. Eliza Lynn Linton, *The Girl of the Period and Other Social Essays*, 2 vols. (London: Richard Bentley & Sons, 1883), II, 110.

2. Adrienne Rich, *Of Woman Born: Motherhood as Experience and Institution* (New York: Norton, 1976), p. 92.

3. Juliet Dusinberre, *Shakespeare and the Nature of Women* (London: Macmillan, 1975), p. 303.

4. The most authoritative studies of Victorian England agree that the age was pervaded by a buried angst stemming from a manifold spiritual crisis. See, for instance, Walter E. Houghton, *The Victorian Frame of Mind, 1830–1870* (New Haven and London: Yale University Press, 1957); David J. DeLaura, *Hebrew and Hellene in Victorian England: Arnold, Newman, and Pater* (Austin: University of Texas Press, 1969); and Steven Marcus, *Engels, Manchester, and the Working Class* (New York: Random House, 1974). These students of troubled Victorians relate this atmosphere of impending crisis only superficially to women, if they speak of women at all.

5. Students of the social history of Victorian women are already perceiving the lives of average women as freer, more buoyant, less suffused by victimization, than was initially the perspective of feminist scholarship. The titles of Martha Vicinus' two important anthologies reflect a major shift of emphasis from *Suffer and Be Still: Women in the Victorian Age* (Bloomington: Indiana University Press, 1972) to *A Widening Sphere: Changing Roles of Victorian Women* (Bloomington: Indiana University Press, 1977).

6. Along with DeLaura, U. C. Knoepflmacher, *Religious Humanism and the Victorian Novel: George Eliot, Walter Pater, and Samuel Butler* (Princeton: Princeton University Press, 1965), provides the most capacious exploration of this complex Victorian ideal.

7. See, for instance, Jerome Hamilton Buckley's classic "The Pattern of Conversion" in *The Victorian Temper: A Study in Literary Culture* (1951; rpt. New York: Vintage Books, 1964), pp. 87–108, and *Season of Youth: The Bildungsroman from Dickens to Golding* (Cambridge, Mass.: Harvard University Press, 1974).

8. T. E. Kebbel, "Diana Vernon," *Macmillan's Magazine* 22 (August 1870), 185–191.

9. Frank Kermode, *The Sense of an Ending: Studies in the Theory of Fiction* (London: Oxford University Press, 1967), p. 72.

10. Samuel Smiles, *Character* (New York: Harper & Brothers, 1877), p. 13.

11. Samuel Smiles, *Self-Help*, rev. ed. (1859; rpt. New York: John W. Lovell, n.d.), p. 416.

12. Wilkie Collins, *The New Magdalen* (New York: Harper & Brothers, 1873), pp. 203, 204, 280–281.

13. Oscar Wilde, *The Picture of Dorian Gray* (1891; rpt. Middlesex: Penguin, 1978), p. 238.

14. Quoted in Richard D. Altick, *The Shows of London* (Cambridge, Mass.: Harvard University Press, 1978), p. 333.

15. Charles Dickens, "History in Wax," *Household Words* 9 (Feb. 18, 1854), 18.

16. See Anita Leslie and Pauline Chapman, *Madame Tussaud: Waxworker Extraordinary* (London: Hutchinson, 1978).

17. Quoted in the National Portrait Gallery pamphlet *G. F. Watts, The*

Hall of Fame: Portraits of his Famous Contemporaries (London: Her Majesty's Stationery Office, 1975), p. 17.

18. H. Schütz Wilson quoting his earlier paean to Millais' "Effie Deans" in "Our Living Artists: John Everett Millais, R.A.," *The Magazine of Art* 2 (1879), 37–38.

19. Thomas Carlyle, *On Heroes and Hero Worship* (1841; rpt. with *Sartor Resartus,* Everyman's Library, London: Dent, 1967), p. 239. Future references to this edition will appear in the text.

20. See *Watts, The Hall of Fame,* p. 8.

21. March 31, 1858; quoted in Gordon S. Haight, *George Eliot: A Biography* (London: Oxford University Press, 1968), p. 254.

22. Richard Maxwell's fascinating essay "Crowds and Creativity in *The Old Curiosity Shop,*" *JEGP* 78 (January 1979), 49–71, locates the roots of this iconography in Dürer and Goya, showing the vulnerability of the dreamer to the dream-creatures who besiege him.

23. Quoted in Edgar Johnson, *Charles Dickens: His Tragedy and Triumph,* 2 vols. (Boston and Toronto: Little, Brown, 1952), II, 911.

24. See Maxwell, "Crowds and Creativity," pp. 49, 58.

25. G. K. Chesterton, *Charles Dickens* (1906; rpt. New York: Schocken, 1965), p. 80.

26. Martin Meisel, "Perspectives on Victorian and Other Acting; the Actor's Last Call, or, No Curtain Like the Shroud," *Victorian Studies* 6 (June 1963), 355.

27. Matilda Betham-Edwards, *Mid-Victorian Memories* (London: John Murray, 1919), p. 42.

28. For more on George Eliot as a covert actress, see Nina Auerbach, "Artists and Mothers: A False Alliance," *Women & Literature* 6 (Spring 1978), 9–14, and "Secret Performances: George Eliot and the Art of Acting," presented at the George Eliot Centennial Convention, Rutgers University, November 1980.

29. See Christopher Kent, "Image and Reality: The Actress and Society," in Vicinus, ed., *A Widening Sphere,* pp. 94–116, and Michael Baker, *The Rise of the Victorian Actor* (London: Croom Helm, 1978), pp. 95–108.

30. October 26, 1896; in *Ellen Terry and Bernard Shaw: A Correspondence,* ed. Christopher St. John (New York: G. P. Putnam's Sons, 1931), p. 82.

31. Quoted in Kent, "Image and Reality," p. 99.

32. Quoted in H. Montgomery Hyde, *Oscar Wilde* (1975; rpt. London: Methuen, 1977), p. 230. From a less gallant, more feminist, perspective, Ellen Moers's witty discussion of "performing heroines" in *Literary Women: The Great Writers* (New York: Doubleday, 1976), pp. 173–210, is a shrewd exposure of covert acting, but its debunking tone does injustice to the complex power and centrality of the female performer in nineteenth-century culture as a whole.

33. " 'Othello' at the Lyceum," *Macmillan's Magazine* 44 (July 1881), 213, 215.

34. Marvin Rosenberg, *The Masks of Othello: The Search for the Identity of Othello, Iago, and Desdemona by Three Centuries of Actors and Critics* (Berkeley and Los Angeles: University of California Press, 1977), p. 228.

35. John Ruskin, *Sesame and Lilies* (1865; rpt. Philadelphia: Henry Altemus, 1894), p. 125.

36. Anna Jameson, *Shakespeare's Heroines: Characteristics of Women, Moral, Poetical, and Historical* (1832; rpt. London: Dent, 1901), p. 25. Future references to this edition will appear in the text.

37. Mary Cowden Clarke, *The Girlhood of Shakespeare's Heroines; in a Series of Fifteen Tales*, 3 vols. (1850; rpt. New York: AMS Press, 1974), I, 311.

38. Ellen Terry, *Four Lectures on Shakespeare* (London: Martin Hopkinson, 1932), p. 151.

39. Andrew C. Bradley, *Shakespearean Tragedy* (1904; rpt. New York: Meridian Books, 1959), p. 13. Future references to this edition will appear in the text.

Epilogue: The Death of Character and the Fight for Womanhood

1. Letter to J. A. Symonds, Spring 1886; *The Letters of Robert Louis Stevenson to his family and friends*, selected and edited by Sidney Colvin, 2 vols. (New York: Scribner's Sons, 1899), II, 23.

2. L. C. Knights, *How Many Children Had Lady Macbeth? An Essay in the Theory and Practice of Shakespeare Criticism* (Cambridge: Gordon Fraser, Minority Press, 1933), pp. 64, 6–7.

3. C. H. Rickword, "A Note on Fiction," in F. R. Leavis, ed., *Towards Standards of Criticism* (London: Wishart, 1933), p. 31.

4. Max Beerbohm, " 'Savonarola' Brown," in *Max Beerbohm: Selected Prose*, ed. David Cecil (1917; rpt. Boston: Little, Brown, 1970), p. 110. Future references to this edition will appear in the text.

5. Thomas Hardy, *Jude the Obscure* (1895; rpt. Boston: Houghton Mifflin, 1965), p. 27.

6. Elaine Showalter, *A Literature of Their Own. British Women Novelists from Brontë to Lessing* (Princeton: Princeton University Press, 1977), pp. 194, 240–262.

7. Vera Brittain, *Testament of Youth: An Autobiographical Study of the Years 1900–1925* (New York: Macmillan, 1937), p. 458.

8. Virginia Woolf, *Mr. Bennett and Mrs. Brown* (1924; rpt. London: Hogarth Press, 1928), p. 4. Future references to this edition will appear in the text.

9. Virginia Woolf, "Modern Fiction," in *The Common Reader* (1925; rpt. with *The Second Common Reader* (New York: Harcourt Brace, 1948), I, 218. In an essay on female poets Catherine F. Smith notes the recurrent image of a grand female personification; she speculates enticingly on the origin of feminist theory in this mystical vision of self-apotheosis. The importance of this paradigm not only to poets but to such feminist novelists and critics as Virginia Woolf, and its urgent life beneath the respectable patriarchal surface of Victorian culture, suggest the larger import of Smith's study. See Catherine F. Smith, "Jane Lead: Mysticism and the Woman Cloathed with the Sun," in Sandra M. Gilbert and Susan Gubar, eds., *Shakespeare's Sisters: Feminist Essays on Women Poets* (Bloomington and London: Indiana University Press, 1979), pp. 3–18.

10. Alain Robbe-Grillet, "On Several Obsolete Notions," *For a New Novel*, trans. Richard Howard (New York: Grove, 1965), pp. 27, 28.

11. Leo Bersani, *A Future for Astyanax: Character and Desire in Literature* (Boston and Toronto: Little, Brown, 1976), p. 212.

12. In the 1970s for example, three major literary journals conducted symposia on the idea of literary character. See Martin Price, "People of the Book: Character in Forster's *A Passage to India,*" *Critical Inquiry* 1 (March 1975), 605–622, and "The Logic of Intensity: More on Character," *Critical Inquiry* 2 (Winter 1975), 369–379; and Rawdon Wilson, "On Character: A Reply to Martin Price," *Critical Inquiry* 2 (Autumn 1975), 191–198, and "The Bright Chimera: Character as a Literary Term," *Critical Inquiry* 5 (Summer 1979), 725–749; "Changing Views of Character," *New Literary History* 5 (Winter 1974); and "Character as a Lost Cause," in Mark Spilka, ed., *Novel: A Forum on Fiction* 11 (Spring 1978), 197–217.

13. Hélène Cixous, "The Character of 'Character,'" trans. Keith Cohen, *New Literary History* 5 (Winter 1974), 387.

Index

Coutts, Angela, 181
Crane, Walter, illustration to *Beauty and the Beast*, 65–66
Cruikshank, George, "How to get rid of an old woman," 110

Daly, Mary, 238 n. 1
Darwin, Charles, 52, 55, 148, 235 n. 10; *The Origin of the Species*, 52. *See also* Evolutionary theory
Death: in *The Old Curiosity Shop*, 83, 86–87, 134, 237 n. 16; and sentimentality, 87, 133–134; in *David Copperfield*, 85, 87, 237 n. 16; the drowning of Ophelia, 94–96; in *Mildred Arkell*, 133–134; in *Buddenbrooks*, 134; in *East Lynne*, 134; of fallen women, 155, 161, 171; of Dickens, 202–204, 205; and post–World War I writers, 220–223; twentieth-century worship of, 226, 228
Defoe, Daniel: *Appleby's Journal* quoted, 110–111; *History of the Devil* in *Mill on the Floss*, 183
de la Rue, Madame Émile, Dickens and, 181–182
DeLaura, David J., 243 n. 4
Demons: women as, 1–4, 7, 9–10, 61, 63–108, 110, 118, 120, 121, 124, 140, 160, 183, 185, 190, 197, 203, 207, 219; as divine principles, 1, 2, 7, 9–10, 75–76, 93–96, 103, 105, 108, 118, 140, 183, 185, 186, 187, 190, 197, 203, 207, 219; traditional, 33–34, 64, 71, 74, 93, 236 n. 5. *See also* Angels; Mermaids; Serpent-women.
Dickens, Charles, 43, 77, 90, 105, 106, 181, 196, 226, 237 n. 17, 238 n. 39; life of, 180, 184, 190, 236 n. 11; and fallen women, 180–183; as Victorian artist, 181–182, 200–204, 205, 206, 220–221; and Madame Tussaud, 195–196. *See also* Acting; Mesmerism
    works of: *David Copperfield*, 31, 82, 84–88, 89, 90, 96, 101, 138, 160, 181; *The Old Curiosity Shop*, 41, 66–67, 82–88, 89, 90, 96–97, 101, 102, 103, 105–106, 107, 134, 196, 236 n. 11; *Nicholas Nickleby* mentioned, 55; *Little Dorrit* mentioned, 55; *Dombey and Son*, 83, 159–160; *Hard*

Times, 100–101; *Bleak House*, 106, 143; *Pickwick Papers*, 109, 143, 190; *Great Expectations*, 114–115, 127, 133, 142–144, 181; *A Christmas Carol*, 143–144; *Oliver Twist*, 171, 182; *The Frozen Deep*, 182; *Sketches by Boz*, 195; "History in Wax," 195–196; *Martin Chuzzlewit*, 200–201
Disraeli, Benjamin, 10, 231 n. 1
Dixon, Thomas, on C. Rossetti, 115, 117
Doolittle, Hilda (H. D.): *Tribute to Freud*, 32–33; *Helen in Egypt*, 33–34
Doubt, in Victorian England, 2, 7, 10, 11, 14, 62, 73, 105, 125, 155, 184, 190, 198–200, 214–217, 235–236 n. 4, 243 n. 4. *See also* Faith; Religion; Religious Humanism
Douglas, Ann, 232 n. 4
Dowling, Linda, 232 n. 7
Doyle, Richard, illustration to his *Fairy Book*, 65, 67
Dumas, Alexandre, his Marguerite Gauthier mentioned, 17
du Maurier, George: *Trilby*, 16, 17–21, 24, 26, 27, 30, 31, 32, 34, 35, 36, 39, 41, 42, 43, 48, 101–102; as artist and illustrator, 18, 20–22, 32, 48; illustrations for *Henry Esmond*, 100–101
DuPlessis, Rachel Blau, 232 n. 3
Dusinberre, Juliet, quoted, 188

Edwards, Lee R., 232 n. 3
Egg, Augustus, *Past and Present* trilogy, 154–156, 157, 159, 161–162, 163, 167, 170, 177–178, 180
Eiseley, Loren, quoted, 52
Eliot, George, 17, 36, 56, 58, 59, 60, 103, 238 n. 39; life of, 55, 94, 122, 125, 180, 189; and spinsterhood, 118, 120, 124; as fallen woman, 174, 178, 183–184, 205; as actress, 205, 244 n. 28
    works of: *Middlemarch* mentioned, 8, 109; *Daniel Deronda*, 8, 64, 205; *The Mill on the Floss*, 41, 94, 183; *Scenes of Clerical Life*, 53, 109; "Silly Novels by Lady Novelists," 53–56; "Worldliness and Other-Worldliness," 53–56; *Silas Marner*, 83–84, 143–144; *Adam Bede*, 143, 168, 169, 170, 172, 174–178, 183, 200